PROSPERITY AND PUBLIC SPENDING

PROSPERITY AND PUBLIC SPENDING

Transformational growth and the role of government

Edward Nell

The New School for Social Research, New York

Boston
UNWIN HYMAN
London   Sydney   Wellington

Allen & Unwin, Inc.,
8 Winchester Place, Winchester, Mass. 01890, USA

Published by the Academic Division of
Unwin Hyman Ltd
15/17 Broadwick Street, London W1V 1FP

Allen & Unwin (Australia) Ltd,
8 Napier Street, North Sydney, NSW 2060, Australia

Allen & Unwin (New Zealand) Ltd in association with the
Port Nicholson Press Ltd,
60 Cambridge Terrace, Wellington, New Zealand

First published in 1988

Library of Congress Cataloging-in-Publication Data

Nell, Edward J.
  Prosperity and public spending.
Bibliography: p.
Includes index.
1. Expenditures, Public. 2. Economic development.
I. Title.
HJ7451.N44   1987   339.5′ 22   87–1383
ISBN 0–04–339044–7 (alk. paper)
ISBN 0–04–339045–5 (pbk. : alk. paper)

British Library Cataloguing in Publication Data

Nell, Edward J.
  Prosperity and public spending:
transformational growth and the role of
government.
1. Economic development   2. Economic policy
I. Title
330.9   HD82
ISBN 0–04–339044–7
ISBN 0–04–339045–5 Pbk

Typeset in 10 on 11 point Trump Medieval by Grove Graphics
and printed in Great Britain by Biddles of Guildford

Contents

For Marsha

Preface

Although this book was written in a relatively short time, its ideas go back a long way, and many of my friends will recognize their criticisms and comments, now absorbed into the argument. For these I thank them, and absolve them for any blame for the results – they did their best.

The book is ambitious in scope, but it is intended to be suggestive rather than definitive. Its central aim is to reconstruct the Keynesian project by approaching the problem of effective demand in the context of a corporate capitalist industrial system – rather than a craft-based economy of family firms and family farms. By doing this we are also able to understand modern economics better: microeconomics is the theory of the craft economy, mixed with a little ideology to give it some spice, while macroeconomics tries to show us how a modern demand-constrained economy works, but can do so only when complemented by a proper account of prices, such as provided by the current revival of Classical economics. So we are forced to rethink both micro and macro, with the result that we come out with a new appreciation altogether of the role of demand.

Many people helped in the preparation of this book. First of all, I would like to thank Rosemary Rinder, who prepared drafts of two chapters for a book on the critique of austerity policies, a project that was finally abandoned. But much of the material she collected found its way into Chapter 1. Next Robert Heilbroner, for reading an early draft and insisting on a full account of the relationships between policy positions and economic theory. A fellowship at the Lehrman Institute supported work on the development of the role of the state, and a Visiting Professorship at the University of Rome supported work on the post-Keynesian theory of the multiplier. Felix Jimenez helped with econometric studies of several important propositions, and Abdelkrim Errouaki collected helpful statistics. Cigdem Kurdas, Ray Majewski, and Christof Rühl read and commented on several drafts, as did a study group they arranged at the New School. These comments proved extremely helpful in sharpening the focus of the book. It is not their fault if I have failed to carry out their suggestions adequately. Next, the highest praise goes to Liz Paton for a skillful, precise and thoughtful job of copy-editing; completing the work of the initiating editor, Walter Allen. Finally, I have to thank my son, Jacob Nell, for a lot of boring typing when he should have been out playing games, and Marsha Lasker for making sure that the project got finished.

Introduction

This is a partisan book, but it is not a party book. It is partisan in the
sense that it has a point of view about the way politics and economics
should interact, and it puts forward that point of view quite strongly.
The argument is that we do not live in a 'free-market' system. This
is not because such a system has become overburdened, or because
labor unions and monopolies have usurped its functions, or because
the market has become tangled in regulations and red tape. It is
because the fundamental institutions of economic society have
changed: crafts have become industries, firms have become
corporations, and markets are administered. These are not
'imperfections' or examples of 'market failure'; as the basic
institutions changed, the market itself came to work differently. An
economy of family firms and family farms might once have functioned
like an idealized 'free market'. But a modern system of corporate
industry does not. It behaves differently in regard both to output and
employment and to pricing: output and employment are adjusted to
current sales, but prices are planned with an eye to the financing of
investment, so are governed by long-term considerations, and tend to
be unresponsive to short-term changes. So, the automatic and
anonymous rule of supply and demand in the market came to be
replaced by a form of private (and therefore largely unaccountable)
administration. Moreover, where the earlier economic system had
grown slowly, and by accretion, so that it functioned according to
static principles, the corporate industry that replaced it depended on
an internal dynamic. It either grew, or collapsed. But this growth was
not a simple expansion – it was developmental. The economic
system was transformed. And when this transformational growth
faltered, as it did in the 1930s and again recently, the system
malfunctioned in a wide variety of ways. Finally, the transformation
from a craft economy to modern industry is world-wide. It cannot be
understood, and policy cannot be planned, on the basis of a single
country taken in isolation. This is especially true with the
development of transnational corporations and international capital
markets.

In theory, idealized 'free markets' will tend to establish full
employment; whether actual markets in the nineteenth-century
system of family firms did is more problematic. It is certain, however,
that the corporate industrial system of today does not. Moreover, the
modern economy has to grow just to stay afloat; if growth falters,

unemployment will break out in the capital goods industries, eventually spreading to the rest of the economy. And industry will not build new factories unless it expects its markets to grow. But after the mid-1960s/ early 1970s crucial US markets 'matured' – stopped growing. The resulting slump affected the whole world.

For the craft economy, laissez faire prevails; there may or may not be a case for regulation, but there is little need to support aggregate demand – the system tends to operate near the full employment level. The industrial business system, by contrast, cannot be left to itself: it not only tends to periodic slumps, but its distress is self-reinforcing, leading to long-term bouts of stagnation. To overcome this the system needs regular infusions of demand, and needs to be controlled and regulated by a democratically elected government, in the interests not only of the people, but also for the benefit of business itself. The growth of modern industry is also the growth of corporate hierarchy, the correlative of which is the growth of the state. Given that the economy is undergoing systematic transformation, the state cannot be continuously under the thumb of any one party or faction; a politically powerful but economically outmoded faction could hold up progress.

However, regulating transformational growth and the development of hierarchy means 'big government', and, moreover, it means using the policy tool of 'deficit spending' to stimulate the economy when demand is slack. But if one aspect of the system is influenced by policy, other parts will very likely react; so policy measures may have to be extended to them, too. All the more so in an interdependent world. A strong and positive policy of government intervention is necessary because the 'free market', left to itself, cannot reliably, and perhaps cannot at all, ensure full employment, whereas government spending – deficit spending – can; and full employment is a crucial economic objective both for ordinary people and for business.

All this has been true for decades, yet nowadays government intervention, and especially deficit spending, has, to put it mildly, a bad press. The 'dangers of the deficit' and the red tape of regulation – which, we shall argue, are largely mythical – have been used to scare people away not only from a full employment program, but also from supporting big government. Liberals who used to support full employment as the number one priority now agree that deficits are a danger to us all. Are they? Are they more dangerous than allowing unemployment and stagnation to destroy whole communities? Or do deficits, perhaps, cause unemployment? Or do they cause inflation? High interest rates? Many will argue that deficits cause some or all of these. But the facts don't show it. Indeed, they suggest the reverse – that deficits tend to promote prosperity when the economy is slack, as it is and has been for a decade and a half. So perhaps the attack on deficits and deficit spending is a disguise, a smokescreen, for the assault on the real target, the government's role and position in the economy, and its associated policies of full employment and regulation of business? As an indication of this, consider the change in the position of the government relative to the economy since the beginning of this century.

In 1890 the ratio of total government spending to GNP (gross national product) was 6.5 per cent in the US. It was the same in Germany, and only 4.5 per cent in Great Britain. By 1982, the ratio had risen to 36.3 per cent in the US, 44.8 per cent in West Germany, and 44.6 per cent in Britain. These were not even the extreme cases; this same ratio went from 5 per cent to 62.2 per cent in Sweden. The rise was dramatic and persistent in every major industrialized nation. This is the background against which the current drama of the deficit and the role of the government is being played. Why has there been such an increase? Is it good or bad? Can — or should — anything be done about it?

Proclaiming the need to cut back the government has been a constant theme of conservative administrations, like that of Reagan, or Thatcher in Great Britain. But, in a surprising shift, the last US presidential election saw the Democrats move a long way towards this position, in many ways reversing the stance they had held since the days of the New Deal. The centerpiece of their new position, at least as far as the election went, was a new-found opposition to deficit spending, and this connected with a more general intellectual rejection of traditional Keynesian demand management, indeed of interventionism in general. We must examine this new alignment of opinion on government and explore its roots both in the current assessment of Keynesian economics and demand management policies, and in the emerging realignment of economic forces world-wide.

Why attack government intervention? Because, from the point of view of business, the changes that have taken place in the world economy imply that stronger controls are now needed in order to manage the system effectively. And this has occurred at a time when the drying-up of transformational growth at home coupled with the emergence of overseas profit opportunities makes it convenient to have no controls at all. From this perspective, then, deficits, crowding-out and market efficiency are not the real issues. What is at stake is the role of the government — more specifically, whether government will control and direct the economy to assure the prosperity of the majority of the people, or whether it will adjust its role so as to provide maximum scope for the free movement of capital in its search for new profits, regardless of the effects on workers and consumers. This is what we shall explore, beginning with the changes in the economy starting in the late 1960s and running through the 1970s, and moving on to a general discussion of the theory and practice of economic policy.

We shall find that the old policy tools will not be adequate and new ones will have to be proposed. Central to this project will be a new wages policy — not one of keeping the lid on wages, but rather one of pushing wages up, both to create new consumer markets and to compel business-men to innovate. But such a policy is dangerous and we will have to explore it carefully.

PART I

The Retreat from Prosperity

When capitalism first appeared on the stage of history it was dressed in the clothes of mercantilism. The guild-masters became the capitalist employers, apprentices and journeymen became wage-laborers, and businesses and capital, like the traditional craft skills, were passed along in the family. But neither the family, nor the small firm, nor the traditional craft technology were appropriate vehicles for the growth of capital. Much of the subsequent history of the system can be read as the progressive transformation of economic institutions, shaping them to the needs of capital.

The early phase we shall call the 'craft economy', the later 'corporate industry'. Transformational growth is the process that connects them. However, it does much more than create corporations and modern industries out of family firms and family farms – although that in itself is a large project. It creates whole new sectors and new technologies, new products and new processes, new jobs and new career prospects. It replaces farms with cities and suburbs, and changes the nature of family life. These changes, in turn, generate the new markets that will absorb the new products. They also bring about a redefining of the relationship between the economy and the political life of the state.

The process is sometimes gradual, and at other times cataclysmic: sectors may be transformed slowly, so that new sectors are added while old ones decline and gradually fade away; or the changes may be abrupt and wrenching, bringing booms and slumps in their wake. In either case this process is the core of investment behavior in the capitalist economy, and one reason that behaviour is so difficult to model.

A craft economy works differently from a system of corporate industry. Although activity in both systems depends on markets, i.e. on the expectation of sales, markets work differently in each. A pure craft economy is governed by the laws of supply and demand (markets respond to incentives, and the price mechanism allocates scarce resources). In such a system, employment tends to be stable in the face of changing aggregate demand – variable costs are low, since much labor cost is fixed, and declines in demand tend to generate offsetting increases, so that, overall, 'supply tends to create its own demand' contains an element of truth. Conventional microeconomics lacks an adequate theory of capital, and therefore of distribution, but it provides many elements for an account of the working of a craft economy. However, it does not apply at all to a system of corporate industry, which works on different principles altogether. Such a system is fully demand-determined: employment adjusts to sales, and is regulated by the multiplier – changes in demand are multiplied, not offset. Prices are set in accordance with the financial requirements of investment, which in turn is adjusted to the expected growth of markets, as governed by the process of transformational growth. So prices will be unresponsive to short-term developments.

The conventional wisdom concerning economic questions is based almost entirely on orthodox microeconomics – that is, on a theory that applies only (and, even then, imperfectly) to the craft economy. Yet we live in a system that is primarily, though not completely, one of corporate industry. The result is a consistent failure of public discourse to address the real issues. This failure works systematically to the benefit of business interests. These points can be illustrated by an example: the debate over the deficit during and after the 1984 US presidential election.

Prudent Democrats and Prodigal Republicans

A funny thing happened on the way to the landslide: the Democrats and the Republicans switched sides on the issue of 'fiscal responsibility'. Traditionally, Democrats have been the big spenders, while Republicans have stood for financial prudence and a tight-fisted attitude towards government borrowing. No longer. Now the Democrats worry that the deficit will raise interest rates and 'crowd out' productive investments, while Republicans argue that tax cuts will stimulate expansion (remember the Kennedy–Johnson tax cut?) ultimately increasing the taxable base.

Perhaps the Republican switch, engineered by the 'supply-siders' is really not so hard to understand (although some conservatives have trouble): an expanding economy is good for business. So what if there's a deficit; growth is more important. Evidently the electorate found this message easy to understand. They had been hearing it for years – from the Democrats!

By contrast, Walter Mondale: 'Here's the truth about the future: we are living on borrowed money and borrowed time. These deficits hike interest rates, clobber exports, stunt investment, kill jobs, undermine growth, cheat our kids and shrink our future.'

But Ronald Reagan was not worried: the economy would grow out of its deficits, so long as the tax cuts remained in place. This was the central conclusion of the 'supply-siders', the young Turks of the new conservative movement. Their argument in a nutshell: work effort is a response to real wages; higher real wages call forth greater effort. (This is textbook price theory, taken very literally indeed.) Taxes reduce take-home pay, so they must reduce effort. Ergo: if you cut taxes you'll raise work effort, and therefore GNP. A similar argument is advanced for savings and interest: taxes reduce the 'take-home' rate of interest, so cutting taxes will raise effective interest and therefore call forth more savings. (Again the microeconomics textbook.) More savings mean more investment, so higher growth and higher GNP. (This idea is the exact opposite of the Keynesian position, which regards saving as simply refraining from spending, i.e. as passive, so that what drives the economy is investment decisions. The contrast between these two perspectives will be one of our main themes.) All in all a very conventional picture, easily derived from ordinary price theory but, for that precise reason, not at all appropriate to the world of modern industry.

In addition, this view holds that government spending should be cut – except the military – because such spending, in the words of former Assistant Secretary of the Treasury Paul Craig Roberts, 'preempts the private sector's use of resources, regardless of whether the government finances its spending by borrowing or by taxing' (*Business Week*, 9 April 1984). The best policy would be to have low taxes and no deficits, because then government spending would be held to the minimum. However, deficits do not raise interest rates, so the next best policy is to have a deficit that results from tax cuts, since the cuts will stimulate growth by increasing the willingness and ability of households and businesses to work and supply goods and savings. Moreover, concern over the deficit will encourage people to think of ways to cut government spending, particularly the 'useless' spending on social services, which free marketeers have always opposed on the grounds that people should be self-reliant.

A balanced budget would be best; but human nature is what it is, so we may have to settle for second best. This is a wholly understandable position. Moreover, it leads naturally to a further position, which is that Congress, reflecting human nature and normal politics, is never going to balance the budget. The only possibility, therefore, is to *require* that it be balanced – by a Constitutional Amendment. Advocating a balanced budget amendment, therefore, does not contradict the Reagan position that deficits, as such, pose no great danger; since a balanced budget almost certainly means reduced government spending, it fits quite naturally into the current Republican position. Being able to have it both ways is the true test of political genius.

The defense of the Democrats has to be that, although their strategy was suicidal, it was noble because it was correct: 'the deficit is a clear and present danger.' According to this view, supply-side economics is nonsense. Tax cuts will not be saved, they will be spent, so the rate of interest will not be lowered by additional savings. Nor will tax cuts stimulate workers to work more or harder. So incomes will not rise, and therefore the deficit will have to be covered by borrowing, which will cut into existing savings and drive up interest rates, aborting the recovery and hampering further growth. These high interest rates will attract foreign funds, thus driving up the dollar, which in turn will weaken US exports while making imports of foreign goods more attractive. Thus the domestic deficit creates the foreign one. A clear-cut argument, perfectly straightforward, but – and this is the key – crucially based on microeconomic, and therefore inappropriate, principles.

Let's look more closely at the argument that deficits cause inflation and high interest rates. If the economy normally operated without slack, as it did in the earlier era, and the government ran a noticeable deficit, then both prices and interest rates would be forced up. Prices would be driven up because, with everything operating at normal capacity, the government's added demands could be met only by bidding resources away from other uses. Similarly, to finance government activity, savings would have to be attracted, and, with the level and distribution of income fixed, this could be done only by bidding up interest rates. This quite reasonable argument shows exactly what is wrong with most current discussions: we are now and have been for over a decade in a period of slack usage of resources. Modern economies do not normally operate at full blast; in fact, genuine full employment is rare. Modern economies normally face a shortage of demand. Yet, because most current discussion rests on mainstream assumptions, the implications of this fact are not widely recognized.

And what of the foreign deficit? Has the government deficit driven up interest rates and so brought about the foreign deficit, as so many commentators seem to agree? We shall see that this runs counter both to the facts and to sound theory: interest rates are determined by monetary policy and by the costs of operating the financial system, not by supply and demand for funds, which adjust in line with the level of activity, whatever the level of interest rates.

The most likely effect of a tax cut (with given government spending, i.e. a deficit) is that households will spend more, in fact will spend almost all of what they get back. In conditions where there are idle or underutilized factories and unemployed workers, such a rise in sales means that output can be profitably expanded, i.e. more workers will be hired, because more goods are being sold, assuming that the increased spending goes on domestically produced goods, rather than on imports! (We shall take up the problem of the foreign balance later.) There will be more savings, not because people are saving more – they will probably save at the same rate – but because more people have higher incomes. For the same reason, tax collections will be up. In other words, a deficit stimulates the economy for good old-fashioned Keynesian reasons. In fact, according to the economics most college students still learn, the government *ought* to run deficits when the economy is operating at less than full employment; indeed the government's budget ought to be in balance *only* at full employment.

This is the basic Keynesian argument. It will have to be redeveloped for the case where transformational growth has slowed or halted, because then spending responds much more sluggishly and pricing can become perverse. Besides unemployment, inflation is now an endemic problem. And the two frequently go together, a possibility not envisaged in the standard Keynesian textbook. Moreover, conditions in the world economy have become a much more important factor in the domestic policies of every major country. The Keynesian argument is none the less fundamentally correct about the way a corporate industrial economy works; the contrary view, embraced both by mainstream theory and its conservative critics, rests on an account of markets and economic behaviour that fits only an earlier era of family firms and family farms, what we shall term 'kinship capitalism'. Yet just as the basic Keynesian argument needs to be revamped, so shall we find a need for new and fundamentally different policies now – *post*-Keynesian policies – adapted to the new conditions.

The first order of business, therefore, is to take a look at what has been happening to the American economy in recent years. We shall see that the 1970s were a period of slack for the corporate economy, but that this has been widely misunderstood because it has been interpreted in terms appropriate to the supply-constrained economy of an earlier era.

1

The Slowdown of the 1970s

In the mid 1960s things looked pretty good, economically, for the US. There had been twenty years of prosperity, of near full employment, with little or no inflation. Growth had been rapid, so that the standard of living of a large and expanding middle class had risen steadily, and a new automobile-centered lifestyle, which became the envy of the world, blossomed in the suburbs. First, a car in every garage, then, for the prosperous, two cars – and a radio in each; one television for the house, then two, one color and one black and white; radios, hi-fis, dishwashers, washer-dryers, blenders, appliances of all sorts became normal equipment, as electronic wizardry advanced by leaps and bounds. The standard equipment of the middle-class household of the 1960s was almost unimaginable to even the richest of the flappers and Great Gatsbys. And things kept getting better and better; 'new and improved' was the order of the day. Then poverty was discovered; in the richest country in the world, there were people going hungry, people who, it emerged, were not only relatively poor, but absolutely so. Such poverty was intolerable to the liberal conscience, as intolerable as communism in Vietnam; so war was declared on both. Guns for Saigon, and butter for the inner cities; Lyndon Johnson thought the richest country in the world could surely afford both.

Something went badly wrong. Within a few years the economy found itself plagued by *both* unemployment and inflation. Worse, the conventional remedies no longer seemed to work. Policy-induced unemployment, which was supposed to cure inflation, sometimes seemed to exacerbate it. Growth slowed down, the dollar, the basis of world trade, turned shaky, and for the first time the US began to import as much or more than it exported. And things then began, not to improve, but steadily to get worse. Inflation intensified, reaching double-digit figures; recessions got deeper and deeper, with unemployment eventually reaching double digits, too. And new problems emerged; productivity, which had grown rapidly and reliably for over twenty years, began to slow down, until by the late 1970s it was no longer growing at all. Manufacturing slumped. What growth there was took place in services. Real wages stagnated, and class divisions widened; migration from the countryside to the cities trickled to a halt, and even reversed one year in the mid-1970s. Construction in the suburbs slowed and housing starts stagnated, while costs soared. The American Dream, owning your own home, began to fade.

Why? What had gone wrong? For most economists and economic journalists, the answer was plain – bad policy decisions (starting with Johnson's misguided attempt to have both guns and butter) came on top of bad luck, a streak of 'supply shocks'. The Vietnam War should have been financed by a tax increase; the failure to impose the necessary taxes, by an administration fearful of making an already unpopular war intolerable, led to inflation, which eroded the US's international position. In this weakened condition, the US found it harder to deal with external shocks, such as bad harvests, the oil increase, and so on. Moreover, each of these external jolts was then followed by a succession of mistakes. Conservatives and liberals disagree about just which policies were mistaken, but both agree that the stagflation of the 1970s was caused at bottom by policy errors, following supply shocks. Monetarists blamed deficit spending and monetary laxity for the inflation, and held that the rising unemployment was the result of 'natural' factors. The decline in the effectiveness of Keynesian policies, on the other hand, was due to the fact that those policies had only worked in the first place by fooling people – and now everyone had caught on. By contrast, Keynesians held a mixed bag of views that ascribed the origin of either the unemployment or the inflation to some external shock or other, and then explained the other member of the unwanted pair by the misguided policies undertaken to control the first. Most Keynesians believed that correct fiscal and monetary policies would rectify the situation, though they frequently disagreed about the exact mix; a small but influential group of 'post-Keynesians' maintained that incomes policies – tying money wage increases to increases in productivity – were necessary to prevent inflation and thus make room for an expansionary fiscal stance. Either way, policy errors were at the root of the matter.[1]

Radicals disagreed. Policy mistakes may well have been made, but problematical policies were nothing new. The question was not whether policy mistakes were made, or even which policies were mistaken; rather, it was why mistakes mattered so much. What had changed in the way the economy worked? Why did mistakes now have such a major impact, and why was it so difficult for correct policies to set things right again? Radicals gave two different kinds of answers. One group argued that the long period of post war prosperity was basically the result of a set of accommodations (somewhat grandly termed a 'social structure of accumulation') between US capital – the major corporations – and US labor – the big unions – on the one hand, and between capital and the citizenry, on the other. These accords, unspoken yet detailed, and arranged through informal channels, provided the foundation for corporate profitability. Oversimplifying a complex argument, the claim is that workers agreed to mitigate labor disputes in return for wage increases that kept pace with rising productivity. Citizens agreed to let the market rule, and to minimize regulation, in return for social security and a full-employment policy. A third accord, the *Pax Americana*, supplemented the other two, providing US corporations maximum scope for their operations world-wide in return for US military protection against indigenous socialist movements. Many other elements were involved in each of these accords, but the central point was simple – the accords permitted profits to expand, so capital could accumulate. And the crises of the 1970s developed, not because of external shocks, or as the consequence of policy mistakes, but because these accords eroded and then broke down.[2]

The great weakness in this story is that it explains the economic crisis by the breakdown of the accords, but it offers no adequate reason why the accords should have broken down. In fact the most plausible reasons, indeed the ones the authors themselves mention, are all economic – tightening labor and raw material markets, environmental destruction, widening income differentials, slackening sales, and intensifying international competition. However, the breakdown of the social structure of accumulation was supposed to explain the economic crisis; it won't do then to turn around and explain the erosion of that structure by the onset of economic troubles.

The other radical approach faced no such difficulties. It explained both the breakdown of such postwar accords and the onset of economic troubles by the tendency of the rate of profit to fall, which in turn is brought about by the working of competition. So this tendency, noted by both Ricardo and Marx, and also (although interpreted differently) by mainstream economics, must be considered inherent in the system. As the rate of profit falls, the tendency to invest weakens; hence, on the one hand, unemployment emerges, while, on the other, monetary relaxation and other Keynesian measures will have less impact. Moreover, faced with sagging profitability, governments will try with increasing fervor to stimulate the economy; the result will be deficits and excessive monetary growth. Businesses meanwhile will try to raise prices wherever possible. Thus unemployment and inflation will develop together, and will appear to be the results of mistaken or excessively lax Keynesian policies, while Keynesians will complain over the economy's unexpected lack of responsiveness to their normal policy tools.[3]

The difficulty here is quite different, but no less serious. There is no generally accepted theoretical explanation for a persistent tendency of the rate of profit to fall, and the main ones offered all seem to contain flaws. The capital theory controversy of the 1960s revealed serious incon-sistencies in the mainstream approach, which held that higher levels of capital per worker would bring about lower rates of return. This was a version of the scarcity principle: abundance of capital reduces its value. The controversy showed that no such regular relationship existed: once business invested in new methods of production, chosen in response, say, to a change in the wage, a new set of prices would (eventually) be established, whereupon capital would have to be revalued. For the mainstream story to hold, the revalued stock of capital would have to be consistent with the 'scarcity' story: a rise in wages, bringing down the rate of profits and causing changes in methods of production, would have to mean a larger invested capital. But it was found that no general rules could be stated, and, worse, that any number of perverse and surprising cases could be devised. Moreover, this critique also applies to the radical theory, which holds that competition will force firms to substitute capital for workers, even when the new methods are less profitable overall. However, when the new methods are installed, new prices will eventually be established, and both capital and output will have to be revalued. Capital may be increased – but the rate of profit may be higher, not lower! The simple parables, derived from the microeconomics of the craft economy, don't work when applied to the problems of an industrial economy.[4] In short, *if* the rate of profit fell in the manner indicated, then the results described by the radical theory would almost certainly follow. But, while profits and the rate of profits have in fact fallen, this fall may well have been caused by, rather than causing, the economic difficulties in question.

The radicals have an excellent point: the issue is not policy mistakes, but why they have mattered so much. Although the economy is working differently, more sluggishly, the fundamental change is not on the supply side. What has changed is that the growth of demand has slowed. Crucial markets have matured and new ones have not opened at the same rate.

As long as growth consisted of the opening of new territories there was no reason to worry about the growth of demand. The development of the new region could be expected to create new demands right along with the new productive capacity. But once growth comes to mean the more intensive development of the existing economy, as it does in the modern economy, the expansion of markets can no longer be taken for granted: markets must be cultivated, demand stimulated. For example, a major redistribution of income, such as happened after World War II with the provision of veterans' benefits by the G.I. Bill of Rights, can create a massive new consumer market.[5] So can a major shift in population, e.g. from rural to urban areas. But if new productive capacity is to be constructed, there must be some reason to believe that new markets will emerge or old ones expand. Up to the mid-1960s, this seemed reasonable; by the beginning of the 1970s the outlook had become bleak.

Twenty Years of Stagnation

These issues cannot be assessed properly until we have a better idea of what took place in the economy after the late 1960s. Nor will it do to confine our discussion to a few sets of numbers representing inflation and unemployment. The economy is a complex of inter-related institutions, involving at least employment and production, finance, marketing and sales, consumption, investment and growth, the payment and distribution of incomes, international relations, and technological innovation. To see how the economy works, we shall have to look at all of these, comparing the way the economy worked in the 1950s and early 1960s with the way it worked later, in the 1970s. It would be nice if it were simpler, but it isn't.

Overall real economic growth

Economic growth overall slowed significantly, from nearly 4 per cent per year in the period 1950–65, to just over 3 per cent per year in the period 1965–80. Hard-to-measure services production rose rapidly in the 1960s and 1970s. If we look only at goods and structures, the slowdown in growth is somewhat sharper – from 3.4 per cent in 1950–65 to 2.5 per cent in 1965–80.

Not only was growth slower in 1965–80 than it had been earlier, it was also more undependable. Between 1969 and 1980, real economic activity declined in four out of eleven years, whereas the record for the 1950s and 1960s showed only two years of decline in a twenty-year period. There was a comparable variability in income and employment growth, and these presented the same problem for households and for business: uncertainty. With real sales falling almost as often as they rose, planning the expansion of businesses became a much more risky proposition. So the slumps of the 1970s seem to have reflected justified uncertainty about the future development of key consumer markets.

Unfortunately, the resultant instability made conservative planning rational for the individual business, reinforcing the trend: when investment falls off, the reduced employment means that household incomes in the aggregate are down, and hence consumer spending also weakens. When the consensus of planning turns risk-averse, then growth falters and, ironically, planners are vindicated. Boom and bust are self-reinforcing. In other words, the degree of optimism or pessimism (the 'animal spirits', to use a Keynesian phrase) of planners will determine the long-term growth of the economy. But these 'animal spirits' are not simply based on crowd psychology and subjective reactions to the news of the day. The consensus of corporate planners on investment is based on good research and hard facts about what will sell and what won't, what markets will grow and how fast, and which ones will slow down or stagnate. We shall come to this in a moment. First, let's consider the rest of the record, starting with the effect of inflation on the prosperity of the majority of people, then turning to consumption and the balance of trade. We shall find a developing pattern of stagnation.

Inflation, Real Wages and Income Distribution

Until inflation hit in the late 1960s and 1970s, real wages rose steadily and both the distribution of earned incomes and the relative shares of total income going to capital and to labor appeared stable. Once inflation steamed up and especially when it took off into double digits in the late 1970s and early 1980s, average money wages began to lag behind, so that real wages stagnated and eventually declined (see Figures 1.1 and 1.2).

Average real wages are only part of the story, however. Median real family income, which rose an average 3.2 per cent per year in 1950–65, stagnated thereafter, and rose not at all during the whole of the 1970s, actually falling during the first four years of the 1980s. But during this latter period real GNP per capita has been rising (albeit more slowly than earlier). How can this be? First, families are somewhat smaller – 3.3

Figure 1.1   *Inflation rate, 1951–76*

Source: Wall Street Journal, 18 October 1976

Figure 1.2   *Real wages, 1967–84 (1967 = 100)*

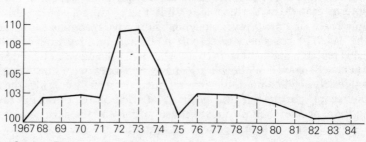

Source: Economic Report of the President 1982

persons, on average, down from 3.7. Secondly, non-family households have risen as a proportion of the population, and their incomes are rising faster than before – this category includes many Yuppies. But, most important, families above the median have done better, while those below have not, which is to say that income distribution has shifted in favor of the relatively well-to-do. This is confirmed by the fact the proportion of American families living in poverty, which declined sharply during the 1960s (from 18 per cent to about 9.3 per cent in the early 1970s), began rising in the later 1970s, until by the mid-1980s it had reached almost 14 per cent. (The same pattern can be seen in the figures for persons, rather than families, in poverty.)

Income distribution figures may be unreliable, but they confirm the shift away from the relatively poor to the well-off (see Table 1.1.).

Table 1.1 *Income distribution 1965–80*

% of population	received % of income		
	1965	1970	1980
top 5%	15.5	15.6	15.3
top 20%	40.9	40.9	41.6
2nd 20%	23.9	23.8	24.3
mid 20%	17.8	17.6	17.5
4th 20%	12.2	12.2	11.6
lowest 20%	5.2	5.4	5.1

Source: US Department of Commerce, Bureau of Census, *Current Population Reports*, Consumer Income', Series P-60.

Income held up better for households headed by white males; black, Hispanic and female-headed households lost heavily (see Table 1.2).

Table 1.2 *Percentage change in real median family incomes, 1970–80*

All families	0.4%
Characteristics of head: White	0.8%
Black	− 4.9%
Hispanic	− 8.7%
Female	− 4.1%

Source: US Bureau of the Census, CPR P-60.

Not only did real income growth stagnate at most levels, with distribution moving against the poorer, the prices of necessities – food, housing and utilities – increased more than those of other goods, and these are items that make up a large part of the budgets of the poor, but only a small part of the budgets of the well-to-do (see Table 1.3).

Table 1.3 *Distribution of family expenditure, 1980*

	% change in prices 1967–80	Low budget families	High budget families
All items	146.8	100.0	100.0
Food	154.6	13.1	20.4
Fuel & utilities	178.6	NA	NA
Housing	163.3	19.6	22.5
Medical care	165.9	9.2	3.9
Rent	91.6	NA	NA
Home purchase	154.3	NA	NA
Home maintainence and repair	185.7	NA	NA

Source: US Department of Commerce, Bureau of Labor Statistics, 'Urban Family Budgets'.

Unionized blue-collar workers were best able to keep up with inflation, up to the Reagan years, when they also fell behind. But non-union workers, whose number rose steadily as a proportion of all workers, fell behind all through the 1970s, and the fastest growing sectors, clerical and services, figured among both the lowest paid and slowest growing (see Table 1.4).

Table 1.4   *Median weekly earnings, full-time workers*

	1979 level $	As % of all workers' median income	% change from 1970	% of all workers
All workers	244	100	88	100
Professional	316	130	75	15
Managers	349	143	84	11
Sales	254	104	91	6
Clerical	195	80	79	18
Craft	303	124	93	13
Operatives, excl. transport	211	86	87	11
Transport operatives	272	111	97	4
Laborers	206	84	87	5
Private household workers	62	25	65	1
Service	164	67	88	12
Farm	157	64	121	1

Source: US Department of Labor, Bureau of Labor Statistics.

Yet another perspective is provided by looking at the relation between compensation, consumption and government transfer payments (see Table 1.5). Without the growth in transfer payments, consumption would undoubtedly have been lower, and the stagnation of the 1970s and early 1980s would have been worse.

Table 1.5   *Compensation, consumption and government transfer payments*

	As a proportion of national income			Transfer payments as percentage of consumption
	Compensation of employees	Transfer payments	Consumption	
1950–65	69.5	6.4	77.0	8.3
1965–80	74.3	11.9	76.9	15.5
1965–70	72.6	8.4	74.8	11.3
1971–75	74.8	12.0	76.8	15.6
1976–80	74.8	13.3	77.9	17.1

Source: US Department of Commerce, Bureau of Economic Analysis.

The inflation of the 1970s was accompanied by stagnating and then declining average real wages and family income, plus a widening of the gap between rich and poor, only partly offset by government transfers. Prices rose faster than money wages on average (particularly for the relatively weak and unorganized), and the prices of the items on which these groups spend the most rose the fastest. These changes all tended to weaken aggregate demand. Let's look at some of the effects.

The slowdown in the growth of consumption

The first thing that stands out in Figure 1.3 is the difference between the behavior of services and that of both durable and non-durable goods. Services grew steadily at a high rate from the late 1950s right on through the 1980s. But non-durables slowed down from the late 1960s until the end of the mid-1970s' recession; they picked up during the Carter years, only to go flat again under Reagan. Durables show a marked sensitivity to the cycle. They grew very fast in the early 1960s, slowed down and slumped in the late 1960s, speeded up in the early 1970s, slumped again, and then went flat after a short rise in the first half of the Carter administration. On the one hand they were volatile; on the other, from the late 1960s to the early 1980s, their growth clearly slowed. (Draw a line from 1958 to 1972, and compare its slope with that of a line from 1972 to 1982. This makes the point quite dramatically.)[6]

A significant implication follows quite directly from these figures: the share of services in total personal comsumption has risen at the expense of manufactured goods. It is important to bear this in mind, for we shall find a similar shift in every major component of aggregate demand, and it signals a change in the nature of the economy. We shall return to this theme.

Figure 1.3   *Annual rate of consumption, 1956–82 (billion 1972 dollars)*

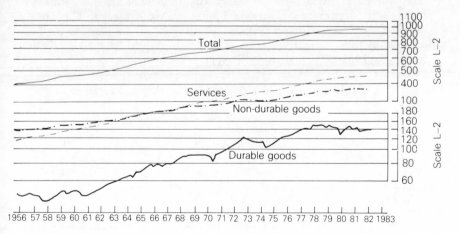

Source: Business Conditions Digest, August 1982

One major element of consumer durables whose behavior is particularly worth noting is the item known as Motor Vehicles and Parts. Its average annual growth rate for five-year periods (with GNP growth for comparison), is shown in Table 1.6. Except for the spurt in the early 1970s (which is misleading since it represents a recovery from a slump), the motor vehicle market has been pulling the growth of the economy down. Moreover, starting in the late 1960s imports began eating into sales quite significantly. In short, after 1965 the automobile sector no longer provided a stimulus to the economy's growth; indeed, it came to be an important cause of the stagnation of the 1970s.

Table 1.6   *Motor Vehicles and Parts*
(average annual growth rate)

		Real GNP
1960–65	7.4	4.7
1965–70	1.9	3.2
1970–75	4.5	2.6
1975–80	2.5	3.7
1980–82	− 4.2	− 0.6

Source: compiled from *Statistical Abstract 1985*.

The change in the balance of trade

As we shall see, investment in US basic structural capacity lagged in 1965–80 and productivity declined, with the result that the competitive position of the US in world markets deteriorated. The favorable balance of trade, previously an important source of stimulus to the US economy, evaporated after the late 1960s. Table 1.7 shows that exports exceeded imports by a wide margin for the entire postwar era until the late 1960s. After that, imports rose more rapidly than exports, so that potential economic growth was sapped, as stagnating individual income (although rising in the aggregate) was used to purchase goods abroad. This shift, moreover, did *not* represent import substitution on the part of trading partners as they 'caught up' with US industry. World trade rose briskly during the 1965–80 period, and US exports rose an average 8.6 per year in

Table 1.7   *Balance of trade as a share of GNP*

	Average annual levels ($ bn.)		BoT as % of
	Balance of trade	GNP	GNP
1950–64	+ 3.756	448.8	0.8
1965–79	− 5.929	1,322.4	− 0.4
Sub-periods:			
1965–69	2.762	812.8	0.3
1970–74	− 2.101	1,203.4	− 0.2
1975–80	− 18.447	1,951.0	− 0.9

Source: Compiled from *National Income and Product Accounts*.

real terms, while increases in economic activity in the major trading partners were somewhat slower: Japan 8–9 per cent, EEC 4–5 per cent, West Germany, 4–5 per cent; Canada 4–5 per cent; developing countries, 7–8 per cent.

Thus, the shift to a deficit in the balance of trade represented substitution of imports for domestic production in the US markets. Imports rose an average 11 per cent per year in real terms over the period. By contrast, real GNP averaged an annual increase of 3.2 per cent. Even without the oil crisis, this pattern would have held: non-petroleum imports averaged a 9 per cent rise per year. In addition, buyers in world markets increasingly purchased goods from countries other than the US. No one worried about the US losing its domestic markets for shoes and textiles. But during the 1970s, major basic industries – autos, steel, electronics, machinery and machine tools – in the US were out-performed by the competition. Better products, at lower prices (despite comparable wage rates and higher social spending and taxes), were offered by German and Japanese producers, not to mention France, Italy or Brazil.

In the 1970s inflation accelerated slowly but steadily, and this, with the weaker balance of payments position of the US, put the dollar in a precarious place, requiring high interest rates and a low level of imports to protect it. By the late 1970s the US could no longer easily manage a booming economy.

From 1951 to 1966 exports and imports as a percentage of GNP remained approximately steady at 4.5 per cent. After 1966 American imports shot up in response to the heated up war economy at an annual rate of 11.3 per cent between 1966 and 1974. This led to decreases in the US current account balance. Whereas in 1965 the US had an $8 billion surplus, by 1972 it had a $5 billion deficit (see Figure 1.4). The US became more dependent upon the international economy at a time when its world hegemony was threatened by defeat in Indochina. By 1974 imports were 9.7 per cent of GNP (see Figure 1.5). Devaluation also brought exports up to 10 per cent of GNP.

However, the worsening of the US balance of trade is not the end of the story. There was, in addition, a shift in the composition of trade. Manufactured exports declined as a percentage of the whole, while services rose. And manufactured imports rose as a percentage of total imports. Thus the net effect was to shift the composition of the balance of trade against manufacturing, a pattern we have seen in consumption, and will shortly find in investment.

Government
Chapter 3 will examine the government's deficit more closely. But it is clear from Figure 1.6 that government spending in real terms ceased to grow at the end of the 1960s, with declining federal spending offsetting slowly growing state and local purchases. Moreover, during the 1970s public construction stagnated and defence spending fell as a proportion of the declining federal expenditure – and, within defence, personnel

Figure 1.4   *Balance of payments on current account, 1951–77*
(billion 1967 dollars)

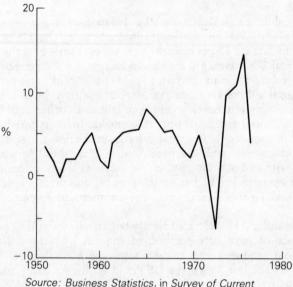

Source: *Business Statistics,* in *Survey of Current Business,* August 1977

Figure 1.5   *Imports/GNP, 1951–77*

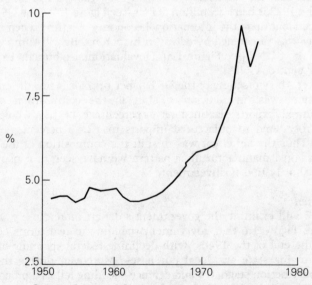

Source: *Survey of Current Business,* May 1977

Figure 1.6   *Government purchases of goods and services, 1956–82*
(annual rate, billion 1982 dollars)

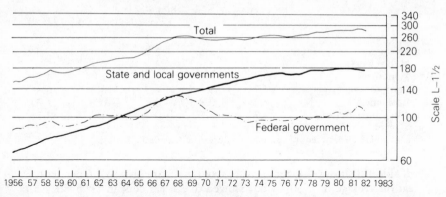

Source: *Business Conditions Digest*, August 1982

expenditure on the volunteer army rose. Hence, in government too there was a shift in spending away from manufacturing towards services.

Now let us turn to the most complex and volatile component of aggregate demand – investment.

Investment growth

Today's investment creates the new factories and offices that, tomorrow, will be able to produce, process and market output, if there is adequate demand. Investment creates potential new employment, which will become actual if and when the new factories are operated. During the time the new factories and offices are being built, the spending on them creates demand for construction materials and labor and for capital equipment. The activity so generated brings employment, and thus additional consumer spending. So, in the long run, investment expands the productive base, while in the immediate term it generates demand. If growth is to be maintained over time, investment has to grow steadily, both to keep the productive base expanding, and to keep demand increasing in step. And this is just what did not happen. In the period 1965–80 the growth of investment slowed markedly. Almost equally important, investment changed in composition, shifting away from factories towards office construction and equipment.

This should not come as a surprise, for we have already seen that market growth in the consumer goods sector was slowing down, and in some cases coming to a standstill. And we have also noted that business was becoming more heavily indebted. Both of these factors would tend to inhibit the growth of investment. And any slowdown in the growth of investment would be reflected in a slowdown of both the growth of output and productivity, because its influence would be felt on both the demand and the supply sides of the market.

Table 1.8 *Real investment*
(average annual growth rate)

	1950–65	1965–80	Sub-periods 1965–70	1970–75	1975–80
Real GNP	3.8	3.2	3.2	2.6	3.7
Gross private investment	3.6	2.6	2.0	0.9	5.0
Non-residential	4.5	3.3	3.2	0.9	5.8
Structures	5.1	1.2	1.6	– 2.7	4.8
Equipment	4.2	4.5	4.2	3.0	6.3
Residential	1.7	0.8	– 0.8	– 0.6	2.7
Public construction	5.7	– 1.8	– 0.9	– 1.7	– 3.1

Source: US Department of Commerce, Bureau of Economic Analysis.

Table 1.8 shows that real private fixed investment rose 3.6 per cent per year on average in 1950–65 but slowed to 2.6 per cent in 1965–80. All of the slowdown came in the structures category. Machinery and equipment investment actually accelerated slightly, but construction of non-residential structures practically levelled off. Within the non-residential structures categories, the mix of structure types shifted (see Table 1.9). The table summarizes the sharp shift in the focus of structural investment. Construction of factories slowed dramatically between 1965 and 1975. In the early part of the postwar period, in contrast, it had led overall investment, rising an average 10 per cent per year in real terms in 1950–65. Factories, it can be argued, provide the basis of a nation's productive capacity, and in the 1950s and 1960s the US was building basic capacity at an impressive clip. After 1965, this building drew practically to a halt. By 1980, real industrial construction stood about 10 per cent *below* its 1965 level. Keep in mind that new construction of facilities (a flow) serves two functions: it provides expansion of existing facilities and replacement for obsolete facilities. Depending on the size and the depreciation rate of the capital stock, a prolonged slowdown in the flow

Table 1.9 *Real investment: non-residential structures*
(average annual growth rate)

	Total	Private Industrial	Commercial office & stores	New public Construction
1950–65	5.1	9.7	8.4	5.7
1965–80	1.2	– 0.6	1.9	– 1.8
Sub-periods				
1965–70	1.6	– 3.4	1.9	– 0.9
1970–75	– 2.7	– 5.1	– 3.7	– 1.7
1975–80	4.8	7.0	7.8	– 3.1

Source: US Department of Commerce, Bureau of Economic Analysis.

of gross industrial investment will end its expansion or even fail to replace scrapped facilities, resulting in a *decline* in the stock of capital.

While the stock of capital is difficult to measure, some samples suggest significant deterioration. The American Machinist inventory of metal-working equipment shows that the percentage of machine tools that are modern has declined steadily since the late 1960s. Only 31 per cent of this machinery was less than ten years old in 1976–78, down from nearly 40 per cent in 1968. Of that 31 per cent, only 10 per cent was less than five years old. Compared with that of major trading partners, US machinery was by far the oldest.

Moreover, sluggish growth in output for industrial *products* suggests that manufacturing productive capacity in basic sectors grew slowly over the period. Steel and auto production were especially weak: steel production rose not at all; auto production rose only half as much as overall GNP.

Public sector construction fell sharply after 1965, threatening deterioration in the nation's infrastructure. By 1980 overall public construction was only three-quarters the 1965 level, while the US economy had grown 60 per cent. The only categories of public construction that rose during the period were industrial projects (a minute amount), and water, sewer, and mass transit projects (including airports). In no case did these expenditures keep pace with overall economic growth. The growing economy created needs for growth in public physical structures and amenities, but these needs were ignored. Deterioration of streets, sewers, and transit systems in the aging metropolises of the North and East were only one side of the coin. Insufficient expansion of public facilities in the boom towns of the South and West left gaps and created headaches. Water supply, sewer lines and sewage disposal, traffic flow, public schools, and public recreational facilities are all insufficient in many of these areas.

As public and industrial construction declined during 1965–80, commercial construction came to the fore. Rising an average 2 per cent per year in 1965–80, this sector continued to expand the nation's stock of office buildings and shopping centers, though at a slower rate than in 1950–65.

By 1980, total non-residential construction (including public construction) was slightly below its 1965 level in real terms. But the changing mix was striking. Government and industrial building were down, and commercial construction up sharply as a share of total (see Table 1.10).

Home-building, another major category of investment, rose more slowly than overall investment throughout the postwar period, even in the much-celebrated construction of America's suburbs during the 1950s and 1960s. But its growth rate dropped by half from the 1950s and 1960s to the 1970s, a further important slowdown in structure building in the US economy.[7]

This pattern of slowing investment growth suggests a picture of maturing markets and decelerating product cycles. This sketch will be filled in as our story unfolds. We shall see an economy that in 1965 had already experienced its fast-growth period of building structures and infrastructure. Investment in these important categories leveled off. Since

Table 1.10 *Value of private and public*
non-residential construction

	1950	1965	1980
Total value (1972 = 100) of non-residential construction ($bn.)	33.7	75.0	74.3
Percent of total			
Industrial	7	12	11
Commercial	9	13	18
Public	43	44	34

Source: US Department of Commerce, Bureau of Economic Analysis.

the economy grew more slowly in the 1970s, we should expect to find investment growth also slowing down. Both, in fact, grew at about 2.5% during the decade. But with the shift in the composition of growth, the structural plant gradually became inadequate to the nation's needs.

Ironically, this has not been apparent. If investment, and thus productive capacity, has been growing too slowly, or in the wrong direction, surely the economy should be straining at the seams, overworking its aging facilities? But the very decisions not to embark on extensive new investment projects have further slowed the growth of the economy, by causing layoffs and unemployment, which cut into demand. Investment, perversely, seems too much for being too little. And, with slower growth, existing capacity – or current growth rates of capacity – seem adequate or more than adequate. Excess capacity, then, emerges in periods of slow growth. So managers congratulate themselves: they were right, growth of demand has been slower than previously, and large new plants would have proved to be embarrassing excess capacity.

So the major components of aggregate demand – consumption, foreign trade, government purchases and investment – have all both stagnated and shifted in composition away from manufacturing towards services.

Let us now look at the results, starting with profits.

The profit squeeze
Measurement of profit is notoriously difficult. There are profits before and after taxes, before and after inventory valuation adjustments, before and after depreciation, and, of course, before and after inflation. Moreover, the cyclical variation in profits is very large, so year to year comparisons can be misleading. Table 1.11 shows growth rates from business cycle peaks (1948–66) and from troughs in recent recessions.

Real net profits fell sharply from 1965 to 1970, staged a moderate recovery in 1970–75, but again fell behind overall GNP growth in 1975–80. Moreover, despite some recovery during the 1970s, the sharp erosion in 1965–70 left corporations even in 1980 below the mid-1960s' level of real net profits.

The rate of profit apparently declined as well (Table 1.12). Again, measurement problems are legion; profits as a percentage of what?

Table 1.11   *Growth and profits*

	Profits ($bn.)		Real (1972 = 100)		Average annual growth rate from previous period (%)		
	Nominal		Real (1972 = 100)		Real profits		Real GNP
	Gross	Net	Gross	Net	Gross	Net	
1948	35.6	17.0	67.2	32.0	—	—	
1966	83.0	51.4	108.1	67.0	2.7	4.2	4.0
1967	79.9	49.4	100.8	63.1	− 6.8	− 5.8	2.7
1970	75.4	37.2	82.5	40.7	− 6.5	− 13.6	
							2.4
1975	132.1	59.9	105.2	47.7	5.0	3.2	2.6
1980	245.5	100.4	138.4	56.6	5.6	3.5	3.7

Note: *Gross profits is before taxes, before inventory valuation adjustment, before capital consumption adjustment. Net profits is after those adjustments.
Source: Statistical Abstract 1985.

Perhaps the best denominator is the current replacement value of depreciable assets. In any case, business peaked in the mid-1960s and weakened after the late 1960s. The rate of profit leveled off in the 1970s at about 8 per cent, down from 12 per cent in the late 1960s and 9 per cent before that.

But perhaps these numbers indicating levels and rates of profits are deceptive. Since profits are highly volatile, even a careful examination of growth rates from comparable business cycle points may obscure the true progress in business profits. However, similar conclusions can be drawn from the average share of income that went to net corporate profits in the postwar period (Table 1.13). Here again we see in the late 1960s a sharp erosion in profits, which averaged 6.6 per cent of income between 1950 and 1965, but fell to 4.6 per cent of income in the early 1970s. Some recovery in the late 1970s still left the profit share significantly below the historical average. Within this overall pattern sectoral differences are striking. Financial and service industries posted respectable profit growth, keeping pace with the growth of the economy. The manufacturing and utilities sectors, however, fell far behind even the lackluster performance of profits in general. Steel and autos were, not suprisingly, at the bottom of the list.

Table 1.12   *After-tax rates of return:*
non-financial corporations (%)

	Return on depreciable assets	Return on stockholders' equity
1955–65	9.2	5.8
1965–79	9.4	7.3
Sub-periods:		
1965–69	12.2	8.4
1970–74	8.1	6.9
1975–79	8.0	6.6

Source: US Department of Commerce, Bureau of Economic Analysis.

Table 1.13   *Profits as a share of income*

	Gross profits	*Average annual levels (current $bn.)* Net profits	National income	*Profits as % of income* Gross	Net
1950–65	50.3	25.3	381.7	13.2	6.6
1966–80	138.5	65.5	1,178.5	11.8	5.5
Sub-periods:					
1966–70	82.7	46.8	720.6	11.5	6.5
1971–75	116.3	52.6	1,064.0	9.3	4.6
1976–80	216.6	95.7	1,750.8	12.4	5.5

Source: US Department of Commerce, Bureau of Economic Analysis.

What did this mean for business? The pool of earnings available for investment became smaller relative to the size of the economy. Businesses scrambled for loans to finance their investment projects; and they planned more conservatively, calculating that the prospective growth of sales and the return to investment were shrinking. While 5.0 per cent (average profit share for the 1970s) may look similar in magnitude to 6.5 per cent, it is really only three-quarters as large!

With the stagnation of profits came a progressive erosion of the financial position of US corporations (Table 1.14). The proportion of investments financed by retained earnings fell from two-thirds to less than 60 per cent during the 1965–80 period. Naturally, this implies a sharp increase in borrowing relative to the growth of capital stock. The level of current assets relative to current liabilities deteriorated significantly after 1965. Corporations had their current liabilities 'covered' only 1.5–1.6 times by current assets in 1965–80, down from 2 in 1950–65. Moreover, in recent years much of the increase in borrowing has been in short-term paper. The increasing financial fragility of the basic economic structure of the US shows clearly.

Table 1.14   *Sources of corporate finance (%)*

	Internal funds	Short-term loans	Current ratio[a]	
1950–64	66.7	6.2	1950–59	1.897
1965–80	57.6	12.1	1960–65	1.981
Sub-periods:				
1965–69	59.4	11.2	1966–70	1.732
1970–74	55.9	13.4	1971–74	1.564
1975–79	57.5	11.7	1974–79	1.608

[a] Current assets divided by current liabilities. 1950–59 for all corporations; subsequently for non-financial corporations. There is a break in the series in 1974. Adjusted to be consistent with earlier data, the current ratio for 1974–80 would be about 1.470.

Sources: Federal Reserve Board, Federal Trade Commission, Securities and Exchange Commission.

Corporate debt

Let's look more closely at the changing debt/equity ratio of American corporations. If funds for increased investments could not be generated internally through profits, then they had to be borrowed. This borrowing continued a long-term trend. Real corporate debts had risen at an annual rate of 5.9 per cent between 1971 and 1975. Corporate debt as a percentage of national income was 70 per cent in 1951, but by 1975 it had risen to 79 per cent. Even more spectacular was the rise in corporate debt as a percentage of total debt: in 1951 this was 32 per cent, and by 1975 it had risen to 47 per cent (see Figure 1.7).

The increased debt to equity ratio of American corporations made them more vulnerable to external shocks. First, a high percentage of corporate income was needed to pay interest on their loans. Whereas in 1951 only 1 per cent of national income consisted of net interest, by 1975 this figure had risen to 6 per cent. The effect of the increased debt structure can best be viewed by looking at the corporate liquidity ratio. This consists of cash and government securities that the corporations possess divided by current liabilities. In 1951 this figure stood at 55 per cent and by 1974 it had dropped to 17 per cent (see Figure 1.8).

The economic structure of American corporations now resembled a house of cards. Any large default could set off a round of loan recalls and further defaults that might cause the whole structure to collapse (a near disaster followed the Penn Central bankruptcy). By the mid-1970s a liquidity crisis had become potentially more dangerous than the problem that increased borrowing was supposed to have alleviated – the crisis in profits. In fact, the potential financial problem made it even more necessary to increase profits, since only by increasing profits could corporations continue to service their massive debts safely.

Capacity utilization: down or up?

Not only did the rebuilding and expansion of productive capacity languish

Figure 1.7   *Corporate debt/total debt, 1951–76*

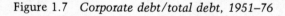
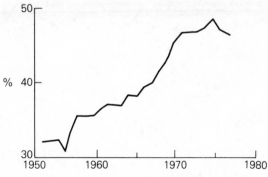

Sources: Business Statistics: 20th Edition and
Survey of Current Business, August 1976

Figure 1.8   *Corporate liquidity ratio, 1951–76*

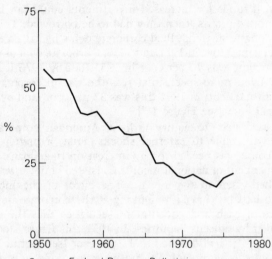

Source: Federal Reserve Bulletin

during the 1970s, but its rate of current utilization also turned down after the high point of the late 1960s. This was probably accompanied by a progressive deterioration in plants and equipment. There is some evidence of a rise in the age of equipment, particularly in machine tools. This helps to account for the decline in the growth of productivity (see Figure 1.9).

However, the two most widely cited measures of capacity utilization do not agree (see Table 1.15). The Federal Reserve Board's measure of capacity utilization shows production intensity peaking in the late 1960s (91.1 per cent in 1966), and levelling off, in the 1970s, nearly 10

Figure 1.9   *Capacity utilization and growth rates, 1955–80*

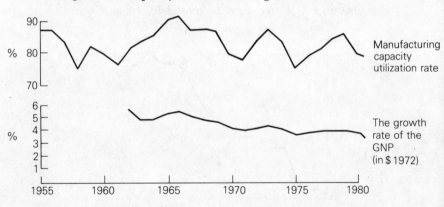

Sources: US Department of Commerce, Bureau of Economic Analysis, Federal Reserve Board, Federal Reserve Board of St. Louis

Table 1.15 *Capacity utilization in manufacturing (%)*

	Federal Reserve Board	Wharton	
1950–59	84.0	83.9	(1954–59)
1960–64	81.6	76.8	
1965–69	88.1	87.6	
1970–74	82.5	87.2	
1975–79	80.8	86.6	
1980–81[a]	78.8	86.0	

[a] 1980–81 levels (business cycle trough) should not be compared to the five-year averages, which encompass entire business cycles. For example, the 1975 level (FRB) was 73%.

Source: Federal Reserve Board; Wharton Econometrics.

percentage points below its late 1960s level. The extraordinarily high level of capacity utilization in the late 1960s, applied to a capital stock that had undergone extensive modernization and expansion during the investment boom of 1950–65, helped generate the very high profits and high rates of profit in those years. The Wharton series, on the other hand, shows no decline in capacity utilization during the 1970s. What do these divergent data series mean?

The Federal Reserve measure of capacity utilization combines three kinds of information. Survey results show business judgements of their utilization of capacity, and data on industrial production fill in gaps between surveys. Then information on real investment is used to corroborate or to revise business estimates of available capacity.

The Wharton series uses only industrial production data. Capacity utilization is estimated to peak when the economy is running full steam, so that backlogs of orders are rising. Though surveyed managers may assert that their factories are not fully utilized, as a practical matter they cannot step up production. For the Wharton series, it is not important whether the blockage comes because of skilled worker shortages, slow delivery of inputs, or obsolete or mismatched equipment (which managers may nevertheless *call* productive capacity). So when business cannot increase production – as shown by the fact that business *does not* increase production despite rising demand – Wharton considers this to be full practical capacity utilization.

There are merits and difficulties on both sides. On the one hand, Wharton begs the question by assuming that business cycle peak production equals full capacity production. Business planners may decide not to expand production because they mistrust the sales indicators, so keep actual utilization rates below potential. On the other hand, counting practically unusable capacity as viable, as the FRB apparently does, is questionable. For example, think back to 1973–early 74, when basic materials shortages and bottlenecks abounded, and production could not in practice be expanded in many sectors of the economy. Capacity utilization measured 87.6 per cent by FRB methods, 92.6 per cent for Wharton. For Wharton, capacity utilization was higher in 1973 than in any year during the 1960s. For FRB, it was down from a 1966 high point of 91.1 per cent.

What is intriguing, though, is the increasing divergence between these two series. It seems that a growing proportion of US productive capacity is practically unusable, for reasons that include the rising age of capital stock, a growing mismatch between available and necessary labor skills, the fact that much capital stock is non-competitive at high energy prices. These trends are ominous for the US economy. And they may all be symptoms of a larger structural problem.

Productivity
Along with the overall slowdown and increasing instability came a sharp slowdown in the growth of productivity. Employment growth accelerated in the 1970s, concentrated in services (employment did not grow at all in manufacturing). So per-employee GNP rose far more slowly in the 1970s than in the 1950s and 1960s. Labor productivity (real output per hour worked) rose an average 3 per cent per year in 1950–65, and slowed to only half that in 1965–80. Over the business cycle 1975–1980, productivity inched up an average 1 per cent per year. Although productivity growth slowed throughout the industrialized world, nowhere (except the UK) was the slowdown so pronounced as in the US.

As investment lagged, productive capacity on average became less modern, and capacity utilization eased; so it is not surprising that productivity growth declined. Indeed, it is remarkable that productivity continued to grow at all.

At this point we can see some of the connections between these various economic variables. In a development capitalist industrial system, productivity growth depends less on worker morale and effort than on new technology and equipment. It is true, of course, that workers can stage a go-slow or strike; but it is usually less true that they can, just by working harder, speed things up. Industrial systems are designed to operate reliably, minimizing human error and variability in performance. In addition, under capitalism, they are designed to control the labor

Table 1.16 *Productivity (average annual growth rate)*

	Real GNP	Total employment	GNP per employee	Productivity (real output per hour worked)[a]
1950–65	3.8	1.3	2.9	3.0
1965–80	3.2	2.3	1.4	1.6
Sub-periods:				
1965–70	3.2	2.0	1.6	1.9
1970–75	2.6	1.8	1.4	1.9
1975–80	3.7	3.2	1.2	0.9

[a] Shifting industry composition accounts for the divergence between productivity growth and the simple measure of growth of GNP per employee.
Source: US Department of Commerce, Bureau of Economic Analysis, Bureau of Labor Statistics.

process and to establish 'work norms'. Hence, so far as capitalism is successful in developing industrial technology along the lines it desires, worker attitudes can be expected to affect productivity growth relatively little, while investment should affect it a great deal.

So, if the productivity of a firm depends on that firm's investments (new plants, embodying superior technology, will be more productive than old, raising the average for the firm), then its *growth* of productivity should depend on its investment growth. So the growth of productivity for the economy as a whole should depend on the rate of growth (not on the level) of aggregate investment. Since this has slowed down since the late 1960s, becoming nearly zero at times in the 1970s, and has shifted away from industrial plant, this could well explain the corresponding slowdown and collapse in productivity growth.

Supply or Demand?

To make a long story short, our investigation into what happened in the 1970s, comparing that decade with earlier ones, shows that the chief feature was a slowing down in the growth of demand – for consumer durables, for US exports, for factories – combined with a shift in the composition of demand away from manufacturing. This led to underutilization of capacity and to a slowdown in the growth of productivity, which combined to squeeze profits, leading to a precarious rise in corporate indebtedness, further inhibiting investment. All of these factors weakened the US vis-à-vis its competitors, and made it more susceptible to supply shocks.

On this interpretation, the chief explanation of the crisis of the 1970s lies on the demand side. By contrast, the accounts we canvassed earlier all found the principal factors on the supply side. For example, monetarists pinpoint labor supply reactions to policy-induced inflation; Keynesians regard supply shocks as the starting point of a chain of misguided policy decisions; Marxists explain the crisis by the falling rate of profit, which results from the competitive response to technological change; and radicals point to the breakdown of the accumulation accords that they consider central to labor supply and productivity growth.

Many of the points made by these schools are surely valid, and must be included in a full account of the slowdown of the 1970s. However, by overlooking the decline in the growth of demand, together with the correlative shift away from manufacturing, all have failed to come to grips with the central dynamic of the era.

How could this happen? How could major schools of thought all fail to bring the core of the problem into focus? If our approach is correct, the core problem is Keynesian: it is a slowdown of the growth of effective demand, leading to a slowdown in investment growth and in technical progress, as manifested in productivity growth. Yet, although the problem is Keynesian, it is located at one of the weakest points in Keynesian theory. For there is no theory of the *growth* of demand, that is, of the growth and development of new markets. Nor is there an agreed-upon approach to the development of new technologies and their influence on investment. Keynesian growth theory explains increments in demand by the multiplier effects of induced investment – where the additional investment is in turn induced by some unexplained rise in spending. So it explains changes in demand by changes in demand. It gives no account, for example, of how markets are expanded by new groups of consumers, or of how new products are brought into the consumption patterns of representative households. If such changes in demand happened on an economy-wide scale they would noticeably affect aggregate demand. But this is an area Keynesian thinking has not explored.

Finally, of course, the major currents of economic thought in the past two decades have been running against Keynes. The fashionable theories left and right, from Marxist to rational expectations, have all been supply-side. These factors could account for a widespread tendency to overlook demand questions, but this just answers one question with another: why has the Keynesian approach been left undeveloped, and then abandoned?

Notes

1 For the Keynesian view, see Blinder (1979) and Bruno and Sachs (1985). Conservative views are presented in Friedman (1973) and in Barro (1986), a textbook that favorably contrasts the work of Lucas and Sargent and the rational expectations school with both Keynesian and earlier monetarist thinking. For a critique see Hahn (1984) or Nell (1984a). The post-Keynesian position is set forth in Weintraub (1978), and in many articles in the *Journal of Post-Keynesian Economics*.
2 For a good presentation, see Bowles, Gordon and Weisskopf (1987).
3 A classic presentation, which, however, also stresses over-production, can be found in Mandel (1978). See also Shaikh (1984).
4 See Steedman (1977) and Nell (1980a).
5 From 1945 to 1949 over $27 billion in Veterans' benefits were paid out, principally to recently demobilized GIs, enabling them to obtain qualifications, take out mortgages, buy cars and other consumer durables and generally establish themselves. This came on top of a substantial increase in the share of private wages and salaries in domestic business product during the war, rising from about 46.5 per cent in the late 1930s to about 50 per cent in the early 1950s, remaining near that level until the late 1970s and early 1980s, when it sinks to about 48.5 per cent.
6 Clear as these figures are, they tell only part of the story. Services overtakes non-durables in the mid-1960s, and by the mid-1980s just about equals the sum of durables and non-durables. But the categories are a little misleading: for example, fast foods, one of the most rapidly growing industries, is classified under non-durables, although from our perspective they should be counted under services. This reinforces the picture of sluggishness in both durables and non-durables. But from the point of view of effective demand the growth of services does *not* offset this sluggishness. The largest component of the category of services in this National Income and Product Accounts series is the imputed value of the services of owner-occupied housing; when this is removed, the growth of consumer demand shows clear weakness starting in the early 1970s.

7 Gross private domestic investment in 1972 dollars reached $237 billion in 1978, and then lay below that for each of the next five years. The value of new construction of all types peaked at $199 billion in 1973, measured in 1977 dollars, and never came within $20 billion of that figure in the next decade. New housing starts of all types peaked at 2.4 million in 1972, and averaged under 1.5 million for the next decade.

2

The Breakup of the Keynesian Consensus

'We are all Keynesians now.'
[Richard M. Nixon]

On the whole, major political parties, even less than people, are loath to commit suicide. Yet, after a decade of economic difficulties, the Democrats tried to win an election by promising to raise taxes! After the New Deal and the Fair Deal, after the New Frontier and the Great Society – they offered the Balanced Budget! Previously liberals had argued that deficits mattered very little, certainly less than full employment, social justice or rapid growth. Even President Nixon learned the lesson well enough to expand the economy before the election of 1972, and he was willing to use controls to prevent inflation getting out of hand. By 1984, or even earlier, everyone favored austerity and cutbacks. What led liberals to adopt a policy stance that was a proven loser? And how did public opinion go from Nixon's position to a widespread agreement that Keynesian economics is outmoded, passé, if not just plain mistaken?

The Keynesian consensus didn't just passively evaporate; events took their toll by interacting with internal tensions that had threatened it even at the best of times. None the less, in the 1970s the consensus theory – 'the grand neo-Classical synthesis' – didn't seem to explain what was happening and the preferred policies didn't seem to work. To understand this we shall have to review the main features of the Keynesian approach to economic policy, and then look at the way economic policy in the late 1970s responded to the slowdown of the economy.

Expansionist Policies and Controls

Underlying the Keynesian approach there has always been a kind of pragmatic liberalism, which centered on the belief that social conflict could be avoided or mitigated by managing the economy properly. First, create prosperity by ensuring full employment; everyone who wants a job should be able to find one, not necessarily their ideal, but decent work for decent pay. And instead of quarreling over income shares – slices of the pie – workers and management should cooperate in order to make the pie grow bigger. That way everyone can have more. So the basic Keynesian objective in managing the economy has always been to produce full employment and growth, even at the risk of a little inflation.

However, this was not to be done through planning or central direction. Keynesians accepted the idea that the economy was basically a market system, and they further accepted orthodox theory as a valid account of how that system worked. Macroeconomics should rest on a firm foundation of microeconomics. Which implies, disastrously, that they accepted the idea that, in principle, a market system produced socially optimal results under ideal, and therefore unrealistic, conditions. In practice, since actual conditions would normally be far from ideal, such a system needed to be corrected from time to time through appropriate government policies. These were of two kinds: on the one hand, there were fiscal policies, i.e. taxing and spending, which could stimulate or dampen aggregate demand (total sales); on the other hand were monetary policies, which involve setting interest rates and controlling bank lending and the availability of credit. Easy money will encourage investment and expansion, and, for that reason, inflation, while tight money will tend to bring on hard times. In addition, direct controls might be used from time to time, but only as a last resort. The market should be respected, and intervention should take place only when clearly necessary. (This left the orthodox Keynesians in an inherently weak position vis-à-vis anyone, e.g. the monetarists, who could plausibly claim that it was Keynesian interventions that, in fact, prevented the market from achieving optimal outcomes.)

Now recall the position of the economy in the second half of the 1970s. Growth had slowed down and unemployment had risen, while inflation seemed out of control. Yet, from the Keynesian perspective, inflation and unemployment should not occur together; inflation results when demand pressure has reduced unemployment to the minimum, so that businesses, because of high sales, are trying to produce more and are competing for additional workers, bidding up wages, which are reflected in higher prices. If this was correct, how could inflation and unemployment both be rising?

Moreover, the dollar, hitherto the basic currency of international trade, had begun to sag precariously, reflecting the new weakness of much American business in international markets. Again something was wrong; the dollar was supposed to function as the reserve currency. It should not itself have become, or have been allowed to become, the target of speculation. The working of the economy seemed in many ways to signal the end of an era. Some argued that the very policies that had helped to sustain prosperity through the 1950s and 1960s had undermined the ability of the economy to function properly in the long run, so that by the 1970s, underlying weaknesses, exacerbated by Keynesian policies, had begun to show through, making the economy now more difficult to control. Government policy could no longer rely on market stimulation, or on 'moral suasion', 'jawboning', and the like. It seemed to presage a choice between well-funded and well-planned controls, or a return to the free market – every man for himself, and hope for the best. (Yet without regulation, liberals argued, the free market would prey upon the weakest, just as has been happening under President Reagan.)

In response to these developments, President Carter, who opposed controls, adopted an increasingly conservative 'pro-business' stance, gradually abandoning the Keynesian position. This brought him into direct conflict with the liberal, Kennedy wing of the Democratic Party.

Kennedy and his allies proposed a strong expansionist program, coupled with wage and price controls, an incomes policy and considerable government direction of investment. But this policy package had no clear-cut formula for dealing with the weakness of the dollar, nor did it have a convincing plan for dealing with the changing competitive position of US industry in the world economy. True, many liberals supported 'industrial policies', schemes for providing help to 'sunrise' industries and relocation and retooling help to capital and labor in 'sunset' sectors. But which industries are sunrise and which sunset? And who is to decide? In addition, the experience with controls under Nixon had not been happy. The Carter–Kennedy primary was fought in large part over the best way to strengthen the economy – to expand or to retrench – and Mondale, of course, firmly sided with Carter: the way to get the economy moving again was to eliminate impediments and interferences, that is to say, to cut back on Big Government, to deregulate. So both Carter and Mondale opposed Reagan, not on principle, but as a matter of method and degree, and both supported tax increases and austerity – in marked contrast to Reagan, who stood for tax cuts and free-market, rather than Keynesian, expansion.

In the conditions of the past decade, a Keynesian expansionist policy would imply regulations limiting the ability of capital to move overseas; it would also mean more controls over banking, especially international banking. Regulation and controls on an unprecedented scale for peacetime would very likely have been necessary to defend the dollar if a traditional, low-interest/easy money, deficit-driven expansionist policy had been followed. Under the inflationary conditions of the late 1970s such an expansion would have sucked in imports, creating a large and growing external deficit, which would have triggered speculation against the dollar. The low interest rates, pegged to stimulate domestic investment, home-building and car sales, would have provided no defense against (and might have encouraged) the flight of short-term capital, because capital movements, and, as we shall see, exchange rates, depend on international interest rate differentials.

Thus a Kennedy-style expansionist program required a willingness to impose controls – price controls, import controls and controls over the movement of capital. Wartime experience has shown that such controls are not only feasible, but when adequately funded and administered can work very well. Of course controls mean government bureaucracy, but, as anyone who has tried to collect an insurance claim knows, private bureaucracies also exist and also require your forms in triplicate. We live in the age of bureaucracy, private as much as public, Big Business as well as Big Government.

Business is none the less adamantly opposed to controls, and not only for ideological reasons: controls limit the scope for profit-making – price controls interfere with the freedom of business to plan its prices and take advantage of the possibilities in its markets; import controls interfere with the freedom to buy the cheapest or best goods; and capital controls prevent business from moving money around to take advantage of the best investment opportunities. Business has always disliked controls, but has put up with them when necessary, in return for expansion and high profits. In the 1970s, however, vast changes began taking place in the international economy. New global markets opened, while new technologies operating in newly industrializing countries made it possible to produce on a global scale. Production processes in Singapore or Hong Kong could be coordinated from Detroit – but without Detroit wage levels. In these new circumstances business felt that it had to be free to experiment and search out the most profitable ways of producing and marketing on a world scale. Thus a traditional expansionist policy meant heading for a major collision with Big Business. Kennedy was apparently willing to try it; Carter instead opted for trying to control inflation by retrenchment and monetary restraint.

Retrenchment came gradually. At first, Carter tried an expansionary program, but this ran into trouble, and so he cut back, to keep down imports and combat inflation. It looked like 'stop–go', familiar from Britain and other European economies. ('Stop–go' is standard political Keynesianism: the economy is set to 'go' shortly before election time, with easy money and a fiscal stimulus, and then after the votes are counted the stimulus is curbed, so that inflation does not get out of hand.)[1] Moreover, Carter's job program under the Comprehensive Employment and Training Act was quite successful and firmly in the tradition of the New Deal. However, the new program in the second half of the Carter Administration in fact marked a major policy shift. Almost without noticing, the traditional liberal commitment to expansion and full employment was abandoned, and fiscal policy was down-played in favor of a redefined monetary policy, in which the pegging of interest rates was set aside in order to concentrate (not very successfully) on the control of monetary aggregates.

The reason: in the policy vacuum created by the collapse of the Keynesian consensus, monetarists had convinced the administration that the key to curbing inflation lay in controlling the money supply; and inflation had come to be perceived as the most serious problem facing the economy. We shall see later that this wholly misunderstood the character of the inflation, but at least it was taking action, and it was clear from the polls that the American public was fed up. The way was open for Reagan and the supply-siders.

The Liberal Compromise with Monetarism

The changes in the working of the economy in the last decade have created problems for an expansionist policy. We shall examine these in a moment. But first let's consider what we can call the 'neo-liberal' compromise: partial retrenchment and monetary restraint – financial prudence, but not full-fledged monetarism, – while maintaining a more than token commitment to fair shares for all. This position is much more important than Carter or Mondale; it is the basis of a new version of liberalism, which would like to move still further in the direction of deregulation and support for entrepreneurial initiatives, affirming a belief in the self-regulating and socially optimal market. It's not that such liberals oppose government initiatives on principle; it's rather that they think, pragmatically, that private enterprise is likely to do the job better. However, the heart of the matter is that the new liberals reject Keynesianism – what economists call 'demand management' – as the cornerstone of government economic policy. Let's see why.

Monetarists have advanced a simple, definite and superficially plausible explanation for the simultaneous appearance of unemployment and inflation in the 1970s: consumers, workers and business people were catching on to what the government was up to. Since the market system naturally tends towards a certain equilibrium, government intervention can push the system to some other point only by creating false expectations; as soon as people catch on the system will slip back to its 'natural' position. Usually governments are trying to reduce unemployment, for example by expanding the money supply, leading to higher prices, which if there are misperceptions and/or false expectations, will lead to lower real wages and an increase in employment – until people catch on. And sooner or later people *will* catch on, and unemployment will go back up again. But there would be one lasting effect: the government intervention (trying to reduce unemployment) would necessarily leave the system with a larger money supply, and therefore a higher price level. In other words, inflation.

So what should be done? First, the budget should be balanced; second, the money supply should be closely controlled, and its growth should be set at a fixed rate; and, thirdly, business should be deregulated, to provide as much incentive as possible to expansion and to innovation. There are many varieties of monetarism, but I think all will agree on these basic tenets.

And what have liberals said to all this? They have responded that, while it may be true that free markets reach a full employment equilibrium (an equilibrium with a 'natural' rate of unemployment, reflecting market 'frictions', e.g. the desire of some workers to change jobs), the forces making for this are weak and need to be helped along by the government. So, in fact, it seems there is no very great disagreement in theory; it all boils down to what works best. In the 1960s this had been enough of a reply, but in the 1970s Keynesian theories did not seem to explain things, and Keynesian policies did not seem to work. So the Carter administration, from a certain point of view sensibly enough, gradually shifted from a Keynesian to a more conservative position, in fact to an endorsement of austerity policies. And this shift had some very significant consequences.

Implications of Neo-liberal Austerity

First, liberals and neo-liberals, left in a 'me-too' position, failed to ask some important and obvious questions. Yes, we must balance the budget (but at whose expense?); yes, we must cut wages to stop inflation (why not prices?); yes, we must lift the burden of regulation off the backs of our entrepreneurs (and let them poison our air, and dump chemical wastes in the water we drink?). The traditional liberal position had always put full employment, progressive taxation, subsidies to deserving (and not-so-deserving) businesses, and the elimination of poverty ahead of the alleged benefits of the free market, let alone those of austerity.

Second, since the New Deal, liberals have appeared as common-sense defenders of the people. Businesses are out to make money, so they will cut corners where they can. And that often means unsafe working conditions, or pollution of the environment that all of us share. But who is going to stop them, if we don't have watch-dog government agencies, well-trained and well-funded, armed with the necessary legal powers? That is how the New Deal Democrats told it; that's what Harry Truman meant when he said 'the buck stops here'; that's why the Environmental Protection Agency and the Occupational Safety and Health Administration were set up. But neo-liberals say regulations will destroy incentives (the traditional argument of their opponents); some even call the former liberal stance 'one-sided'. (One-sided? it was the liberal side – conservatives supported the other side!)

Third, concern for fairness in the distribution of income and wealth sometimes seems to have disappeared in the thinking of the neo-liberals. Everyone wants to be a character in *Dallas* or *Dynasty*, super-rich, super-exploiters; fair shares and equality of opportunity are boring. Certainly the climate of opinion has changed. But the ideal of fairness is deeply rooted in the American psyche. And so is distrust of the rich and powerful. Moreover, great inequalities engender great social frictions, and ensure a great waste of natural talents. Yet nothing much can be made of these points if the liberal position on the economy uncritically accepts the need for retrenchment.

Fourth, the neo-liberal position simply abandons the traditional interests of the established and hitherto prosperous industrial working class. Of course, it usually favors an industrial policy, government planning to assist 'sunrise' industries, while helping 'sunset' industries to shift their resources into other areas – retraining and relocating labor, converting factories to newer uses, and so on. And some neo-liberals even advocate limited protectionist measures – domestic content rules, for instance. But they draw the line at full employment brought about by government stimulus whenever the market sags, i.e. deficit spending along with controls to prevent inflation and runs on the dollar.

By embracing traditional sound finance and fiscal rectitude, liberals left open the possibility of a Republican pro-business *expansionist* position, which could capture a large part of their common-sense, pocket-book appeal: if there's a deficit because government is spending on important things, or cutting taxes for good reason, then the deficit will probably stimulate the economy, and eventually make it possible to grow out of it.

Growth had been the province of liberals once upon a time, when it had meant growth in incomes, employment and standards of living (not to romanticize: what they stood for and what they actually did often diverged). By contrast, when the conservative talks about 'growth', he usually means growth in *profits*, accumulation of capital. Of course, the rationalization is that, if business is profitable, then (eventually, somehow) everyone will benefit. With profits up, there will in the long run be more output and more employment, since with higher profits savings will be greater, so investment can be increased. And so on. This 'trickle-down' theory rests on the mistaken view that savings governs investment, which is not the way a modern industrial economy works. However, it is hard to argue this starting from the position that government must be cut back in order to liberate the forces of the market, and that retrenchment is necessary to restore the economy's health.

Now let us turn to the question of why such an about-face in liberal policy thinking should have such appeal today, when it clearly has considerable political costs. One major reason is simply that it has seemed correct, the right or responsible position to take. Keynesian thinking had come to seem outmoded, out of touch with the new realities of contemporary capitalism. The main Keynesian gurus no longer seemed invincible; they suffered a major defeat at the hands of the left in the 'capital theory controversy',[2] and they didn't appear to have their fingers on the pulse of the economy any more. New issues had arisen, new themes sounded, and the old ideas seemed full of cobwebs, ready to be swept away. On top of this, changes in the world economy led business to some new concerns, which did not fit at all comfortably with Keynesian interventionism. Let's first consider the decline of Keynesianism, and then the changes in the world economy.

The Weakness of the Keynesian Position

In the late 1960s, monetarists mounted a major attack on Keynesian theory, basically centering on the idea that, if prices are flexible, free markets will necessarily reach equilibrium by themselves. (We have seen that orthodox Keynesians accepted this.) Every market can be described by a supply curve rising from left to right and a demand curve falling from left to right, so they will intersect, determining absolute quantities and relative prices. (A full explanation will be given in Chapter 4.) This means that total output and total employment are determined. The Quantity Theory of Money then tells us the general price level, once we know the policy of the central bank, which fixes the money supply. With all this being settled by the market, there is very little left for the government to do. Hence government intervention will either be trivial, just helping the free market along, or it will actually make everyone worse off by forcing the system to some disequilibrium position. In fact just this was happening, monetarists claimed: government intervention was pushing the system to over-full employment, setting off an inflationary spiral. The battle was intensified by the emergence of the Rational Expectations School, who argued that rational agents would be motivated to discover the underlying economic theory and would then move at once to the equilibrium position (if it existed), so that there would be no need at all for government to help things along. Government policy would be completely ineffective, even in the short run.

The Keynesian response to this has to be judged weak. The trouble lay in the fact that the Keynesians wanted a compromise that would avoid an open break with the dominant theory, allowing them to stay in the fold, so to speak. They wanted to accept the main conclusions of traditional price theory – for example that prices adjust when demand changes or that in a competitive equilibrium welfare will be at a maximum – while arguing that in practice government intervention will be necessary.[3] Keynesian theory then became a kind of disequilibrium economics. It consisted in more and more elaborate analysis of the basic model, showing again and again that various special but realistic circumstances and features – transaction costs, long-term contracts, search time – would make it possible for government policies to have a significant impact, in spite of the points raised by conservative critics. Many of these analyses were brilliant; most were correct, theoretically. As a practical matter, it was obvious that government policies usually had their intended impact, although it became more and more apparent that they had unintended ones, too. But while the conservatives may have lost most of the battles, they won the war. The political or ideological component of economic theory remained intact: a free-market capitalist system, under perfect conditions, would indeed be optimal (actually, careful analysis qualifies this conclusion nearly to death). In free competitive markets, as traditionally conceived, prices will adjust so as to bring output and employment to their full employment levels. Unemployment must be due to one kind or another of imperfection, and the effectiveness of government policy therefore depends on that imperfection. But the need for any intervention at all could be eliminated by removing the imperfection.

This leads to the important and very traditional proposition, already mentioned (and first set forth by the Benthamites, then fully articulated by John Stuart Mill): government intervention should take place only where it is apparent that there has been a clear failure of the market. The presumption is that the market will work, and that if it does the outcome will be superior (in some sense) to what government or a planning agency would do. Both orthodox Keynesians and their monetarist opponents share this view, although they differ in their interpretations both of 'market failure' and of the relative effectiveness of different policies, among many other things.

This compromise has both left Keynesians vulnerable to the monetarist counter-attack, and prevented them from understanding the decline in the growth of demand. Indeed, since mainstream Keynesian thinking has largely accepted the traditional theory of supply and demand, it has never considered the problem of the long-term growth of markets. By default, therefore, the mainstream position on growth has prevailed; and the neo-Classical approach holds that, in the long run, capital accumulation depends on saving! That is, in the long run savings will determine investment. But why should businesses build factories or set up offices, to the value of a certain amount of money (or proportion of GNP), just because households and institutions have refrained from spending that amount of money (or proportion of GNP)? Saving is refraining from spending; it is just as passive in the long run as it is in the short. Investment is undertaken because business needs more productive capacity, not because it has more savings on hand. But why is more capacity needed? There's no point in building additional factories unless there's good evidence that what they produce will be sold; so business will invest only if it thinks that the market is going to expand or that the new factories will out-perform the old so well that they can capture their markets. In other words, the reason for an investment is that capacity is needed because it is expected that the market will be larger. If accumulation falters in the long run, it is because businesses no longer expect their markets to grow or new ones to develop at the same rate as before. But what makes a market expand, and at what rate will an expanding market grow, and why? These are the questions that a theory of market growth should answer, and the answers would clearly help to explain investment.

So we shall argue that the basic insights of Keynesian thinking are fundamentally sound: saving is passive, investment determines output and employment, which are flexible, while prices are governed by long-term considerations and are sticky in the short run. But the Keynesian approach is incomplete – it lacks an account of the growth of markets in relation to the accumulation of capital. So it has not been able to deal adequately with the questions of the long-run development of the system. Both its theory of investment and its account of prices have been borrowed from the orthodox approach – and both borrowings have been inappropriate. This is the defect we will try to remedy in the discussion of transformational growth. But at the outset it is essential to understand the true relationship between 'Keynesian' thinking – the theory of effective demand – and traditional price theory. So long as macro-economics is burdened with the requirement that it rest on, or at least be compatible with, microeconomics, it will make very little progress. In particular, investment cannot be understood unless it is grasped in conjunction with pricing, which in turn has to be examined in connection with the growth of markets. If the perspective is that of scarcity in static conditions, as in conventional micro-theory, the problems cannot even be posed. Moreover, until there is a clean break there will always be a tendency to fall back on neo-Classical methods when difficulties arise, rather than developing new methods for the new problems. More of this later.

Changes in the World Economy

Intellectual weaknesses are only a part of the story. The most evident weakness of the economic policy of the 1970s was its inability to do anything significant about inflation. Even worse, the normal demand management measures could not seem to get rid of unemployment. The two problems were connected, of course, since the cure for inflation was supposed to be a dose of unemployment. But the doses got larger and lasted longer, and the inflation just got worse. If anything destroyed popular confidence in the established, Keynesian, economic policy tool-kit, it was the decade-long inability to handle stagflation.

Moreover, there was something very unsettling about deliberately creating unemployment in order to control inflation. This meant inflicting major disaster on part of the electorate, and also giving up growth, in order to control prices. Surely, there must be a better way – and monetarists proposed one: controlling the money supply. In practice, the monetarist solution turned out to involve even worse unemployment, but in public debate their position sounded attractive and technocratically precise.

If the unemployment–inflation connection undermined the general public's confidence in the Keynesian approach, international developments were at least as important for business. The development of international competition radically affected the business world. American business was both forced and encouraged to begin to think on a world scale. The position of the dollar became crucial, but in different ways for different sectors. A cheap dollar helped sell goods overseas, and protected US industry (and therefore labor) from the competition of imports. But it was not so good for banking, or for those who wanted to invest abroad or buy into successful foreign firms. For them, a strong dollar became the cornerstone of sound policy. However, the value of the dollar was no longer determined by the US alone.

The US domestic market remained the world's largest but, starting in the late 1960s and early 1970s, it became apparent that it was no longer growing so rapidly. In particular, a number of major consumer durables appeared to be approaching saturation, most strikingly automobiles, television and household appliances. The pace of urbanization also slowed, bringing with it some slack in the growth of construction. By contrast, in what have come to be called the 'newly industrializing countries' (NICs), growth in all these areas speeded up. It also became clear that, taken together, the NICs constituted a huge potential market. Who would supply these markets, where would the factories be located? Who would control these markets, and the firms supplying them, in whose interests?

The very least that can be said is that businesses might be tempted to move some (or most) of their capital abroad, if they thought that profit and growth prospects were better there – if markets were growing faster, and if labor costs were lower . . . But *controls* could prevent this. If a Keynesian expansionist program required controls on capital movements to protect the balance of payments, then profit and investment opportunities could be lost forever. As the domestic market declined in importance in regard to growth prospects, and as the danger of controls and regulations became more apparent, the business community's latent hostility towards Keynesianism was aroused once more.

Costs of Full Employment

Full employment tends to make people first complacent, and then assertive; a little unemployment goes a long way to make the campuses docile and the public receptive to the needs of business. A lot of unemployment goes even further. And a lot was needed after the combined shocks of Vietnam and Watergate. It is hard to say that this was ever an explicit motive for any particular policy stance, but as an attitude it fits with the general anti-Keynesian tenor that began to emerge in business and banking circles in the mid-1970s and found expression in the monetarism of the Thatcher government in England. The idea was often expressed in metaphors: the economy needs to be 'trimmed down', 'streamlined'; labor is 'too fat'; we need to become more fit and competitive; we need a 'shaking out'. Unemployment was seen as a kind of medicine, unpleasant but necessary, which would both cure inflation and re-establish discipline over, even punish, the unruly social elements that had arisen to challenge conventional morality.

In addition, the commitment to full employment and growth came under attack from an unexpected, and largely liberal, quarter. The environmentalists saw danger in further unregulated and unplanned growth. Uncontrolled industrial growth cannot help but add to the pressure on supplies of non-renewable resources and to pollution. According to this perspective, the pragmatic liberal's commitment to growth as a way of resolving social conflict had to be revised. Social conflict, especially over the distribution of income, should be faced directly; trying to expand to avoid the fight is just running away from what will have to be faced some day anyway. Slowing down the economy, even creating unemployment, might be acceptable, then, since it would reduce the pressure on the environment.

The Loss of Perspective

All these elements combined to create a climate of opinion in which conventional Keynesian thinking gradually evaporated. There were serious intellectual reasons for doubting its validity, against which the mainstream defenses were weak because of their acceptance of traditional price theory. This also prevented the development of a theory of the growth of markets. In addition to these intellectual flaws, conventional Keynesianism didn't seem either to explain what was happening or to provide effective policies. On top of which, as a result of new developments in the international economy, the normal Keynesian policies were increasingly unacceptable to business. And the underlying political program – make the pie bigger to avoid the fight over how to slice it fairly – had come to seem not only escapist, but also costly in environmental terms.

But by abandoning the Keynesian perspective, rather than rethinking it, modern political thought has inflicted a serious wound on itself. It has lost both a realistic theory of the way the system works, and an essential insight into its basic absurdity. To appreciate this paradoxical nature, consider how often we hear that there is not enough money to pay for social security, for cleaning up the environment, to have both a strong defense and a good educational system, or decent welfare – all at a time when both factories and workers are idle. It is perhaps *the* central insight of the Keynesian perspective that when there are idle resources, idle productive capacity, the real cost of spending on an additional project is *less* than zero. To put it in a less paradoxical way: when there are unemployed workers and factories, spending on an additional project not only pays for itself but actually generates additional income. From a social point of view, these costs are a gain.

Keynes was acutely aware of this, and also of the implication that, as a result, the system did not really make sense. No doubt it had its good points, as present-day rhetoric regularly assures us, but some of Keynes' remarks are as fresh and relevant today as they were in 1936:

> It is curious how common-sense, wriggling for an escape from absurd conclusions, has been apt to reach a preference for *wholly* 'wasteful' forms of loan expenditure rather than for *partly* wasteful forms, which, because they are not wholly wasteful, tend to be judged on strict 'business' principles. For example, unemployment relief financed by loans is more readily accepted than the financing of improvements at a charge below the current rate of interest; whilst the form of digging holes in the ground known as gold-mining, which not only adds nothing to the wealth of the world but involves the disutility of labour, is the most acceptable of solutions.
>
> If the Treasury were to fill old bottles with banknotes, bury them at suitable depths in disused coal-mines which are then filled up to the surface with town rubbish, and leave to private enterprise on well tried principles of *laissez-faire* to dig the notes up again (the right to do so being obtained, of course, by tendering for leases of note-bearing territory), there need be no more unemployment and, with the help of the repercussions, the real income of the community, and its capital wealth also, would probably become a good deal greater than it actually is. It would, indeed, be more sensible to build houses and the like; but if there are political and practical difficulties in the way of this, the above would be better than nothing. (Keynes, 1973, vol. xiv, p. 129)

Supply-side Theory, Military Keynesian Practice

With the breakup of the consensus on the management of the economy, new proposals surfaced. Demand theories were out of fashion. Budget

deficits could be defended on 'supply-side' grounds, but not because of
their demand effects. However, these supply-side grounds were, at the
very least, intellectually weak, and for many liberals it must have seemed
a golden opportunity to attack Reagan: his program was incoherent. And
so it was – as stated. But how it was presented was irrelevant; in fact,
it was military Keynesianism – stimulate the economy with deficits,
concentrating the spending in the military industrial complex, and try to
control inflation, but above all protect the dollar by tight money. (Indeed,
it can be argued that if Reagan had stuck with his tax cuts, he might not
have had such a deep recession – but then he might not have had such
success in reducing inflation.) The tight money was supposed to hamper
inflation; in fact it helped to cause the recession, and it has been the
fundamental reason behind the over-valued dollar. But, arguably, this is
not a mistake; a high dollar was considered desirable, for it facilitated
investment overseas and enhanced the world position of US banking. And
it reduced inflation by cheapening imports. Of course, it caused problems
for many manufacturing companies, but these were also receiving fat
Pentagon contracts, which could be considered a kind of compensation.

Consider what has happened. The recession cut demand for raw
materials and for oil; non-oil raw materials fell 15 per cent from 1980 to
1982, and the real price of oil declined even more. The rise in the dollar,
and the increase in imports, both helped to reduce business costs and to
keep the cost of living from rising too fast. The military spending helped
to keep up activity in the manufacturing sector. The deficit provided a
strong and growing stimulus, although this has been partially offset by the
growing trade deficit. But the recovery basically came about as a result of
the stimulus the deficit provided to consumption. And it came in time for
the election. What could be more Keynesian? And what could be more
exclusively short run in perspective?

Yet it has been dressed up and presented almost wholly in traditional
terms, a move that has distracted many critics and diverted them into
harmless attacks on the misuse of traditional ideas in supply-side theory.
Of course, traditional theory has been misused, but the issue is not the
academic sheepskin but the predatory wolf barely concealed beneath it.

The liberals have abandoned Keynesian thinking, then, because it has
lost intellectual credibility, on the one hand, and because its practical
failures have discredited it in the eyes of both the business and the larger
community, on the other. Keynesian measures appear likely to require
difficult, politically dangerous, and unpopular controls and regulations.
Something new seemed to be called for – but not something so new that
it would endanger the consensus that government intervention should be
kept confined to those cases where a definite market failure could be
demonstrated. And the genius of modern politics has produced exactly
what is required: old wine in new bottles, the traditional theory now
doing battle on both sides, here labeled 'supply-side', there labeled
'financial prudence'. In the resulting clamor the wolves may be able to
make off with everything in the cupboard.

Notes

1   The locus classicus for this idea is Kalecki (1943). Besides inflation there are other reasons that dampen the stimulus after elections. Full employment increases realized profits, but it tends to erode potential profits by strengthening both the labor movement and consumer/citizen opposition to business practices. Short-run profits are no bargain if obtained at the cost of control in the long run.

2   The neo-Classical theory of distribution takes the position that the wage rate is the price of labor and the rate of profit the price of capital. According to the principle of scarcity, then, a rise in the equilibrium capital/labor ratio should be accompanied by a lowering of the profit rate and a rise in the wage rate. Market forces, in other words, would allocate capital and labor – and distribute incomes – efficiently. In the mid-1950s this proposition emerged as central to the newly developing theories of growth and technical progress, and was at once challenged by economists skeptical of the market. A decade-long controversy followed in which the skeptics quite decisively showed that, in general, the principle of scarcity could not be applied to capital and income distribution, owing to the fact that the changes being studied imply the need for revaluation of capital-produced means of production – leading to all sorts of irregularities and discontinuities. See Harcourt (1972); Nell (1980b). Prior to the controversy it had seemed that the 'grand neo-Classical synthesis' of Keynesian aggregate demand and pre-Keynesian price theory could be extended to encompass the long-run problems of growth, technical progress and income distribution. The controversy not only showed that this was not possible, but also raised fundamental questions about the adequacy of the basic synthesis itself, leaving the liberal Keynesians on the defensive. And this was the position when the monetarists attacked.

3   The great weakness in the 'grand neo-Classical synthesis' lay in its attempt to accept the pre-Keynesian approach to prices as a matter of theory while rejecting it in practice. If prices are flexible when demand falls then, when unemployment begins to emerge, both money wages and prices should fall *pari passu*, leaving the real wage unaltered. But the decline in money wages and prices should bring a proportionate decline in the interest rate, on the one hand, and the rise in the real value of cash holdings – the celebrated 'Pigou Effect' – should directly increase consumption demand, on the other. In other words, the system always has, and tends towards, a full employment equilibrium. But, then, how is persistent unemployment to be explained? Answer: by wage and/or price 'stickiness', for which various ad hoc explanations are advanced – unions, or long-term wage contracts, or 'implicit' contracts, or monopolies make wages or prices inflexible, so that the price mechanism cannot do its job. Hence, Keynesian policy measures must be brought into play. Such a justification is inherently weak. It leaves open an attractive alternative, which is to eliminate the impediments to the free working of the market. This has the added advantage, from the orthodox perspective, of moving the system towards competitive equilibrium, which maximizes welfare, whereas an interventionist policy must move the economy away from the optimum.

4   In the standard neo-Classical growth model the capital-output ratio adjusts to bring the rate of growth that will first balance aggregate demand and aggregate supply into line with the given rate of growth of the labor force. So the equilibrium (or 'natural') growth rate is actually a given. More advanced models modify this; the important point, however, is that only saving is ever considered. There is no long run theory of investment or of investment-saving interaction.

3
The Impact of Government Deficits

With the slowing down or ending of the postwar phrase of tranformational growth, the usual Keynesian policies became less effective. Stronger medicine was needed − more, rather than less, government intervention. But popular opinion ran the other way. Aggressive internationally oriented business, faced with maturing markets at home, wanted the option of moving its capital investments abroad, where growth promised to be faster, and did not want to be hampered in this by the kinds of regulatory controls a conventional expansionary program would have needed in the present era. Nor, of course, would it want to be stopped by labor or community concerns; it will decide to leave Vermont for Singapore on the basis of the bottom line, not the welfare roll. And managers can hardly be blamed for this; their job, after all, is to make profits.

However, if the stagnation of the 1970s and early 1980s reflects the slowdown of growth in aggregate demand (investment, consumer durables, government, net exports) that we explored in Chapter 1, a strong expansionist program was called for. The slowdown in the growth of aggregate demand needed to be offset either by higher (and growing) government deficits or by increases in real wages or real transfer income, which would have led to an expansion of consumer markets followed by induced investment, in order to maintain employment levels. The policy mistake, on these assumptions, would lie in failing to provide adequate stimulus. But that is not what the traditional theory tells us; quite the contrary. According to it, the danger lies either in government spending, or in deficits themselves, which are alleged to 'crowd out' more productive spending. Echoing this, the popular press has attributed many of the economic problems of the past decade and a half to government deficits. By contrast, of course, Keynesians have always argued that deficit spending, or, more generally, manipulation of the government budget, can keep unemployment down. However, the Keynesian argument has been hampered by acceptance of the traditional theory's account of prices, and by the associated belief that savings determines accumulation in the long run.

In the past decade and a half, five countries have avoided unemployment almost completely. Japan, Austria, Norway, Switzerland

and Sweden have suffered relatively little inflation, and by the standards of the US almost no unemployment. To be sure unemployment in Sweden went up to 3.5 per cent in 1983 (down to 3.1 per cent in 1984), from a norm of under 2 per cent during most of the postwar era. And Japan was up to 2.7 per cent in 1984, from a little over 1 per cent in the early 1970s. Norway had an unemployment rate of less than 1 per cent in 1970, but it hit 3.8 per cent in 1983. Switzerland's official unemployment rate in 1970 was 0.0; it rose to the spectacular height of 0.9 per cent in 1983 – although this is misleading in that Switzerland also sent home a large number of 'guest workers'. And Austria went from 2.0 per cent in the mid-1970s to 4.5 per cent in 1983. All five countries felt the effects of the world recession, but all kept their unemployment levels far below what is counted as 'full employment' in the US. And all practiced systematic counter-cyclical fiscal policy.

What does this show? Can Keynesian measures, like deficit spending, substantially counteract a world depression? Does this mean that no one need suffer unemployment if adequate policy measures are taken? That is the extreme form of the traditional Keynesian position, with which both left and right disagree. It is not our purpose to analyze the policies of these countries. Yet it does seem that their governments, all labor-oriented and with a strong commitment to full employment, did manage to protect themselves from the worst effects of recession. So, evidently, it can be done. However, some of their methods went beyond traditional demand management, and, in any case, what can be done by relatively small countries, or, in the case of Japan, a newcomer, may not be applicable to the largest country of all.

These cases are suggestive, then, but we must now undertake a close examination of the central ideas of demand management. To begin with, we've got to understand how the budget is drawn up. Exactly what *is* the deficit, and how is it measured? It is important to remember that the government is not a household or a business, so we must beware of falling into easy analogies. Once we understand the budget, we can then turn to what economic theory has to say about the causes and effects of government taxing and spending.

Concepts and Definitions

So let's see what the deficit actually is, and what has been happening to it. This is not going to be so simple. The 'size' of the deficit depends on what kind of dollars we measure it in – 'constant', that is deflated, dollars, or current ones. But there is a way of avoiding all the problems associated with measuring inflation: instead of talking about the deficit in terms of any kind of dollars, we can consider it in relation to GNP. We form the ratio, deficit/GNP, and, so long as both are expressed in the same dollars, they cancel out.

Of course, this makes very good sense, because it doesn't matter how big the deficit has got if GNP has got even bigger. The size of GNP shows what we have produced each year, which is what is available to finance the deficit. So it is actually misleading to complain that the deficit this year is, say, twice the deficit of twenty years ago, if GNP is three times as big as before. Moreover, GNP is not the only thing we could compare the deficit to. We could also compare it to total investment spending, the spending by businesses to build factories and offices and showrooms. Another significant ratio might be the deficit/private debt ratio, showing how much government borrows compared to the private sector. This can take in all levels of government, or just the federal, and it can combine business and consumer borrowing or treat them separately. Another illuminating figure would be the per capita deficit or national debt.

Before we look at these ratios and how they have moved, however, we've got to explain just what the deficit is, a surprisingly complex question, as it develops. (And important, for some widely held views will turn out to be groundless.)

The government spends – on education and police and the military and roads and highways, rivers and harbors, and courts of law, and many, many other functions. It also makes payments to individuals, such as social security or pensions. On the other side, it takes in money from taxes, many different kinds of taxes, and it also makes money from the sale of certain goods and services. And it has income from its assets – leases, rents, holdings of bonds and shares, etc. The simplest idea then is that the deficit arises when payments exceed income in the current period. But this has to be understood carefully: we have to be sure that both income and outgoings are properly credited to the right periods of time. Clearly we needn't get excited about a deficit that has arisen just because some payments have been bunched up, or because we have chosen an arbitrary period with only payments, although the next week, say, there will be only income.

However, there is a deeper yet related problem. Ordinary businesses, and households, keep separate capital and current accounts. Such accounts distinguish between spending for current consumption, and investment for the future. Think of a business: the current expenses will be for wages and materials; the purchase of a building or new machinery will be a capital expense. If the two are lumped together, then every time a new machine or building is bought there will be a huge deficit, while the rest of the time, as funds are saved up to pay for it, there will be surpluses. Such a situation is not only very misleading, it also doesn't answer the all-important question of whether the surpluses add up, during the right amount of time, to what is needed to offset the deficits. This is the question the capital account deals with, while the current account shows whether current operations can generate the surpluses that are needed to service debt and still leave a profit.

Amazingly, the government does not keep its accounts this way! Everything is lumped together. (In fact, the 'consolidated budget' even lumps together payments that are funded, like social security, with expenditures from general revenues). When we see figures for the annual deficit, we cannot assume that current tax collections (and other income) are not sufficient to meet current expenses; it may be that a large payment is being made this year on a long-term project, which properly ought to be amortized over a number of years. (To some extent this takes place in military contracting: payments are stretched out, beginning before delivery, while the weapons systems are still being developed. But this is done for the benefit of the contractors, not to rationalize the government's accounts.)

Some will immediately argue that a capital account for the government does not make sense because government activities are 'unproductive', and the idea behind a capital account is that a long-term asset will pay for itself over a number of years. This mixes up two quite different distinctions – productive and unproductive, and marketed versus non-marketed. To see the absurdity consider: cigarette manufacture is productive, but highways are unproductive? (what about freeways versus toll-roads?) public schools are unproductive, but private schools are productive? private eyes are productive but the FBI isn't? The point is that government activities are not (usually) *marketed*, which is quite different from being unproductive. So they do not earn a monetary return, directly. This doesn't mean that a return isn't obtained, or that it cannot be calculated reasonably precisely. The benefits, however, do not flow to individuals or to spending units; they are spread out, often imprecisely, to the nation or some other collectivity taken as a whole, and they are also paid for by the group as a whole.

Think of it this way. Suppose the government sets up a flood control system in a previously unprotected, and so sparsely inhabited and poor, area. A set of dams will be built, rivers channeled and banked, a large reservoir/lake will be created, and so on. Big spending, all at once. And the return? With flood control established people can move there and live safely. The cheap land values will attract new families and new business. The dams will provide cheap electricity, and the reservoir and newly channeled rivers will provide opportunities for recreation and vacation businesses. So economic activity in the region will increase, raising the tax base. (One way of calculating the return on the project would be to balance the later increased taxes against the cost of the project. But many economists would object that this underestimates the value of the project. If just the increased taxes are counted as the return, projects that would pay for themselves in terms of additional total income would not be considered worth-while. Instead, the whole of the new activity should be counted as the return on the project.) Clearly, then, government activities can be valuable and productive – and often benefit everyone – even though they are not marketed like toothpaste and cigarettes and calculating the return may pose problems.

In fact, there's more to the story. What about the private ('investor-owned') power companies that were supplying the region with expensive electric power before the project? They've not only lost their market, but will now have to meet the competition of public power. And what about the small construction companies that provided flood clean-up services? They'll be out of business altogether. In other words, besides yielding benefits, the project also causes some people losses, and these have to be considered, too.

Though this example concerned something relatively easily to measure, the principles are the same for other forms of economic activity, except transfers. However, in the absence of a distinction between capital and current items, we don't know whether any actual deficit is genuine or just the result of inadequate accounting. So it *would* make sense to draw up a capital budget for this kind of government activity. Moreover, a capital budget for the government would also take account of changes in the values of government assets. The federal government owns buildings, land, equipment, and gold, securities, mortgages and obligations of foreign governments – in 1980 adding up to more than $1,430 billion! And, of course, these assets change in value with changes in economic conditions, so they should be periodically revalued and any capital gains or losses should be entered into the calculation of the current deficit, just as we do on our income tax. Inflation, changes in oil and mineral prices (federal land), and changes in interest rates all affect the values of the kinds of assets the federal government holds. In recent years these changes have been important.

Besides the federal government, state and local governments have budgets (which also are not normally divided into capital and current) and they, too, may run deficits or surpluses. Since we are going to contrast public and private activity, we had better bring them into the picture, too. If interest rates are driven up, and private investors crowded out, it doesn't matter whether the deficits that do this arise from federal or state government spending. In fact, however, state and local government have tended to run surpluses. In 1978 and 1979, state and local surpluses were just over $30 billion, offsetting the 1978 federal deficit of $28.5 billion, and swamping 1979's $16.1 billion. In the 1980s, state and local surpluses have risen to about $50 billion, about a quarter of the 1985 federal deficit.

Finally, a more complicated concept: the full employment deficit or, since nobody agrees on what counts as full employment any more, the high employment deficit. Instead of looking at what the deficit is now, this calculates what the deficit would be if the economy were operating as it should be, at full employment. Why? Because then incomes would be higher, so taxes would be larger, and welfare and unemployment compensation payments would be lower. Ideally, the full employment deficit would be zero – that is, if it were calculated correctly over an appropriate period of time it would average out at zero. Below full employment, there should be a deficit, since deficit spending tends to stimulate the economy. Above full employment, in an inflation, there should be a surplus, to reduce the pressure of excess demand – that is, *if* the inflation is due to excess demand, which, we shall see, has not been the case.

Numbers

Now let's look at the numbers. How big is the deficit, how has it grown, how is it financed, what are its causes and effects?

To begin with, it looks as if we are dealing with big numbers, very big numbers as far as most people are concerned (although actually not so big compared to interstellar distances, for example). People are often uncomfortable with such numbers, but many attempts to explain them only make it worse. Before he became President, Ronald Reagan used to try to give people a feel for the size of the national debt (about $1 trillion in 1980) by explaining that to equal the debt a pile of $1,000 bills would have to be 67 miles high! (What if there were a windstorm while you were stacking them?) The President doesn't use this particular image any more, perhaps because he has added another 60 miles or so during his first administration. Here's another one, this time to give you a feel for the size of Ronald Reagan's fourth-year deficit of $181 billion: if you spent money continuously at the rate of $100 a minute, day and night, it would take you nineteen years to spend an amount equal to the deficit. Now what do these images actually tell us?

The fact is, they are misleading and direct our attention in the wrong way altogether. What's much more relevant is that the total *assets* of the federal government add up to $1.433 trillion, as against $1 trillion in debts. Almost 1½ to 1, assets over liabilities. Again, more relevant than the mere size of the almost incomprehensibly enormous pile of bills representing the total national debt is the ratio of that pile to another even more enormous one representing total business and household borrowing. In 1950, federal debt was 45 per cent of total debt, so the private pile was only a little taller. By 1980, federal debt had *fallen* to only 19 per cent of total debt, so the pile of bills representing private sector debt must now be over 250 miles high. Again the crucial point is simple: federal debt has been growing more slowly than private debt, and the latter is now four times as big. (And per capita federal debt has been falling until recently, so that today it is less than half its 1946 level, while per capita private debt has been rising.) The point can be shown very dramatically on a graph (see Figure 3.1).

Next let's look at two graphs that present the story of the budget over the period 1956–83. Figure 3.2 gives the actual sizes of surpluses or deficits; note that Reagan's deficits go off the graph. Figure 3.3 plots the actual deficit or surplus as a percentage of GNP, and contrasts this with the high employment surplus or deficit as a percentage of GNP. The first isn't really all that helpful. The absolute size of the deficit is going to change because of inflation and because the economy is growing – the same percentage deficit will be larger when GNP is larger. What it does show is that, before Reagan, the largest deficits came in recession years. The second graph shows some more interesting things. First, the two series tend to move together and to reach peaks and troughs at about the same time. Second, from the late 1950s to the early 1970s the cyclically adjusted deficit stays very small; the surpluses don't cancel the deficits altogether, but the deficits in relation to GNP are very low – under 2 per cent except in 1959. Moreover, it fluctuates less than the actual deficit in relation to GNP. (This indicates that in these years opponents of deficits would have done better to advocate stimulating the economy, to move it

Figure 3.1 *Federal debt/total debt, 1951–76*

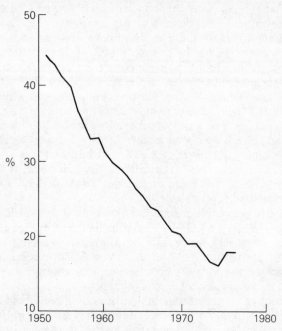

Sources: Business Statistics: 20th Edition and *Survey of Current Business,* August 1976

nearer to full employment, than to push for, say, a Balanced Budget Amendment.) After 1973, by contrast, the cyclically adjusted deficit/GNP series is more volatile than the actual, and both deficit series tend downwards, that is, both deficit/GNP ratios increase. The decade from the early 1970s to the early 1980s is clearly different from the late 1950s and the 1960s. We shall come back to this point later on.

Now let's take a closer look at the high employment deficit, and see if it makes a difference to make adjustments to it for changes in the value of government assets that have occurred because of changes in prices and interest rates. Table 3.1 shows the figures from the mid-1950s to 1981. From 1955 to 1965 the adjustments change the annual magnitudes but do not affect the way these magnitudes stand relative to one another; in other words the adjustments don't make much difference – not surprisingly, for inflation was very low and interest rates were fairly steady. After the Vietnam escalation, however, and especially in the 1970s, the adjustments change the picture dramatically, converting a decade of high employment deficits into one of surpluses!

Stop and think about this for a moment; which are we to believe? It really makes a difference: the inflation of the 1970s cannot be blamed on runaway budget deficits if in fact, by a clearly reasonable measure, the true federal budget was in surplus! And the same goes for the spectacular

Figure 3.2 *The federal government budget surplus, 1956–83*

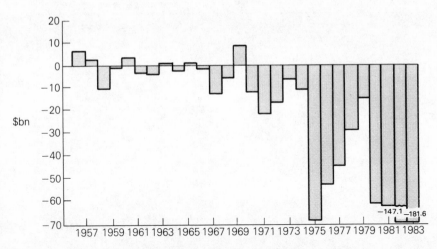

Source: Department of Commerce, Bureau of Economic Analysis,
        Survey of Current Business
        Prepared by the Federal Reserve Bank of Boston

Figure 3.3 *Actual and cyclically adjusted surplus, 1956–83*

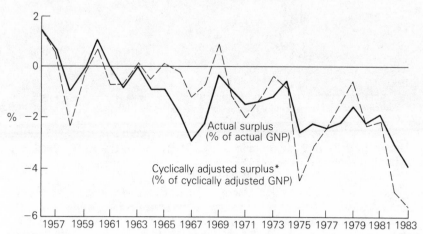

*Adjusted for the effects of economic fluctuations by estimating the surplus consistent
with a mid-expansion trend level of employment
Source: Department of Commerce, Bureau of Economic Analysis, *Survey
        of Current Business*
        Prepared by the Federal Reserve Bank of Boston

Table 3.1 *High employment deficit: official and adjusted (% of GNP)*

Year	Official	Adjusted for price effects	Adjusted for price and interest effects
1955	1.30	2.81	3.71
1956	1.87	3.83	4.63
1957	1.37	2.47	1.26
1958	0.00	0.93	2.21
1959	1.11	2.09	2.90
1960	2.39	2.84	0.98
1961	1.35	1.99	2.44
1962	0.53	1.29	0.91
1963	1.24	1.79	2.26
1964	0.17	0.78	0.73
1965	0.13	0.98	1.42
1966	− 0.74	0.34	0.09
1967	− 1.89	− 0.89	− 0.38
1968	− 1.26	0.06	0.20
1969	0.52	1.95	2.68
1970	− 0.46	0.77	− 0.64
1971	− 1.05	0.12	− 0.21
1972	− 1.02	0.02	0.42
1973	− 0.72	0.89	1.13
1974	− 0.02	2.16	1.97
1975	− 1.88	− 0.37	− 0.55
1976	− 1.01	0.22	− 0.52
1977	− 1.13	0.39	1.27
1978	− 0.70	1.30	2.16
1979	− 0.09	1.74	1.81
1980	− 0.81	1.31	1.63
1981	0.15	1.92	1.97

Source: *American Economic Review*, March 1984.

rise in interest rates at the end of the 1970s and in the early 1980s. But which is the true measure, the official one or one of the adjusted ones? On what grounds do we choose?

The adjusted deficit takes changes in wealth into account, and therefore gives a better picture of the solvency of the state, but such changes in the state's wealth don't affect flows of spending much. So let's look at a different sort of ratio – the ratio of the deficit, as conventionally defined (i.e. without considering the revaluation of government assets) but adjusted for inflation, to investment spending, also adjusted for inflation. This is what might be called 'the flow of spending' concept of the deficit (since capital gains are not spent and so don't affect demand for goods and employment), and is therefore the concept most closely related to the

economic slowdown and stagnation that developed in the 1970s. Table
3.2 shows the figures for investment, the rate of growth of investment,
the deficit and its ratio to investment.

Two things stand out very clearly. First the rate of growth of
investment slows down dramatically, and this slowdown is characteristic
of the whole period from the mid-1960s on. Notice that these rate of
growth figures are percentage changes from one five-year period to the
next; to get the (approximate) *annual* average rate, divide by five (except
for the 1980s). Second, the ratio of the deficit to investment rises steadily,
quite dramatically by the 1980s. And this is exactly what we would expect
in a situation where investment growth is slowing down, because such a
slowdown brings stagnation, and stagnation in turn means higher
payments for unemployment compensation and welfare, on the one hand,
and lower tax collections on the other. So the deficits will rise.

Of course, the conservative position will be that the rising deficits –
due, presumably, to willful and wanton overspending – have 'crowded
out' productive private investment, causing the slowdown in the growth
of investment. But look again at the figures: investment growth slowed
down markedly in a period like the late 1970s when the federal
deficit/GNP was declining, and the overall (federal, state and local)
government deficit was small or non-existent (depending on how it is
measured). By contrast, investment grew most rapidly in the late 1960s,
when there was a growing deficit due to Vietnam spending (with
government spending directed towards manufacturing). In any case, as we
shall see, the idea of 'crowding-out' just doesn't make any sense when
there are underutilized factories and unemployed workers. The
government and private business are both demanding goods and services,
competing for them, yes. But when there are unused resources, the goods
and services are not scarce; more can be produced just by hiring more
workers and opening up plants that have been closed down for lack of

Table 3.2   *Federal deficit and capital investment*

Year	Fixed investment[a]		Federal deficit[b]	
	Annual average (1972 $bn.) (1)	% change from preceding period (2)	Annual average (1972 $bn.) (3)	Deficit as % of fixed investment (3)/(1) (4)
1960–64	111.0	—	2.6	2.3
1965–69	148.4	+ 33.7	3.5	2.4
1970–74	177.9	+ 19.9	14.0	7.9
1975–79	197.8	+ 11.2	31.2	15.8
1980–83	214.2	+ 8.3	51.9	24.2

[a] Fixed investment includes investment in residential construction, non-residential
structures, and producer's durable equipment.

[b] The deficit data are for calendar years adjusted to be consistent with the national
income and products accounts deflated by the implicit price deflators for government
purchases of goods and services.

Source: *Economic Report of the President*, February 1984.

Table 3.3   *Capacity utilization in manufacturing (%)*

1965–69	88.1
1970–74	82.5
1975–79	80.8
1980–81[a]	78.8

[a] 1980–81 levels (business cycle trough) should not be compared to the five-year averages, which encompass entire business cycles.
Source: Federal Reserve Board.

Table 3.4   *Investment growth (average annual growth rate)*

(a) *Investment in gross private domestic fixed capital (including residential construction, excluding inventory)*

Years	
1960–66	6.3%
1966–73	4.6%

(b) *Excluding residential structures (including office, shopping center and factory construction)*

Years	
1960–66	8.3%
1966–73	3.6%

(c) *Equipment only (excluding all structures)*

Years	
1960–66	9.5%
1966–73	1.3%

Source: Economic Report of the President.

markets. The stagnation of the 1970s manifested itself in extensive unemployment of both workers and factories (see Tables 3.3–3.5).

Of course, as most readers of the business press know, both unemployment and capacity utilization can be measured in several ways, which don't always give the same answers. The main issues are simple: should we count 'discouraged workers' (workers who have given up trying to get a job) as unemployed, or should we treat them as no longer members of the labor force? How should we treat part-time work? Similarly, should we continue to count capacity even if it is never used? How long should it be carried, after it has been retired or mothballed? If we add in discouraged workers, we raise the unemployment rate about 1½ points. If we cease to count capacity that is never used, we raise our measure of capacity utilization about 5 or 6 percentage points. But the important conclusion is that, *whatever* measures are chosen, the decade of the 1970s shows up as a period of widespread slack in the economy.

Again, conservatives and others will blame or try to blame the deficit: the deficit has caused inflation and high interest rates, and these in turn led to a

Table 3.5 *Average rate of unemployment*

Years	Average rate of unemployment as % of civilian labor force
1965–69	3.8
1970–74	5.4
1975–79	7.3

Source: US Bureau of the Census.

Table 3.6 *Transfer payments as a proportion of consumption*

1950–65	8.3%
1965–70	11.3%
1971–75	15.6%
1976–80	17.1%

Source: US Department of Commerce, Bureau of Economic Analysis.

slowdown of spending by both consumers and businesses. Who's going to buy when prices are rising? Who's going to borrow when interest rates are so high? And the deficit in turn is caused by excessive welfare spending and (although conservatives won't stress this) excessive military spending.

Yet welfare spending is not that large, although it has risen in relation to consumption (see Table 3.6, which shows all transfers, not just those concerned with welfare). As times have become harder, and as the aged population increased, transfers have funded a larger and larger proportion of consumption; if they were cut back, consumption spending would have to be curtailed. In Keynesian terms, these payments are a counter-cyclical stabiliser.

Figure 3.4 shows that defense spending fell during the 1970s in constant dollars, and so fell even more as a percentage of GNP. This undoubtedly contributed to the slump – but it had nothing to do with the deficit or with inflation.

And how could the deficit have had such alarming effects if in fact it did not even exist, as the adjusted figures show? Moreover, the deficit is quite clearly not the cause of changes in nominal interest rates in the 1970s and early 1980s (see Figures 3.5 and 3.6). The deficit in relation to GNP rose from 1970 to 1972, while nominal interest rates fell; then the deficit fell in the next two years while interest rates rose to record levels; next the deficit rose from 1974 to 1976, while interest rates fell again. Finally, interest rates climbed to all-time record levels at the end of the decade, as the federal deficit sank once again. Far from the deficit causing high interest rates, as far as the 1970s are concerned, contrary to all the newspaper stories, high and/or rising deficits are associated with low and falling interest rates. In the early 1980s, the federal deficit reached record heights, while interest rates first rose and then fell.

However the nominal interest rate is of only limited interest. If there

Figure 3.4   *Federal outlays as a percentage of GNP, 1960–86*

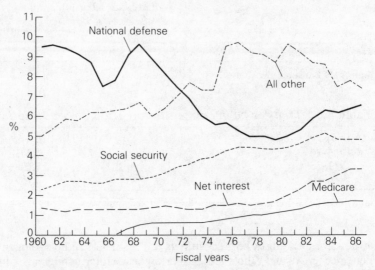

Source: Economic Report of the President 1987, p. 70

Figure 3.5   *Federal budget receipts and outlays, 1970–84*

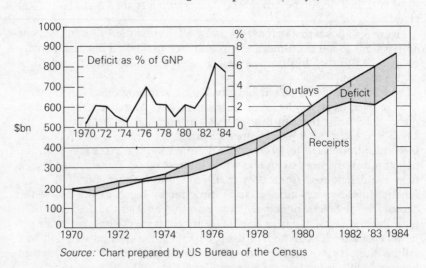

Source: Chart prepared by US Bureau of the Census

is inflation, then the money you repay is worth less than the money that you borrowed; hence the real interest rate is the nominal interest rate minus the percentage rate of inflation. Once we take this into account the picture of the 1970s looks very different; some of the very high interest rates turn out to be very low indeed (see Table 3.7). Once again, we see no obvious correlation with either the federal or total government deficit. For example, 1975 was a year of record deficit, both in actual terms and in high-employment terms. Moreover it was a year in which the *adjusted* deficit was also exceptionally high. But the real interest rate turned negative. On the other hand, 1979 was a year of no actual deficit and a very low high employment deficit, with a substantial adjusted surplus. But the real interest rate, though positive, is extremely low.

What about inflation? Perhaps inflation can be correlated with the deficit? According to the traditional theory it ought to be, since deficit spending puts extra money into circulation, pushing up prices in order to bid goods away from private buyers into the hands of the government. However, inflation and the total deficit do not move together in any reliable way. In the late 1970s, the federal deficit was declining while inflation was accelerating. The highest ever deficits in relation to GNP were recorded in World War II, when there was almost no inflation (see Figure 3.7) – of course, there were price controls, too. So we have to admit that price controls work, which indeed they do, although it has become an article of the free enterprise faith to claim that they don't. In the early 1980s inflation again declined, while deficits expanded to record sizes.

So, to make a long story short, blaming the deficit for the problems of

Figure 3.6 *Money market rates, 1970–83*

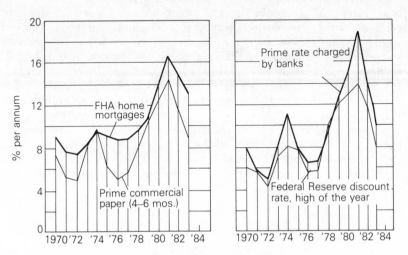

Source: Chart prepared by US Bureau of the Census

Table 3.7 *Real interest rates (%)*

	Prime bank rate (1)	Consumer price index (2)	Real Interest rate (1) – (2)
1970	7.91	5.90	2.01
1973	8.02	6.20	1.82
1974	10.81	11.00	– 0.19
1975	7.86	9.10	– 1.24
1976	6.84	5.80	1.04
1977	6.83	6.50	0.33
1978	9.06	7.70	1.36
1979	12.67	11.30	1.37
1980	15.27	13.50	1.77
1981	18.87	10.40	8.47
1982	14.86	6.10	8.76
1983	10.73	3.50	7.23

Source: *Statistical Abstract of the USA*, 1984.

the economy in the 1970s just won't work. For a start, it's not clear what concept of the deficit is under discussion. Let us review the possibilities: the federal deficit; the overall government deficit; a deficit based on distinguishing current and capital accounts; the high employment deficit; the federal deficit adjusted for revaluation of federal government assets; the total government deficit adjusted for revaluation of assets. It's hard to avoid the conclusion that a lot of public discussion of 'the deficit' is carried on by people who literally don't know what they are talking about. In any event, adopting one or another of the usual concepts, the two most common claims – that deficits cause inflation, and that they cause high interest rates – are clearly false, as a matter of fact. (We'll see shortly that they don't make sense either.) As for what the federal deficit does do: it constitutes additional net demand, so it increases sales. In the craft economy of the nineteenth century an increase in sales to the government would generally have meant a diminution of private sector sales – 'crowding-out' – but, as we shall see, this is not the case in an industrial economy. As for what has caused the high official deficits of recent years, it's important to remember that there was a general slowdown and stagnation during the 1970s, accompanied, to be sure, by inflation, of which more later.

Now it is time to try to understand the relationship between the government budget and the working of the economy. This will not be easy, but it will make it possible to clear up a number of very common questions. So the next chapter will take us right into the center of economic theory.

Figure 3.7   *US experience during World War II*

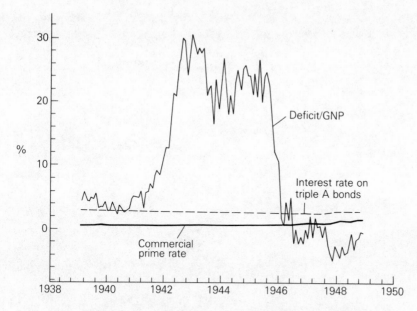

Source: Paul Evans, 'Do large deficits produce high interest rates?'
American Economic Review, 1985, vol. 75, no. 1

PART II

From Kinship Capitalism to Corporate Industry

Since its inception in the sixteenth and seventeenth centuries, capitalism has acted as a powerful catalyst to the development of technology. In turn, technological developments have reacted back on capitalism, bringing changes in its mode of functioning. We shall consider two such parallel and interacting developments: the emergence of mass production from craft industry, and the transformation of the family firm into the modern corporation. These have often been noted before, but what has been overlooked, and what we will focus on, is that these developments, taken together, imply a major change in the way the system works.

Important aspects of the earlier system of family firms and craft production can be described usefully, if not very realistically, by Marshallian supply and demand functions, especially if the long-run position of the system is interpreted in terms of a uniform rate of profit. The simple orthodox theory of supply and demand does focus on genuine features of the craft economy. For example, in such an economy, since employment is held fixed, output is limited by the labor and resources available, which means that efficient allocation is important, so that prices may reflect relative scarcities. It also implies that whatever is produced can be sold. As we shall see, this is not a simple matter; demand is maintained by a complex interaction, which will be explored carefully. The later system of mass production, organized by modern corporations and financed by a modern banking system, works very differently. It runs according to effective demand, which means that resources may be underutilized, so that efficiency is not an urgent matter. Such an economy must be analyzed by a multiplier/accelerator theory, since it is demand-constrained. Output is characteristically limited by the ability to sell, not by the ability to produce, so that no scarcity problem exists. The earlier system of craft production and family firms (and farms!) thus presents conditions corresponding, in many respects, to the assumptions of orthodox microeconomics, while the later system of corporate industry and mass production operates more in accord with the principles of macroeconomics. We shall see that these two imply very different approaches to state intervention.

This is not to imply that orthodox microeconomics is an *adequate* theory of the craft economy – or macro of the corporate system, for that matter. The reason the textbook account isn't very good is that textbook writers try to treat two different theories, which apply to two different economic systems in different historical periods, as if they were two *branches* of one unified theory. By trying to make microeconomics a universal theory of rational behavior under any possible circumstances, its supporters have in fact robbed orthodox theory of much of its practical content. (To restore this it will be necessary to reinterpret the system, especially in regard to the way it reacts to changes in the overall level of demand.) And by trying to make macro compatible with micro, the unique insights of macro have been lost. However when each has been relegated to its proper place, as the theory of the working of the central mechanisms of a particular kind of economic system, the explanatory power of each can be appreciated.

In Chapter 4 we shall explore the orthodox theory of prices and opportunity costs, which will tell us how supply and demand supposedly set prices so as to reflect forgone opportunities, and then, in Chapter 5 we shall contrast this with the working of the system of modern industry, in which employment and output, rather than prices, vary with changing economic conditions. This means looking at the theory of effective demand, the core idea of Keynesian economics. We will find that we have to be careful: most presentations of Keynesian economics, to some extent including that of Keynes himself, try to make it compatible with traditional theory, but, as we have argued, traditional theory applies to one kind of economic system, the modern theory of effective demand to another. This will be one of our main points. So what we say won't be quite the same as the textbooks. Of course, both theories will have to be expressed in a simplified form. But the contrast will still show why traditional microeconomics cannot be combined with macroeconomics: all attempts at a synthesis simply result in distortion.

However, what we finally want, of course, is a practical understanding of how we deal with economic problems in the present-day world, which means understanding the changes in the role of the state as the economy has evolved from the craft to the corporate system. So, after comparing and contrasting the two types of theory, we shall look in Chapter 6 at the development of the modern interventionist, corporate state out of the 'nightwatchman' of the last century. And, finally, in Chapter 7 we shall try to examine some of the forces involved in the transformational growth of the system.

Yet when we come to policy we seem to be in trouble. For our approach not only runs against the current of popular thinking; the policies it suggests seem to run counter to the common sense of everyday business. For example, in a recession it certainly seems paradoxical to propose government pressure to increase wages – though perhaps no more so than running deficits. But, on closer inspection, the element of paradox appears to be inherent in the system itself! This will have to be examined carefully.

Further, adequate policy requires a little more insight into the changing international relationships, both between developed countries and between the developed and developing. Most contemporary problems seem to be world-wide, so the solutions must likewise be global. Demand management and controls cannot be applied by any one country alone; they must be implemented in concert. A revised theory of effective demand is not enough; in the modern world, we cannot have Keynesianism in one country. These questions will have to wait for Part III.

4

The Traditional Craft System: Family Firms and Family Farms

Conventional economic theory proceeds from a simple starting point: the rational individual with given, limited resources and multiple objectives, deciding how to allocate the resources to best achieve the objectives. Prices and outputs follow from the interaction of large numbers of such individual calculations mediated by the market, which converts them into expressions of current costs and demands. This may make sense in a largely static world, or a world in which growth takes place only in the form of conquest and geographical expansion, where the same system covers more space. In an economy growing in all sectors, however, especially when the growth is transformational, business has to plan its prices with an eye to covering the capital charges required by its projected investments. It also has to plan its prices so that it can expand into new markets.

It is from traditional economics – the theory of supply and demand – that we derive the conventional wisdom about the evils of government intervention and deficit spending. Less government is better government, for both economy and citizens. This was the message of nineteenth-century liberalism. And, as we have seen, in the last century the role of the state in the economy was slight. Indeed, it was cut back from the mercantilism of an earlier era to make way for the development of capitalism and modern markets. But conventional theory, grounded in a system of family firms and farms operating with given resources, can actually tell us very little about the economic costs and benefits of modern government, nor can it explain why its share of GNP should have increased so dramatically.

Everyday life in the modern world provides examples of both the dangers of government and its advantages. Both households and businesses suffer from red tape, but both benefit from police and pollution control. Both suffer from taxes, but both benefit from subsidized research in everything from medicine to communications to space flight. Recently, both have suffered from high interest rates – while some have benefitted from the high dollar.

Thus, the conservative argument that, in the long run, intervention harms everyone doesn't come from everyday life, which is ambiguous, and it certainly doesn't come from the statistical record. So, to understand the roots of these beliefs, we will have to look at textbook economics and its relationship to free market ideology.

The Traditional Economics of Supply and Demand

If you open an average economics textbook today and look for the sections on price theory, what you'll find is not very different in substance from what you'd have found in 1929, just before the Great Depression. And that, in turn, was usually based on Alfred Marshall's *Principles*, first published in 1890. Of course, there are more and better diagrams, and, even in elementary textbooks, nowadays the attempt is made to present the central propositions of the theory in mathematical terms. Moreover, the theory of the household and the firm, and the theory of single market equilibrium, will usually be set in the context of general multi-market equilibrium. So the approach looks different – much more impressive and scientific. The core account of how the economy works is none the less pretty much the same. Most practically applicable results derive from the 'partial equilibrium' models, although today many economists, apart from conservatives, are less sanguine about the ability of free markets to work smoothly, precisely because of the difficulties in deriving any clear answers from general equilibrium theory (Hahn 1973, 1981; Arrow and Hahn 1971). More of this in a minute; but now let's think about what prices do and how they are established, according to the orthodox account.

Here's the story in non-technical terms. The resources available to each household and business are assumed to be given, as are the preferences of consumers and the possible methods of production. At the outset, market conditions are assumed to be competitive; later on, refinements can be introduced, allowing for 'imperfections' which give rise to monopolies, etc. Traditional price theory says that people (households) will buy more when prices are low, and less when they are high – and that this is a regular sort of relationship, explainable in terms of individual preferences. The more one has of any one thing, the less intensely a person will want additional units of it; it would be better or more useful to have something else. Hence the more one has, the less one will pay for still more. Businesses, on the other hand, will supply more when prices are high, less when they are low. When prices are high, business will push workers and equipment hard to produce; when they are low, they won't. Additional output thus increases with price; and so does its cost, since hard-pushed workers and equipment will need extra compensation (although, in the long run, additional capacity will be built, and unit costs may very well fall back to their previous level).

When supply and demand balance, everyone is happy; neither suppliers nor customers will be under any pressure to change what they're doing. So the market will tend to settle there. That is, the prices the market establishes will be the ones at which supply and demand balance, which means that the (rising) cost of an additional unit of output is just offset by the (falling) usefulness of that unit, measured in terms of the alternative goods the consumers could have had. So prices and the amounts of the various goods that will be produced and traded are settled simultaneously, by the balance of supply and demand. By extension, this means that the market settles pretty well everything, because we can draw up supply and demand schedules for all different kinds of things – goods, services, labor, savings and investment, whatever you like – and the same market processes will fix both the prices and the amounts produced and marketed.

But if the market settles everything, more or less, what role is there for the government? Pretty clearly, not much. Moreover, the point at which supply equals demand is the point at which everyone is content; they're as well off as possible, given the situation they started off with (provided, of course, that markets are competitive). So if the government changes anything, people will be made worse off. If it regulates, it will have to push the economy away from equilibrium, and if it spends it is going to have to take goods away from somewhere else. It is generally agreed that the government may intervene when markets are imperfect, for then intervention can move the system towards the competitive, optimal point. But consider spending. If, *without* the government, supplies and demands are equal everywhere, and then the government gets into the act, it's going to have to upset something somewhere. The government doesn't produce and sell anything for a profit. So whatever it buys has to be taken away from some other use, and the purchase has to be financed by funds that are also taken from some other use. In short, government spending bids goods away from private purchasers, and government borrowing bids funds away from private borrowers. Taxes, of course, reduce demand so, if the budget is balanced, government spending needn't push up prices. If there is a deficit, however, then the government's borrowing to finance it will bid up interest rates on the one hand, and the spending itself will have to bid up prices on the other.

So there it is. As a matter of theoretical necessity, government regulation moves the economy away from optimality and deficits reduce everyone's economic well-being by crowding out desirable private activities, and in the process causing inflation and high interest rates. But this conclusion is only as sound as the theory from which it derives. The next section lays out the foundations for this argument in more detail, after which we turn to the contrast between the nineteenth-century craft economy and the modern industrial system.

The Economic Theory of the Price Mechanism

When you go into a store in a competitive market and buy something, the price you pay, according to this theory, reflects the *relative scarcity* of what you're buying. And this in two senses: first, you must want more of that particular item, relative to other things you consume, because you could have used all or part of that money to buy other things; secondly, its producers could have used their labor and capital and raw materials to produce other things, so the price the good fetches has got to compensate for the alternative ways these factors of production could have been used. This idea is the heart of the textbook (or neo-Classical or marginalist) vision.

The idea is expressed technically by saying that 'prices measure opportunity cost', which means that the price you pay measures the value to you (your subjective estimate of what it's worth to you) of whatever you've bought, and this in turn has to be (if you're rational) just barely equal to the value of the next best use you could have made of that money (what economists call 'opportunity cost'). In the same way, the price the sellers receive has to measure their opportunity cost – the next best thing they could have made and sold using the resources available to them.

Let's follow this a step further. The reason that prices measure opportunity costs for both buyers and sellers is that each is conceived of as rational; hence each will choose to make the best use of their scarce funds and/or other resources. So buyers will make up a purchasing plan that *maximizes* the satisfaction or 'utility' that can be obtained from spending their income, while sellers will draw up a production/sales plan that will maximize the profit they can obtain from the use of their resources. Notice the important implication: if everybody is (successfully) maximizing, then everyone must be as well off as possible, given their preferences and the available resources and technology.

When consumers and producers make their plans they are assumed to face the current prices on the market (over which they have no control when the market is competitive). The market situation, the initial holdings of resources, and the available technologies are all taken as given. So the next step is to consider (hypothetical) variations of those market prices, calculating the corresponding plans on both sides of the market for each possible set of prices.

Let's go over this carefully. We consider a whole lot of different possible price configurations, and for each we calculate what the best purchasing plan would be for a consumer with given preferences (including preferences for work), and given skills and other assets; and we also calculate the best production plan for suppliers with given resources, etc. Then for each set of prices we add up all the demands of consumers and supplies of producers for all the various goods. What we are looking for, of course, is a set of prices at which the total demands will just match the total supplies for every one of the different goods. It can be shown mathematically that under certain conditions, which are pretty complicated, such a set of prices will exist. It can also be shown that many, sometimes infinitely many, such sets of prices may exist, and it turns out, finally, to be very difficult to describe how the market, unaided by regulations or government directives, can manage to settle upon one or another of these 'market-clearing' sets of prices. So, in fact, when the story of supply and demand is laid out in full, the 'free market' doesn't come off so well. (This is not very surprising when you think about the way everyday markets work, even traditional ones, but it certainly undermines the case against government intervention.)

There is another problem. The theory is meant to tell us what would happen if everyone acted rationally on the best available market information. It is no objection that, in practice, consumers often act on whim and fancy, that workers are sometimes slipshod, and that accountants subtract when they should have added. In the *long run*, these all wash out. That is, the theory tells us what would happen if there were enough time for everyone to adjust fully to the dictates of their preferences and the constraints of their endowments. This leads to the difficulty that some endowments, for example of capital goods or of acquired skills, are themselves produced. So why can't they be altered 'in the long run'?

Not only does it seem natural to suppose that stocks of capital, human and non-human, could be changed in the long run, that is exactly how Marshall and other early theorists told the story. But it led to trouble. If there were increasing returns to scale in the production of such goods, the system would no longer have an equilibrium; and, if there were constant returns, prices and quantities would be determined independently of one another. (When returns are constant, a downward-sloping demand curve will cut a horizontal supply curve, the level of which is fixed by costs. So costs determine prices, and demand determines quantities; Nell, 1980c.) Only if there were diminishing returns would long-run supply curves rise to meet a falling demand curve – Marshall's famous 'scissors', in which the forces of supply and of demand jointly determine price and output. But in this case, if factors are paid their marginal products, aggregate factor pay will fall short of total output. There would have to be a 'residual' factor whose remuneration could not be determined by the usual forces of supply and demand. Only in the constant returns case will aggregate market-determined pay (at rates equal to factor marginal productivities) exactly equal total output (Nell, 1980c). In short, none of the three possibilities was satisfactory. Produced means of production could not be handled by the theory of scarcity.

Finally, and most seriously, a problem emerged over the rate of profit. When businesses employed several capital goods, the total capital of a business could only be determined when the prices of these goods were known (since they had to be added up), but to know the prices it was necessary to know the rate of profit. But the rate of profit was supposed to be determined by the supply and demand for capital, for which the aggregation of capital goods was required. To this day there is no satisfactory resolution of this problem, and modern neo-Classical theorists tend to by-pass it by ignoring the determination of the rate of profit, and assuming that endowments of capital goods and acquired skills can be taken as given – even though this leaves the idea of the 'fully adjusted' position in an awkward state (Harcourt, 1972; Garegnani, 1970; Laibman and Nell, 1977; Nell, 1988b).

But to avoid all the mathematics, and also to simplify the complexities of the long and short run, the story is usually told in a Reader's Digest abbreviation – supply and demand in a single market – where everything works out neatly. Demand curves slope down, supply curves up, they cross in a single point, which is the equilibrium. If the quantity is below equilibrium, competition among the buyers will force the price up, which will encourage suppliers to offer more; if the quantity is too large, then competition among sellers will depress price, and supply will be withdrawn. So in the simplified version there is a unique, stable equilibrium, which satisfies everyone, and is the result of optimizing behaviour on the part of both suppliers and demanders. Since this is the basis for the belief in the efficacy of free markets, let's explore it further.

We'll assume that all other markets are in equilibrium, or at any rate that nothing is changing in them. So we concentrate on the demands and supplies for a single good, say, widgets. ('Widgets'?! Yes, a favorite textbook example. Why? Because if any actual good were chosen, automobiles or refrigerators or sports jackets, it might be too obvious that the theory doesn't account for what happens in our everyday lives.) When the price is high, consumers will not plan to buy so many – the opportunity cost is too high. But when the price falls they will buy more. Why? The answer is that the amount of a good will be proportioned to other goods, by considering the ratio of the good's usefulness to its price. The more you have of a good the less the usefulness of still more, moving down a smooth curve. (This is a postulate, and is supposed to be intuitively obvious.) When all goods have the same additional utility/price ratios, the consumer's plan will be optimal. On the other side, when the price is low, producers will not wish to produce so much; other uses of their resources may be more profitable. But when the price is higher, producers will turn out more widgets. So we can draw the famous curves, a downward-sloping one relating price (on the vertical axis) to quantity demanded by the market (on the horizontal), and an upward-rising one, showing the quantities producers taken together will supply as price increases. So long as the opportunity cost of widgets to consumers is higher (when they don't have any) than the alternative use of widget-producing resources (when no widgets are being produced), the two curves will intersect, and at that point the market will clear. (This last sentence explains why the starting point of the downward-sloping demand curve will lie above the starting point of the rising supply curve.)

Now what have we got? The supply and demand curves determine the market price and the quantity. This must be interpreted carefully: the price is not the *money price*; it is the relative price, or the real price. It is the price *in terms of the real resources given up to acquire the good*. That is what is meant by saying that prices reflect opportunity costs. So the system of supply and demand determines relative prices and absolute quantities. If we now go back to all markets taken together, then all relative prices and all absolute quantities will be determined – including real wages and employment, and interest rates and saving-investment. This conclusion has been reached by considering only the preferences of consumers (which define usefulness or utility), the initial holdings of resources, and the available technology.

Now let's consider the implications – and some of them may be surprising. To begin with, if the system is in equilibrium *there cannot be any underutilized resources*, and in particular there cannot be unemployed labor or idle factories. (Of course, if the system were out of equilibrium, or if it were less than fully competitive, this conclusion would not necessarily hold – this has been the basic reply to those who have charged that such a conclusion shows the theory to be absurd.) Notice also that equilibrium, and the working of the system in general, has been described without *any reference to government*. The system establishes a full employment equilibrium, which, because it is reached on the basis of maximizing behaviour on the part of all agents, can be said to be optimal. If we now introduce the government, its activity will have to be underwritten at the expense of some other activities, which will be 'crowded out', since there were no underutilized resources. Government demand just adds to the total demand, but since the government produces nothing, supplies stay the same. So prices will rise, and private activities will be squeezed to make room for the government. If the original position was optimal, the effect of introducing government must be to create a sub-optimal condition.

Since the system of supply and demand determines only relative prices, the general price level (or value of money) is left out of account. At this point traditional theory introduces the Quantity Theory of Money, which says that the price level is governed by the quantity of money in circulation. Notice the dichotomy: the monetary system (or the banking system, whichever determines the quantity of money) sets the price level, and therefore is responsible for inflation, *but has no effect of any kind on the equilibrium levels of output and employment*. Those are determined by the system of supply and demand, that is, by the rational, maximizing decisions of consumers and producers.

Now we have it all in front of us, both the reasoning and the main conclusions. Here is why we should fear the deficit and cut back the government: the government's activities are a drag on the economy; government intervention reduces everyone's well-being; government spending crowds out private; inflation is due to 'too much money'; and the quantity of money necessarily affects the price level, and nothing else. So, a government deficit must crowd out private activity, simply because any government spending does. This is obvious when taxes reduce private consumption to make room for it. If it is financed by borrowing, then it adds to demand for private savings, so it will raise interest rates, simply by the law of supply and demand. But if it is financed by money creation, then it will push up the price level; it will fuel inflation, since the money supply determines the price level and only the price level. These dangers are the clear and unmistakable implications of the theory of supply and demand.

Why have we spent so much time on this abstruse and difficult subject? We have argued that the study of supply and demand won't tell us much about the world we live in – although it may describe important aspects of the earlier pre-industrial system – but it is absolutely necessary to understand the theory of supply and demand in order to make sense of current discussions about the dangers of the government, particularly of the deficit, and especially to understand why most economists (certainly most conservative economists) completely disregard the facts. Remember what we saw earlier: the greatest boom the American economy ever experienced, the mobilization of World War II, was fueled by gigantic deficits, larger in relation to GNP than any before or since. More recently, the Reagan recovery, complete with declining inflation and falling (nominal and, though later, real) interest rates, has been driven by the Reagan deficits, more 'military Keynesianism'.

If the theory of supply and demand does not describe the modern economic system in which we live, especially if it mis-describes it in important ways, then the entire discussion rests on a mistake. And that is just exactly what we will now try to show.

The Craft Economy vs Modern Industry

First a short summary. The nineteenth-century system of family firms and family farms differs importantly from the modern capitalist industrial system, and these differences are not 'imperfections' in the market. They are differences in the way the two economic systems work and relate to other aspects of the society.

In the craft economy, workers are members of households who cannot easily be laid off when sales fall. Output and employment thus tend to be fairly stable, while prices and wages are flexible. Markets are static, not because the system doesn't grow, but because growth takes place through the creation of new firms in new regions, leaving established relationships unaffected. In the modern system, by contrast, all markets grow and all firms invest regularly. Modern firms have very large fixed costs (fixed in money terms), which make it dangerous to cut prices, but mass production technology makes it relatively easy to lay off workers and cut back on purchases of materials. So output and employment are flexible but prices and wages are not.

The craft economy is a static economy, with low variable costs, and substantial fixed charges set in real terms, and the traditional price theory, what the textbooks call 'microeconomics', applies to certain aspects of it. Modern industry works quite differently, since it is based on growth, which entails monetized capital charges, and substantial variable costs, so that it is described (although not very well) by textbook macroeconomics.

The theory of rational maximizing behavior is probably questionable as an account of *any* actual economy. On the other hand, the system of supply and demand equations does not have to be strictly grounded in maximizing; looser interpretations are possible. The theory can be treated as a rough approximation, and many special cases can be allowed for. In the short run, there will be many rigidities and obstacles; virtually every factor of production is fixed. But, as longer and longer periods are considered, it becomes more possible for business to react to price signals. Household demand is more adaptable than business supply; so in the short run output will be fixed at the level of existing capacity and prices will be largely set by demand, while in the long run, when the scale of production can be adjusted, prices will reflect costs, including profit at the normal rate, and the role of demand will be to determine outputs. (Economists will recognize Alfred Marshall.) This is a kind of compromise between the Classics (Smith, Ricardo, Marx), and the marginal utility theorists. In other words, even if agents did not exhibit strict rational behavior, supply and demand, working together, might determine relative prices and absolute quantities in the short run, while supply conditions would determine prices and demand would determine quantities in the long. If we adopt such a view, it can be argued that the theory then provides a reasonable description of the system of family business, operating traditional crafts and farming smallholdings, that characterized the American economy during most of the nineteenth century.

Small family businesses, operating traditional crafts, do not have employees in the modern sense – workers who can be laid off or put on short time. The workers are the family members, or hired hands and very often apprentices, who live with the family. The accounts of the business and those of the family are often not easy to separate. The costs of the business will be materials, or seed, or tools, and the like, on the one hand, and labor on the other. But the basic cost of labor will be the family's subsistence, including that of hired help and apprentices. And this labor cost will be fixed, but it will not be fixed, as under capitalism, in monetary terms; it will be fixed in *real* terms. Moreover, unlike the fixed costs of later capitalism, it will be a current item, not a capital charge.

So this implies a fixed total number of workers. But this does not mean that the quantity of labor supplied does not vary: the fixed number of workers will supply a variable amount of time and effort, precisely as described by the traditional theory of the marginal disutility of work. And changes in demand for goods will lead to changing demand for labor. Wages will tend to be fixed by custom, but prices will vary more readily with market conditions. Hence with high demand, rising prices will raise the value of additional output.

Now let's consider what these points imply. In the traditional theory, agents are assumed to be 'given' – to exist, and somehow to go on existing, independently of whatever is happening in the markets. The reproduction and maintenance of these agents, households and firms, is not considered explicitly in the analysis (though why it isn't is never explained). This question is passed over lightly in textbook accounts, but it has received attention in mathematical models, because special assumptions have had to be introduced in order to ensure that the crucial behavioral functions of the model would be continuous – an important factor in guaranteeing that the model will always have at least one solution. (If there are no solutions, then the system of free markets *cannot* tend towards a social optimum.)

To see what is involved, suppose a group of workers had no other endowment than their particular kind of laboring ability, and then that the price of that fell from just above to just below the cost of living. In the short run, they can no doubt make all sorts of temporary adaptations, but in the long run the cost of living is what it costs to live – so they will have to emigrate or die. So this group of workers would no longer be able to continue consuming, and so the demand for goods would have to shift sharply. A small continuous change in a single price would thus lead to a large and discontinuous change in the demand for a wide variety of goods. For mathematical reasons this could prevent there being any equilibrium at all, or, equally disastrously, render any equilibria unattainable. Hence, these cases have been ruled out by assumption, in spite of the obvious fact that the only 'endowments' most workers actually have is their particular or general working ability. That, in fact, is the traditional definition of the working class – those who possess no income-yielding property or assets other than their own ability and willingness to work.

The traditional theory has been criticized for being 'unrealistic' on this account, but if we think of it as applying to a craft economy, rather than to an industrial one, then this assumption is perfectly all right. Craft workers and small farmers did tend to be self-sufficient. Their wives and children gardened, the women sewed and made preserves, the men developed a variety of skills, journeymen owned their own tools, and master craftsmen their establishments, and so on. When times were good they concentrated on their craft work and bought their domestic supplies with their earnings. In bad times they retreated as far as possible into self-sufficiency. The traditional theory, in other words, is reasonable enough when applied to the craft economy of pre-industrial times.

Now let's look at the way the system works, before comparing it to an industrial economy. In a craft economy, resources can be taken initially as given, or at any rate fixed. Of course, workshops and tools had to be produced, mines dug and land cleared. But once these projects are complete, their economic influence is over – 'sunk costs are sunk'. Unlike a modern system, the craft economy is not primarily driven by accumulation. Growth of capacity will take place largely through the founding of new businesses in new geographical regions, where the new capacity will serve new customers, rather than through the expansion of existing businesses to serve an increasingly affluent existing market. Growth is largely 'extensive' rather than 'intensive'. So the question for any business is how to make the most of what they've got, rather than how to fund the construction of new capacity. Employment will depend on the number of establishments and on how much and how hard people want to work, which in turn will presumably depend upon what they're paid. The list of households and businesses can be taken as given at the outset. Households will buy more of cheaper goods, and less of more expensive ones, and so on. All businesses will tend to be small in relation to the market as a whole, so none can set or fix the prices. But because the fixed costs are both real and current, the crucial prices for business will be relative prices; hence, as we shall see in a moment, monetary prices will be competitive and flexible. Thus when nominal demand falls, say because investment spending falls off, money prices will tend to decline, but, because employment is fixed, money wages will remain steady. So prices will tend to be more flexible than money wages and, as prices fall, real earnings will tend to rise. As a result, consumption will rise, offsetting the initial decline in demand. A drop in demand from some external effect on investment or exports, then, will be automatically offset, so that output will tend to stay steady. By exactly analogous reasoning, we can see that in a boom the rise in demand will bid up prices more than money wages, constricting consumption. This kind of price flexibility, with prices significantly more flexible in monetary terms than wages, tends to support a stable level of output and employment – justifying Say's law – in contrast to an industrial economy, where money prices and wages are tied together by a stable markup, set by the need to finance capital charges, and variations in demand are met by layoffs. In a craft economy, then, consumption varies counter-cyclically, so as to offset fluctuations in investment or exports, whereas in an industrial economy, as we shall see, the multiplier entails that consumption varies pro-cyclically, reinforcing fluctuations in demand.

A Technical Digression

Think of the economy as consisting of two sectors, one producing capital goods, the other consumer goods, plus a labor market, and a financial market, which mobilizes savings and channels them into investments. Long-run 'normal' prices are set by supply conditions (Marshall's long-period supply curve is flat), the capacity sizes of firms depend on technology and, in particular, on diminishing returns to management, and the number of firms in an industry depends on expected long-period demand. Actual or current prices fluctuate around the long-period norms, varying with changes in conditions of supply and demand. To see how the adjustment pattern works, let's start with the savings – investment market and trace the effects of a change in investment demand as it works its way through the system.

The prospective returns on various investment projects can be computed and compared with their costs, using long-period prices in the calculation. In this way a 'marginal efficiency' schedule can be constructed, based on a given state of long-term expectations, showing that, as more funds are invested, projects with progressively lower rates of return will have to be undertaken. At normal prices and normal levels of operation there will be a normal rate of profit, which will provide a normal quantity of loanable funds, after the expenses of the capitalists have been subtracted. (The ratio, loanable funds divided by capital, is the rate of net earnings; if this is to be maintained in the long run, the loanable funds have to bring in interest at this rate – otherwise the earnings from interest will differ from the net earnings from the business.) Thus, when the normal rate of profit prevails, savings out of such profits will be loaned at a 'normal' rate of interest, which lies below the profit rate by an amount that reflects the average expenses of capitalist families. From the marginal efficiency curve, similarly adjusted for capitalist family consumption, we can then find the amount of investment the marginal efficiency of which just equals that rate of interest. If the marginal efficiency curve is in its 'normal' position, that amount of investment will just equal the saving out of normal profits.

But what is the meaning of the 'normal position' of the marginal efficiency curve? It means that the normal capacity output of the capital goods sector can be sold at normal prices; but this says nothing about the position or shape of the curve itself. Given the Keynesian emphasis on the volatility of investment and the possibility of sudden shifts in the state of long-term expectations, the 'normal' position for this curve may only be realized by accident. How then does the system respond to its shifts?

Starting from the normal position, consider a shift out and up, which means an increase in expected profitability for all investment projects. More investment, in nominal terms, will be undertaken at every level of interest. So initially, at the normal interest rate, there will be a rise in the demand for investible funds; with only normal savings available as supply, the interest rate will be driven up, which will reduce the rise in investment somewhat.

The higher level of investment spending will bid up the price of capital goods, and will lead to harder work and increased output. (But since investment spending was set in nominal terms, the price increase means that less actual output will be needed to satisfy demand.) With higher prices and output, the rate of profit will rise in the capital goods sector. This higher rate of profit will lead to larger savings, which in view of the higher rate of profit will be loaned only at a higher rate of interest, thus reinforcing the effect of demand on the rate of interest.

The higher price of capital goods will be reflected in higher costs, both actual and anticipated, in the consumer goods industries. Hence the price of consumer goods must increase. Such an increase will also be needed to keep the rate of profit in that sector in line with the profitability of capital goods.

But employment and the money wage rate have not changed. So total wage income and consumer demand will not have changed. With higher prices, consumer output can actually decline. Thus resources can be shifted to capital goods; moreover, the initial increase in profitability there sets up incentives to make such a shift.

Notice further that, with money wages and numbers employed given, the rise in demand, raising prices, has led to a decline in the real wage at the same time that the amount of labor being demanded and performed has increased. Thus the variations will trace out an inverse relationship between labor demand and the real wage.

So the rise in the demand for investible funds leads to adjustments in each market around the normal positions, making it possible to match the increased demand with increased savings, but at a higher rate of interest. This increases output in the capital goods sector, reduces consumption, and, simultaneously with the demand for more labor services, lowers real wages, thus permitting higher profits. The striking point is that all the relationships in this adjustment pattern resemble the corresponding relationships in the traditional theory – though, in fact, they don't have the same meanings.

A word on the quantity of money: before the development of modern banking, an important influence on the price level may be the volume of money in circulation. If the supply of money rises, e.g. with a discovery of gold, or through a boom in earnings from foreign trade, or from the government's printing presses, then the price level will tend to rise. If the economy grows, and the money supply doesn't, then the price level will gradually fall. But if relative prices don't change, and money wages and prices move together, then employment and output will tend to stay the same, too, regardless of the amount of money.

A cautionary note must be sounded, however. The supply of money in circulation is neither the only nor the most important influence on total monetary demand – contrary to traditional theory. Even though relative prices stay fixed and the supply of money is given, monetary demand may fluctuate as a consequence of a more rapid or slower pace of spending and producing, which, should a shortage of money develop (as in a boom), can be financed by innovations in borrowing and lending practices. If business prospects look rosy, trade and mercantile credit can always be granted; if prospects are bleak, money will be held back even from normal channels of credit. So the money *available* is at best only one, and perhaps never the most important, determinant of monetary demand; the willingness to circulate that money more or less rapidly is always crucial. And if the supply of money is inadequate to the needs of circulation, the resulting pressure leads to modern banking.

Comparison with the Modern Economy

What we should expect, therefore, is that an economic system of family-run businesses (both in urban and small-town crafts and in agriculture) will be relatively stable in terms of output and employment, but will exhibit a large degree of flexibility in money prices and wages, which will vary in the same direction as changes in total monetary demand. We would also expect to see a long-run (but not a short-run) connection between the general price level and the quantity of money.

And these relationships are exactly what we do find. In the nineteenth century, fluctuations in total demand did take place, and as a result money prices and wages fluctuated in the same direction, but output and employment varied much less.

Let's now consider how we should expect a capitalist industrial system to behave. In what ways is a modern system different from the nineteenth-century craft-and-smallholding economy?

The modern economy is based on large-scale technology, organized into a system of industrial factories, operated and managed from large offices, with retailing handled through chain stores, based on a massive transportation and warehousing system. Relics of the older craft system remain, particularly in agriculture and retail trade, but even in those areas corporate farming and franchising, respectively, are taking over. It has been argued that the efficiency of mass production is a myth; craft production was just as efficient, but in a different way. Perhaps, but there is no doubt that mass production became the dominant system. Yet the skeptics have a point: conventional historians stress the greater efficiency and cheaper costs of the new system – in spite of the fact that many studies show quite a different picture.

The historian's picture is based on traditional theory – if output and employment are fixed, the only possible reason to prefer a new system of production is that it is cheaper per unit. But in fact a chief advantage of mass production is that it permits flexible output and employment on the basis of a fixed product design, in contrast to the pre-industrial system which required fixed output and employment in order to produce products with a flexible design. In the traditional system, the very qualities that make flexible design and customized (therefore efficient in a different sense) production possible, make it impossible to adjust employment to current sales; output can be adjusted to sales only by lowering productivity. Workers cannot be laid off because they have specialized and highly developed skills, which they use in teamwork with others. Morale and human relations are essential to top performance and ingenuity; workers are bound to their firms by personal loyalty and emotional ties. Moreover, if workers were laid off because of a general slump in the industry, their specialized skills would be hard to apply elsewhere. Mass production, by contrast, requires only general skills; workers laid off in one industry can apply their skills in many others. Because workers have standardized skills, and because the pace of work is determined by machinery (and controlled by bureaucracy), production teams, teamwork and morale are comparatively unimportant; layoffs will save more than breaking up production teams will lose. Output can therefore be adjusted to sales without reducing productivity; employment, and so costs, can be reduced instead.

Now, what are the implications of the change from the craft economy to the modern industrial system?

One is that a job can be said to exist only if it has been created in a corporate table of organization. A worker works with machinery or equipment – a drill press, or a typewriter, or a cash register. Whatever it is, it has to be acquired and set up in an appropriate workplace – a factory, an office or a salesroom. So there has to be an investment in capital construction before a job can be offered. (If there are not enough places in the factories for all the potential workers, full utilization of plant will not mean full employment.) By contrast, a traditional small firm or farm can often be operated on the same premises in which the family lives.

This leads to a second point: these fixed costs are amortized. They are capital costs, not current costs, and so they are spread out over a number of years. This requires the development of a sophisticated banking system, but it also means that these fixed charges will be fixed in monetary terms, not in real terms – in contrast to the traditional system in which the fixed costs of the family's subsistence are current, not amortized.

Now consider the effects of these differences when the monetary demand facing a producer falls off. (We take this case because in the postwar world the government has been responsible for maintaining full employment, through deficit spending, when monetary demand slackens). In a traditional craft economy, with many small producers, slower sales will have to be met by cutting prices. In many cases it won't be easy to store the goods – either because they are perishable, or because there isn't storage or warehousing space. Moreover, since labor costs make up the great bulk of current charges, and they are fixed, there is very little point in trying to cut back on output. Hence, with markets competitive, output the same and demand lower, prices will tend to fall. Firms will continue to produce at the normal level so long as prices stay above prime costs. Once prices fall to the level of prime costs, firms will shut down; output in other words will either be normal or zero. In the face of a general shortage of demand, other prices and wages will also be falling, hence relative prices may not change all that much. However, because money prices will generally be more flexible then money wages, real wages (and so consumption spending) will tend to rise, offsetting the initial decline. Consumption demand thus moves counter-cyclically. This is exactly what the traditional theory of supply and demand would lead us to expect; in the short run, supply will tend to be fixed, so that prices will be determined by demand. (Notice that if output and employment hold up, the government does not need to stimulate the economy through deficit spending. However, this does not mean that the state should be reduced to a 'nightwatchman', for there are many other economic functions that it could perform, for example protecting the rights of workers and consumers.)

In a modern capitalist industrial economy, by contrast, the capitalist feature means that fixed costs will be amortized and set in monetary terms, while the industrial feature means, on the one hand, that almost all kinds of goods can be stored, and, on the other, that labor costs, and hence a large part of total current costs, will be variable. An industrial technology can be operated at many different speeds. In other words, production can be slowed down, so that output per period is cut, and in that way workers can be laid off or put on short time while inventory is stored during a period of slower sales. However, prices will not be cut, or will be cut very little, and in any case will be tied to money wages by a fixed markup, determined by the need to cover capital charges. So real wages will not change. Workers who are laid off will have to reduce their spending; hence consumption will vary in the same direction as overall demand. (And in some cases, where a few producers know that they have a market heavily dependent on them, prices may even be *raised* when demand falls, in order to maintain a satisfactory cash flow.)

Why are prices held fixed when demand falls? Why not cut prices? Surely each firm will want to try to attract demand from others? But price cutting is dangerous. When sales have slowed down, fixed costs per period of time are a higher percentage of total monetary revenue per period. To cut price is *certainly* to reduce unit revenue in the *hope* of selling more units. If competitors do not follow suit, then perhaps more sales will be attracted. But if they also cut prices, then no one will gain. (For, characteristically, industrial products are price-inelastic in the short run, but income-elastic. That is, a price cut won't bring much extra demand, but a rise in income might, because it would bring new households into the market. The reason: industrial goods, including household products, tend to be *complementary*, so a change in the price of one kind of good won't attract much extra demand.) Moreover, in an industrial system goods are seldom quickly perishable; technical progress has seen to that. So orders come in now for many different dates in the future – but the same prices must be quoted to all. Changing prices requires renegotiating contracts; but, since the goods can be stored, they should be kept until demand picks up.

On top of it all, everyone will find that price cuts have made a bad situation even worse; their fixed costs are now an even higher fraction of their current revenue. How can they be sure that when variable costs are subtracted there will be enough left to meet the fixed charges? (As a safeguard, corporations will try to raise capital funds through sale of equity; unlike debt servicing, dividends can be cut when sales are down.) Moreover, when sales do pick up, to restore dividends and provide funds for internal finance it will be necessary to raise prices again, even before demand rises enough to press against capacity. This will not be easy unless everyone coordinates; but if they can coordinate to raise prices, they could surely do so to prevent them falling.

In general, faced with a drop in demand, far better to sit tight, reduce output and variable costs by laying off workers, and wait for sales to pick up. In a modern economy, then, output and employment will be adjusted to changes in demand, while both money prices and wages will tend to remain fairly stable. Note that this conclusion does not depend on assuming that markets are imperfect, or that there are monopolies and trade unions that prevent the 'free market' from functioning. On the contrary, the way the market works in the modern system is exactly what we are talking about. A capitalist industrial system is fundamentally different, institutionally, from a traditional craft economy. In consequence, it behaves differently when faced with changes in monetary demand.

Now how does this square with the facts? Most of us know well enough that output and employment vary with demand. We all read the unemployment figures, and many of us have figured among them at one time or another. We also know that, even when slumps are bad, prices don't tend to fall; if we're lucky they just stop rising so fast. So it makes sense in terms of our everyday experience; let's take a look at some more systematic figures.

Table 4.1 Wages, prices and production

	Prices	Industry Production	Wages	Agriculture Prices	Agriculture Production	Variability of output A Expenditure for industrial commodities	Variability of output B % in the fall of A imputable to that of production
Great Britain:							
1873–79	−29%	−5%	−10%	−18%	moderate increase	−33%	15%
1929–32	−21%	−16%	−4%	−44%	stationary	−34%	43%
United States:							
1873–79	−33%	−5%	−35%	−31%	moderate increase	−36%	13%
1929–32	−23%	−48%	−18%	−54%	slight increase	−60%	67%

Source: P. Sylos Labini, *Social Research*, Vol. 50, Summer 1983.

Table 4.1 compares the behavior of prices, wages and output in agriculture and industry in the United States and Great Britain during two
major downturns. The first slump lasted from 1873 to 1879, and the second
is the Great Depression of 1929–32. In both countries the first period is one
in which the traditional system of production by small family firms
predominated, while by the second period the great corporations and trusts
had become ascendant, and mass production was coming to dominate the
leading markets.

Because the theory of supply and demand gives a wrong account of the
way the markets of a modern system work, it cannot tell us anything about
the impact of government spending or government deficits in the modern
world. Before we go on to consider a theoretical approach that can give us
some help, however, we might pause to ask, can't we turn the clock back,
couldn't we restore the earlier system of family firms? Not as it was, of
course, but operating a modern 'soft' technology, on a small scale, in
competitive conditions, so working in the same way?

Restoring the Flexible Price System

Surely, it will be argued, we could break up the big industrial giants and
restore the competitive system of small firms? The new flexible techniques
made possible by computerization will strengthen the market position of
the small firm offering personalized services. Why not pursue an anti-trust
strategy and forget about the industrial system? A few giants might have to
remain, but they could be run along competitive lines.

This completely misconceives the situation. The industrial economy
succeeds the craft economy because it displaces the production system of
the former. It produces better goods on a larger scale, much better goods on
a much larger scale. Perhaps even more important, industrial capitalism is
inherently dynamic, whereas a capitalist craft economy could continue to
function for long periods without any internal change, as family farming did
until industry revolutionized it. The craft economy grows by adding new
regions and new population; the industrial economy grows by investing in
existing firms, by intensifying and transforming present systems of
production. Price adjustments to changing demand must be replaced by the
adjustment of output and employment, without effects on productivity.
Mass production technology makes this possible. The result is significant
changes in the way markets work, in particular, a tendency for variations in
demand to be exacerbated, which in turn seems to call for government
stabilization policies. So modern corporations are not family firms.
Breaking them up just makes small corporations; it won't restore the pre-
industrial pre-corporate system. And the smaller corporations will
immediately set about growing big again, perhaps in different ways in
different markets. Corporations and large-scale industry are here to stay,
and with them the modern financial system, with its monetary fixed costs.
In addition, the combination of social and economic changes has
permanently altered family structure. The extended family has given way to

the nuclear, and even that is under stress. Family firms and family farms cannot operate in the absence of a stable extended family.

The hope that a craft-type system will be revived by the fact that modern high-tech will make possible flexible customized production, in place of the long production runs characteristic of older heavy industry, is quite misplaced. Computerized production systems are dependent on highly sophisticated equipment, which, in turn, has to be produced by highly sophisticated processes that draw heavily on electrical energy, and depend on the whole structure of institutionalized scientific research. Long production runs and unskilled labor may be less important in the future than in the past (though high-tech certainly seems to create plenty of unskilled and semi-skilled jobs, e.g. assembling chips), but that is not the point. High-tech production will be both highly capital-intensive and science-intensive, and will continue to show variability in output and employment in conditions of high, fixed monetary costs, which imply an inflexible relationship between prices and money wages. So modern financial conditions will require lay offs and short time when sales fall; costs will have to be cut. Thus worker incomes will be cut back, and so, therefore, will consumption spending. High-tech simply means that we can now have flexible output and employment together with flexible product design; it provides no route back to the traditional system. So let's now examine the working of the modern economy.

Note

1 The argument of this section is developed more fully – with appropriate mathematics – in Nell (1988a). The functions derived *mimic* a neo-Classical system, but none of the price relationships can be given a scarcity interpretation. Yet they could be used for analysis or even prediction.

5

Corporate Industry: Demand-Determined Production

We turn now to what textbook macroeconomics ought to deal with – the working of a demand-determined system – which it sometimes does. But only sometimes; a lot of effort is wasted trying to make it seem that macroeconomics is compatible with microeconomics. But, if our argument is correct, they cannot be. The traditional theory of supply and demand (in its practical or Marshallian, not its esoteric, 'general equilibrium', version) describes the resource-constrained craft economy; macroeconomics, the demand-determined economy of modern industry. Of course, special cases can be found where these two do fit together, and special assumptions can be made to try and smooth over discrepancies. Yet the difference is fundamental: in one case, output and employment are fixed, but prices and wages are variable, while in the other it is just the opposite – prices and money wages are fixed, while output and employment are variable. That is a difference that will be hard to smooth over!

What we want to examine now are the causes and consequences of changes in the total sales of the economy. This is the same as asking, why does total demand change, and what does it mean? In rough and ready terms we know a good deal about this: when total demand changes, so that, for example, sales fall off, employment usually falls as well. (And this is where Keynesian government policy comes in; deficit spending boosts demand, and therefore sales and employment.) We also know a good deal about why total demand changes – and it is pretty disturbing. Because what we know is that total demand depends in part on non-rational, or even irrational factors, what Keynes called 'animal spirits' and journalists refer to as 'business confidence', the psychological state of mind of the business community. Changes in this can lead to sudden and pronounced shifts in investment spending. If this is so, then the state of the economy at a given time cannot be explained purely in terms of rational calculations of the best courses of action in given conditions. Nor can it be presumed that the system will settle for any length of time at full employment.

The traditional theory's answer is that any such shifts will quickly be corrected, for two reasons. First, when there is a slump due to a falling off of business confidence, the demand for saving will fall, bringing down the interest rate, and lower interest rates will stimulate investment. Secondly, a slump will lead to a decline in wages and prices, but lower wages and prices mean that household and business holdings of money – bank balances, cash holdings, and the like – are now worth more. In other words, a fall in money wages and prices will mean private wealth has increased, and this will tend to stimulate spending. The first of these, however, assumes that the pool of savings is fixed, which we have seen is a mistake. If savings and investment *both* decline, there need be no effect on the interest rate. (In the standard textbook model the decline would reduce interest rates by reducing the transactions demand for money. But this overlooks the fact that the 'money supply' for transactions purposes is largely *determined* by demand. Activity level changes need not affect interest rates. The second overlooks the fact that the decline in prices and wages *increases* the real burden of debt – and debts normally outweigh cash holdings. Indeed, as we shall see, a 'pure' system of corporate industry could operate without cash, using only bank advances. Hence the total effect of the wage/price slump will be to decrease rather than to stimulate spending.

Textbook accounts of macroeconomics do try to analyze the causes of fluctuations in total sales, but in ways that are frequently quite misleading. For instance, to fit into the 'supply and demand' framework of households and businesses, the mainstream approach sets everything out in terms of household saving/consumption decisions, on the one hand, and business investment decisions, on the other. But many households do not normally have the luxury of making rational decisions about saving and consumption; they are hard-pressed and have no choices. Even more important, the great bulk of the saving in the US economy is *business* saving, and has nothing whatever to do with households, rational or otherwise. And finally, business investment decisions are not made the way the textbooks picture it – the information required is not available, business rationality is limited, inter-divisional conflicts within companies often play a major role, and so on. Also, and crucially, investment decisions are closely tied to decisions about technology and long-term pricing policies. Pricing decisions are integral to capital budgeting. They are also basic to sales and marketing campaigns. A decision to invest is a decision to expand productive capacity, and that will not be done unless there are good grounds for expecting sales to expand also. But we know much less about the causes of the expansion of markets than we do about other facets of the economy, a fact that is obscured in orthodox presentations by making investment depend largely on financial conditions. Instead of giving a good and simple account of how a capitalist industrial system works, macroeconomics is set out in a distorted form, to make it appear compatible with traditional price theory, which is based on rational calculation. But there is another way to look at it.

The starting point is that a modern industrial economy is highly interconnected. A rise in production in one sector will mean using more products from other sectors, so an increase in activity (and likewise a decrease) will be transmitted to other parts of the economy. Or again, the wage bill that results from employment in the heavy machinery sector will be spent on consumer goods, establishing a level of demand there, to meet which employment will be offered, resulting in still further consumer demand as the wages of workers in the consumer goods industries are spent on consumer goods. So we shall want to explore this inter-connectedness and tie it up with the impact of government taxation and spending. Here the key will be what kind of goods or services the government spends on, and what kind of incomes it taxes. Why? Because different kinds of spending have different effects, and taxes that fall on incomes that are being withdrawn from circulation, wholly or in part, have a different impact than taxes that fall on incomes that would otherwise be spent. So let's take a preliminary look, and then a more technical one.

The Theory of Effective Demand

Modern industrial technology, which is the technology of mass production (even when computer-driven), can be operated at many different levels, which means that output can be adjusted to varying sales. (Computer technology makes it possible to adapt product design to customer specification, but remains industrial in all other respects.) In other words, the level of sales will set the level of output; but a certain level of output will require only so many workers, for such-and-such an amount of time. So if output adjusts to sales, then employment will be adjusted to output. We'd better try to examine this more carefully.

First, let's recall that prices won't normally vary with changes in the current level of sales. Prices will be set in the light of costs: variable costs (mostly labor and materials) will be marked up enough to cover the capital costs, including interest, of building the factory, and also to generate the profits needed to provide internal funds for expansion and product development. This means that prices will be planned to generate earnings over the lifetime of the investment; which means taking into account the expected development of the market for the product. Prices, in other words, will be set in the light of long-term considerations, involving the balance between the growth of productive capacity and the growth of the market.

With prices set in this way, they will be kept as stable as possible, usually changing only as market expansion permits economies of scale. So short-term fluctuations (which may last as much as a year or so) will be met by adjusting output and employment. But this means that, when one market experiences a falling off of sales, then the effect will be transmitted throughout the economy since, in the modern world, products are used in the production of each other. Coal is used to make coke, which is used in making steel, which goes into the manufacture of coal-mining machinery. More important than this effect is the impact of layoffs and short time, for this reduces take-home pay, which in turn will be reflected in reduced consumer spending, i.e. in further reduced sales. In this way a change in the level of spending in one area is not only transmitted to many other areas of the economy but its impact is multiplied.

This is the basic idea. For government to affect the level of employment it will have to increase or reduce total demand, i.e. spend more than it taxes, or vice versa (but we have to be careful: different kinds of spending and taxes have different impacts). There is no way to avoid another cold bath in economic theory if we are to criticize what has become the Conventional Wisdom about the government. For we now have to try to understand this inter-connectedness more precisely, and then look more closely at government taxing and spending.

Income, Output and Expenditure

To understand how the economy works we will need to see how these three aggregates are related to each other. And to do this we will have to simplify. Let's group all different kinds of earned income together (salaries, piece rate earnings, overtime, tips, and so forth), and call them *wages*, while all different kinds of returns to capital or to ownership (such as rental income, royalties, interest, stock dividends, undistributed corporate profits, partnership bonuses and dividends, and so on) will be grouped together as *profits*. So total income will be total wages plus total profits. (Notice that, from the point of view of the corporation, 'wages' correspond to variable costs, while the items in the 'profit' category correspond to capital charges.)

In the same way we will group together all the different kinds of goods used to make other goods (raw materials, energy, machinery, factory buildings) and call them *capital goods*, while the products that go to support households, which make up the community's way of life, we will call *consumer goods*. Then total output will have to equal the total amount of production (during one year) of capital goods plus the total amount of production of consumer goods. Aggregate expenditure will be composed of the spending (mostly, perhaps wholly, by households) on consumer goods, plus the total spent (except for residual family businesses, by corporations) on capital goods. Note that capital goods are not simply long-lasting goods, like automobiles or houses; they are produced goods used in the production of other goods or services, i.e. produced means of production. So buying a home is not investing; capital formation means investing in means of production.

Now let's consider the relationship between these two groups of income categories and the corresponding categories of output. First, there are some simple points. Wages will for the most part be spent on consumer goods. Some wage income may be saved but, as a practical matter, the bulk of saving (not counting saving up for a home or for buying big-ticket consumer goods) can be considered as coming from business, out of profits. Indeed, as a first approximation, we could say that all wages are consumed, and all profits saved. So the market for the consumer goods sector will be the working class, while the market for the capital goods sector will be corporate decision-makers.

These are big over-simplifications. But let's follow the argument through for a moment. It will make it easy to see our point, and we shall then explain how to deal with more realistic cases. Let's suppose that business decides on a certain level of investment spending. Why? Because businessmen figure that certain markets are going to grow, and that they should build enough capacity to supply them with certain kinds of goods at a price that will make it possible to build up and sustain sales over a certain foreseeable future. So they will design an appropriate set of products and plan to produce them in certain kinds of plants, on a certain scale, and so on. However, just laying plans doesn't get you anywhere; they've got to be carried out, and there's many a slip, etc. In other words, if the factories and salesrooms and so on are going to be built, money has got to be raised and spent, and this had better be done when the circumstances, e.g. interest rates, stock market, current retained earnings, are best. Now back to the point: business decides on a certain level of spending on investment, and it makes this decision in two stages – it plans its investment projects, and then it decides actually to spend money step by step implementing these projects. (Why distinguish these two stages? Because different factors influence the two kinds of decisions. The expected growth of markets is most important for the first, but the current level of profits and the cost of capital funds are most important for the second.)

So business spends on buying capital goods, factories. How is this financed? Remember, we said that capitalist industry required a sophisticated banking and credit system – and that's how the finance will be provided. The capital goods sector, like any other business, will have its operating credit lines with the banks, which will enable it to produce. Its customers, in turn, are engaged in the implementation of investment plans, which they have presumably costed out in a rational manner. So they ought to be able to convince bankers to provide them with funds. Now what are the effects of such spending by business?

The sector producing capital goods will have to employ just enough labor to produce the capital goods that correspond to that level of investment spending. So the level of output and employment in the capital goods sector will be set. But since wages are spent on consumer goods, this means that the consumer goods sector will simultaneously face a definite level of demand, namely that generated by the wage bill of the capital goods sector. So the consumer goods industries will have to hire at least enough labor to produce the output of consumer goods that corresponds to the demands of workers in the other sector. But that alone will not do; for the workers in the consumer goods industries will themselves spend their wages on consumer goods, thereby generating more sales, and so requiring still more workers to be hired. And so on. For how long? It can be shown that the rounds of spending and re-spending converge to a definite value, for at each stage only the variable costs are passed along: the capital charges are withdrawn. So the impact is directed primarily towards the consumer goods sector, and will be a multiple of the original expenditure, the size of which will depend on the ratio of capital charges to variable costs. Although complicated, the point is straightforward: a certain level of business demand for capital goods will *generate* both a primary level of employment and output in the capital goods sector, and a secondary level of employment and output in the consumer goods sector.

Let's see if we can now draw some conclusions. First, look more closely at the relationship between the wage bill in heavy industry and the corresponding activity in the consumer goods sector. Revenue in the capital goods sector is equal to total investment spending by business; take away wages (neglecting any other current charges) and the remainder is the gross profit in that sector. Now that wage bill is spent on consumer goods and, to produce that level of consumer goods for sale outside the consumer sector itself, the industries there will have to employ a certain number of workers, whose pay will be spent on consumer goods, of course. The total revenue received by industries in the sector will equal the total wage bill, that is, the wage bills of the two sectors combined. But again, the consumer sector's revenue minus its wage costs (again neglecting other current charges) equals its profit. Hence, our first conclusion: *the wage bill of the capital goods industries provides the profit of the consumer goods industries.* A second conclusion follows at once. Since the profit of the consumer sector equals the wage bill of the capital goods sector, and the revenue of that sector equals total investment spending by business, total profit equals investment spending. (This was once stated as an aphorism by Michal Kalecki, the famous Polish economist: 'Business gets what it spends, workers spend what they get.' That is to say, the profits that business actually realizes depend on business's own investment spending, while the consumption of workers is governed by the wages they receive. It does *not* mean that a particular business will get back what it spends – it means that business in the aggregate will earn in proportion to its spending.)

The Circulation of Money

Notice that these two propositions provide the basis for an account of the circulation of goods by means of credit money. Suppose that banks grant businesses lines of credit equal to what will be needed to finance the production of their normal full capacity output. (The negotiation of such lines of credit will be part of the installation of plant and equipment; business would be foolish to try and build a plant the operation of which the banking system would be unwilling to finance.) Consider an increase in expected sales from a low to a high level of operation. Businesses draw additional credit to hire more labor and/or pay overtime. The wage payments are deposited, and then spent and redeposited as sales proceeds. The consumer goods sector draws credit, pays wages, sells consumer goods to its own workers (along with others), and repays the credits. The circulation of the wage funds of the capital goods sector is more complicated. Since the wage bill in the capital goods sector generates the profit in the consumer goods sector, the additional wage spending in capital goods means additional consumer goods profits, which finance that sector's additional investment spending. The extra profits of individual firms may be more or less than what they need to finance their own further investment, but profit for the sector as a whole equals the borrowing of the capital goods sector. Hence this profit can finance the investment spending by the consumer goods sector, so the additional profit will finance additional purchases of capital goods. The additional sales receipts enable the capital goods sector to repay its borrowing from its line of credit. Circulation can be financed at any level of activity by bank deposits, which automatically adjust to the level required. There cannot be any problem of shortage or surplus of funds, unless financial constraints are imposed as a matter of policy, or financial institutions fail to mobilize funds rapidly enough or make mistakes in the granting of lines of credit.[1]

Now consider the financing of a government deficit. Suppose the deficit consists of government purchases of capital goods. The government order will be met by production financed by drawing on lines of credit, to cover wage costs, which in turn result in increased profit in the consumer goods sector. This additional profit, if borrowed, will finance the wage costs of the goods the government is purchasing. The capital costs will have to be borrowed from the capital goods sector, but the government purchase will provide that sector with additional revenue, over and above wage costs, of exactly the amount required. Hence the purchase can be effected by borrowing the extra profit of the consumer goods sector, equal to the wage bill of the newly produced goods, and covering the remainder by credit from the capital goods sector itself. The borrowing here is exactly offset by the creation of additional earnings; hence the transactions need have no effect on interest rates. But borrowing to finance the government deficit does set up a permanent flow of interest payments from the general public to the financial institutions wealthy and liquid enough to lend to the government.[2]

Alternatively, the government deficit could be monetized, that is, financed by money creation. The usual objection is that money creation is inflationary: money, once created, continues indefinitely in the system, whereas debts can be wiped out by repayment. But government currency issue offsets debt and private bank advances. Consider a government deficit not financed by taxation or by borrowing. Suppose the government proposes to spend on wages for its employees. It creates money and pays wages, which are spent on consumer goods. Employment, output and profits in the consumer industries will therefore be increased. These industries' receipts in currency will be greater than their advances by the amount of the government's spending; hence, after paying off their advances, they will still have cash in hand. (If they use this to pay dividends it will return as capitalist consumption.) In the next period, therefore, they will be able to reduce their use of their credit lines by the amount of new cash. (The consumer industries might increase their purchases of capital goods, in view of their increased sales to the government. In this case some of the new currency would end up in the coffers of the capital goods sector, which would reduce its use of credit lines in the next period.)

But surely this cannot continue indefinitely, from period to period?

Eventually all advances will be displaced, the currency in circulation will come to exceed the requirements of working capital, and inflation will result – or so the paragons of financial prudence would have it. But each period investment takes place, so potential output grows from period to period and so does the finance required for its circulation. If the government deficit were just equal to or less than the increase in the wage bill due to growth, then it could be regularly monetized without any problem – the additional money would circulate the additional goods. A larger deficit could be partly monetized on a regular basis.[3]

Investment and Wages

What we have just gone through is an essentially mathematical argument boiled down into prose (and none the worse for it). Now let's take stock and see why it was worth going through all this. Total realized profit (what firms get from the actual sales of current production) is not only equal to, but is governed by, *investment spending* – not by wages, not by consumer spending, not by saving or interest rates, or any of the other things business leaders commonly worry about. (Investment spending means purchases of capital goods and construction of factories, and also offices and shopping places.) Now this has to be understood carefully; many of these other things, particularly the level of wages but also the cost of materials, will enter into fixing the level of *potential profit* (the profit that could be earned with the given prices and real wage rate, using the presently installed capacity at the level of operation for which it was ideally designed). This is the profit you would get if everything ran the way it was supposed to, and your sales were what you had always hoped they would be. *Investment decisions* are made in the expectation of potential profit. Such decisions are complicated, involving nothing less than the whole future of the firm – what kinds of products to produce and how they should be designed and marketed, what methods of production to adopt, and on what scale to operate, how both investment and current operations should be financed, and how the new plant capacity should be fitted into the firm's table of organization. Virtually all features of the economy are relevant to investment decisions, but one thing stands out as *sine qua non*: no decision to build new productive capacity will be made unless the firm thinks its market is going to expand, or can be expanded (perhaps at the expense of rivals). Overall, then, the growth of capacity will be very likely to follow closely on the path of the expected growth of markets, a topic we will examine in a later chapter.

However, because the current level of actual profits depends on investment spending (assuming no government deficit), we can expect a slowdown in growth to show up as a crisis in profitability, as well as bringing a slump in employment and output. Note a further implication: the total amount of current profits does *not* depend on the level of real wages (although the level of *potential* profit is inversely related to wages), but higher wages do mean higher demand for consumer goods, which in turn leads to higher employment and output in the consumer goods sector. In a slump due to a slowdown in investment spending, an increase in real wages will not affect profits, but it will lead to an increase in employment. (There is an effect on profits, however. Higher real wages in the capital goods sector reduce profits there, but raise profits in the consumer goods industries. So changes in real wages will shift the proportion of total profit actually earned from one sector to another, although the total amount stays equal to investment.)

Two things now stand out. First, there could hardly be a more dramatic contrast than between the implications of the two theories for employment when real wages change.[4] According to orthodox supply and demand, when wages rise, offers of employment will be reduced: high wages squeeze profits and mean fewer jobs. According to the theory of effective demand, when wages rise there will be more consumer spending, and consequently employment will increase. (At full capacity the higher wages would push up prices rather than output. However, capacity is more flexible than is often realized; firms might be able to speed up or reorganize, so output and employment might expand even when the wage increase comes at normal 'full' capacity. Higher wages, in other words, may stimulate growth in productivity. More of this later.) Realized profits will be unaffected, unless the higher wages affect current investment spending. (Certainly higher wages might reduce investment spending; but notice that, if the new wage levels bring a new set of households into certain important consumer markets, this could lead to additional investment in production and sales facilities to service these new consumers. So the effect on investment could go either way.)

The second point follows directly. When there is a slump in employment, traditional theory, and conservatives everywhere, argue that real wages should be cut back. The Reagan administration wants to lower the minimum wage;[5] 'givebacks' have been the order of the day for a long time now in collective bargaining. However, the economy does not work according to the traditional theory – except in various small pockets, by-passed by history. The way the modern world works is explained by the theory of effective demand: output and employment are governed by current and expected sales, which take place at prices that have been established on the basis of a markup over current (variable) costs, where the size of the markup is determined by the monetarily fixed capital charges required to finance large-scale technology. So cutting wages will make things worse; it will reduce consumer goods sales, and so worsen, rather than improve, the employment situation, and it will most likely have no effect on the level of realized profits. Instead, real wages should be *increased* – if investment is down, then consumption should be raised, and one of the best ways to do this is to increase people's incomes. Of course, just how to do this, without upsetting many other arrangements or setting off an inflationary wage – price spiral, raises many difficult questions, requiring a comprehensive policy analysis, which must wait until Chapter 10.

The argument none the less does suggest that under some circumstances it could be appropriate for the government to lend its weight to attempts to raise wages. For example, in a prolonged slump, government policy might be directed both to raising minimum wages and to increasing government wages and salaries, so that competition would force private employers to follow suit, and so on. It could be objected that this would be inflationary, and yes, it would be; business would certainly try to maintain the traditional markup by raising prices. Hence, a policy of this sort would have to be accompanied by price controls; but controls have worked before, and they can be made to work again. More of all this later.

A Tendency to Stagnation

The working of the multiplier means that changes in investment spending engender corresponding, and larger, movements in the same direction in consumption spending, so long as output is below full capacity. This leads directly to a crucial insight: the economy of advanced capitalism has a built-in tendency to stagnation. A simple formula will show how this works. Let w be the real wage rate, n be labor per unit of output; then $z = 1 - wn$ will be the share of profit in output. Assuming wages to be fully spent, by the analysis earlier (amplified in the Appendix), $1/z$ is the multiplier, since all profits in a corporate economy are withdrawn from the circulation. Let I stand for investment spending, K for the capital stock, and v for the capital/output ratio. Then, ignoring many complications, aggregate demand will be I/z and aggregate capacity will be K/v. The argument, then, is that there will be a persistent tendency for $I/z < K/v$. Let's see why.

First, capitalism is competitive, so firms must build and carry excess capacity for precautionary and strategic reasons. A firm must be able to expand quickly when its market expands, or a new one opens. If it could not, but its competitors could, it would lose its market share, while the competitors would reap economies of scale, leaving it a relatively high-cost producer. Also, markets fluctuate; a firm that keeps its capacity at the level of average demand will be unable to service peak demand, and will lose customers to those who can deliver any time. Finally, firms with reserve capacity will be able to adapt their underutilized plant to new ventures or new product designs; they can plunge right in and still keep their normal operations running. Firms without adequate reserve capacity will have to shut down current operation or build a whole new plant to engage in a new venture. Hence competition dictates that each firm should always carry some excess capacity.

But each firm will choose the amount it will carry on the basis of the best market position – the largest share – it could reasonably hope to secure and defend. Not all firms can have their best position; however, winners imply losers. So when all firms are taken together, the aggregate reserve capacity will be excessive. When there is excess capacity there will be a tendency to cut back on investment spending. Why bring more capacity on line, when what you already have is not operating full blast? Projects will be put on hold, plant openings delayed, and capital spending generally will be cut back. So I will decline. But that is not all: carrying excess capacity is costly, hence firms will try to cut back on operating costs. Wages will be pushed down, corners will be cut, and efforts will be made to raise productivity; hence z will rise. The decline of I may be temporary; if the projects are sound, spending on them will eventually pick up. But the effect on z is likely to be long term. Moreover, technological innovations will require modernization of plant, and v will fall. Hence whenever $I/z < K/v$, the system will set up forces that will tend to worsen this inequality. (If z rises a great deal, many more investment projects may come to seem potentially profitable, and would this not raise investment? But potential profit cannot be realized without a market; if the system is in a slump, if demand is not actively growing, investment decisions will not be converted into spending.)

Competition for sales requires cutting operating costs, improving product design, and preventing delays in delivery. The result is techno-logical improvement – but at the cost of stagnation and waste for the system considered as a whole. We shall return to this point later.

Moreover, as income per capita grows due to technical progress, per capita savings, taxes and imports can be expected to grow also, as with-drawals from a given wage bill. This strengthens the tendency to stagnation: not only does an equiproportionate increase in labor productivity and in wages reduce employment for a given level of investment; but, since household savings, taxes and imports depend on per capita income, the average rate of withdrawals is raised also. Thus, for a given level of investment plus government spending plus exports, the balance with profits plus savings plus taxes plus imports will be struck at a lower level of employment and output.

Conventional Wisdom as Practical Folly

We can now begin to appreciate the radical contrast between the conventional wisdom on the economy, based on the traditional theory, which treats the system as if it were resource-constrained, so that prices would reflect relative scarcities, and in which government activity could expand only at the expense of private, and the practical notion of effective demand, the core of Keynesian economics, which tells us that the system basically responds to – sales! What else would we expect? Do businesses want to make money or not? And this, of course, is where government deficit spending comes in, according to the Keynesian view: because it adds to sales. By contrast, the conventional wisdom would have us cut back the government as much as possible, thereby reducing sales.

The basic idea is very simple. There are two kinds of demands, those like business investment spending that are largely independent of other current economic activity, and those that are possible only because of other current activity, such as consumer demand by working-class families, which depends on wages from current employment. The dependent demands pass along the impulse generated by the independent ones, but at each stage the variable costs are separated out from the total revenue received, and only they are passed along. The part of revenue corresponding to profits, or capital charges, is withdrawn from the circuit of expenditure. And the proposition we looked at earlier (that investment equals and governs realized profits) can be put in this way: employment and output have to adjust until total withdrawals from the stream of spending equal the total of independent inputs, or injections, into it. Withdrawals and injections have to balance. Intuitively this is easy to see – if either were greater there would be pressure to contract or to expand, for a net balance one way or the other would set up movements of the dependent expenditures. (Withdrawals, like saving or corporate retained earnings, refer to funds pulled out of circulation; that is to say, not spent. So an increase in withdrawals means a fall in sales.)

So now we can see what effect government taxing and spending have. Government spending figures as an injection, an addition to the stream of expenditures, which will normally result in additional consumer demand. Taxation, at least of wages and salaries, will normally count as a withdrawal. When these two balance, the net effect will be nil; when there is a deficit, there will be a net impulse to expenditure; when there is a surplus, there will be a drag. So much is common Keynesian doctrine, and can be found, though usually distorted, in almost any textbook. But there is a point to our redrawing of the picture: neither taxation nor government spending is as simple as the picture of mainstream Keynesian theory presents it. So let's take a closer look.

The government budget can impact either on capital goods or on consumer goods, or on both, or, of course, on completely different kinds of things if we introduce a more complicated set of categories. But let's keep it simple (remembering that we are neglecting foreign trade for the time being). Even with only two categories of goods – those for consumers and those for investment – the impact of government spending becomes complicated to analyze, because its effects in the two cases are not the same. For example, government spending on capital goods will increase output, employment and profits in both sectors, but government spending on wages and salaries affects only the consumer goods sector. An even more dramatic contrast can be seen in the case of taxes. Taxes on wages and salaries reduce expenditure in the consumer sector. (If there is no worker saving, they reduce it by the full amount of the tax; otherwise they reduce it by the proportion of income spent.) But taxes on profits, or more generally on capital income, fall on what is largely a withdrawal. So such taxes do not *add* to withdrawals.

And this leads to a major point: government spending financed by taxes on profits will have a net stimulative effect; in fact as far as the net impact on sales is concerned, it will have virtually the same effect as if there were no taxes at all.[6] Of course, taxes on (future) profits may reduce business's willingness to spend on new plant and equipment, although this effect is often exaggerated. But taxes on the profits from present operations are quite distinct from taxes that will fall on the profits from plant and equipment currently being planned or built. These can be exempted if it is feared that investment in them will be curtailed. (There are other reasons for taxes and government spending, we must repeat; but this book is concerned only with the overall or aggregate economic impact.) To put the point dramatically, it is possible to conceive of a fully balanced budget that would have the same impact as a deficit budget with government spending and no taxes at all. All that is necessary is to raise the taxes from profit income, that is, income that would be withdrawn.

Now, finally, we can sum up. Here's a basic conclusion: neither the concepts of the deficit that we discussed earlier, and that figure in the current debates, both technical or popular, nor the commonly used analytical models are adequate, or even appropriate, to an analysis of the impact of the government budget on output and employment. Why not? Because they are based on the assumption that the corporate industrial system can be studied using a theoretical approach that assumes it to be resource-constrained rather than demand-determined. An exception would be studies based on the 'flow' concept of the budget, but, even there, the usual format does not distinguish taxation of capital income items from taxation of wage and salary incomes, nor do the corresponding models analytically distinguish between the categories of spending, to examine the way they impact on the different sectors.

In short, not only is the accounting concept of the government budget confused, as we saw earlier, but there is no adequate version that makes it possible to analyze its macroeconomic impact. The whole discussion is almost hopelessly at sea. In the current discussions we are not primarily dealing with a scientific question or even with an intellectual one. What we have on our hands is a matter of ideology, doing yeoman service in the interest of conservative politics. In Chapter 9 we will take a hard and critical look at the current discussions, but first we should join our account of effective demand to an analysis of the growth and development of the state's activities that has taken place as the system changed from a craft economy to one based on corporate mass production. Then we shall have to look at the underlying pattern of capital development in the post war era, to see what brought about the slump of the 1970s.

Notes

1   Financial constraints can be policy imposed, or they can arise from the normal working of the system during the downswing of the business cycle. Contraction leads to a shortage of profit; hence to difficulties in debt-servicing. Financial institutions find they have to write off a larger part of their loan portfolio as bad debt, and consequently restrict their lending and call in short paper. This can severely dampen investment, that is, the decisions to undertake projects; but that has nothing to do with financing the production and sale of capital goods, which is a matter of the *circulation* of current output by means of money. For further discussion and references, see Nell (1986).

2   Marx's comment on the financing of the Napoleonic War is instructive:

> Is there anything more crazy than that . . . the Bank of England, whose notes only had credit thanks to the state, then got paid by the state, i.e. by the public, in the form of interest on government loans, for the power the state gave it to transform these very notes from paper into money and lend them to the state.
>
> (*Marx*, 1981, p. 675)

3 An excess quantity of currency in circulation need not result in inflation – certainly not directly. If the reason for the availability of excess currency is a depressed level of business activity, it may be hoarded in anticipation of falling prices. Or it may be loaned, in which case it could lead to downward pressure on interest rates, which might tend to stimulate investment. If there were excess currency and the economy were operating at full capacity, such a stimulus could be inflationary. But the economy would have to be operating only with currency; otherwise contractions of bank advances could offset the excess currency and eliminate the pressure. No modern economy could operate that way.

4 According to conventional theory, a rise in the real wage is both required and sufficient to induce households to offer more labor; the labor supply curve rises from left to right. But in the 1970s for many groups real wages and household incomes were stagnant or falling, while their labor force participation rose. One explanation is that they sought to maintain their standard of living by working more when wages or earnings fell. This suggests a downward-sloping supply curve of labor, at least over some ranges. Cf Appendix, § VII, below.

5 The *New York Times* (14 January 1987) argued in an editorial that the minimum wage should be abolished altogether.

6 For a given level of government spending and a given level of taxation, then, the more the taxes fall on corporations, the more stimulative the budget, and the more they fall on households, the less the stimulus. In 1960, corporate taxes accounted for 23.2 per cent of federal revenue in the USA; by 1983 this had fallen to 6.2 per cent and the new tax law reduces it even further.

Appendix: The Post-Keynesian Theory of the Multiplier

I Short Run and Long Run

First, some terminology. The word 'equilibrium' has come to have the connotation of 'market-clearing'; since we shall argue that the labor market does not necessarily clear, it will be best to use a different term. So, I will speak of 'fully adjusted positions', meaning positions which satisfy the relationships of the model, and which are reached as the result of a convergent sequence of adjustments. A *long-run* fully adjusted position is one in which industry sizes are such that growth is balanced, prices are such that the rate of profit is uniform, capacity is operated at the planned level, and profits provide the savings required for actual investment to equal planned. This is Lowe's 'dynamic equilibrium'. In the same vein, a *short-run* fully adjusted position is one in which the aggregate profit currently realized from actual sales just equals the aggregate investment spending businesses currently plan to undertake (plus business consumption costs). The levels of capacity operation and of employment vary with spending, and the position is reached as the result of a convergent sequence of adjustments. These two definitions clearly differ from the usual ones, so will now have to be explained.

But first the distinction between short-run and long-run analysis requires clarification. The object of both is to determine fully adjusted positions; in both, there may be positions of *incomplete* adjustment at which, nevertheless, for various reasons, the economy may come to rest. But – it must seem – the short run is really just another position in incomplete adjustment. We 'abstract from' the adjustment of the capital stock, restricting the analysis to a period in which plant and equipment can reasonably be treated as given and unchanging. Awkward questions follow: can such a period be long enough for the multiplier to work? What happens if new factories come on line before the multiplier process is complete? Since the process is infinite how can it ever be completed in a finite time? Morever, since new equipment is *continually* being brought into operation – and old retired – what determines *how much* of this change can 'reasonably' be neglected? Why should it be the same in all sectors of the economy?

These questions are essentially unanswerable, and indicate that the distinction was developed in a neo-Classical context, from which it has been carried over into a different framework, where it no longer fits.

Neo-Classical theory determines value, which, for it, is equivalent to relative price, according to the principle of substitution in the light of consumer preferences, on the one hand, and technical possibilities on the other. With factor endowments given, the distinction between long run and short run then simply means that in the long run all factor usages are variable, i.e. substitution applies universally, whereas in the short run some factors (capital factors) are fixed, limiting the scope of substitution. This is the definition which Keynes, following orthodox theory, adopted. But it makes no sense in a context in which investment is taking place continuously.

So, a new formulation of the distinction is needed. At any given moment a certain amount of new plant and equipment is in the pipeline; such plant and equipment was planned in the expectation that when it was complete there would also have taken place a corresponding growth in markets. Not only does capacity grow; markets also grow. So the capacity currently in the pipeline was planned to develop at the same rate as the growth in markets – which can also be thought of as 'in the pipeline'. The distinction can therefore be defined, not so much by the length of time, as by the kind of management decisions involved. Long-run decisions are decisions to undertake a project, to put it in the pipeline. Short-run decisions concern moving things along – how fast to bring to completion projects to which the firm is already committed. These are therefore decisions on how much to spend on investment now, in the current bookkeeping period. Long-run decisions, then, are decisions about new commitments, which will translate into investment spending in future periods. Short-run decisions will characteristically be influenced by expectations of the state of market demand at the anticipated completion date of the project, and by the current cost or opportunity cost of funds, together with considerations of the risk involved in making major expenditure commitments in the light of current and immediately future sales. Long-run decisions will be influenced by expectations of the long-term growth of the market, by technical developments in product design and in the manufacturing processes, and by the firm's beliefs about its ability to increase its market share. Once a long-run commitment is made, a firm is locked in; not absolutely, of course, but changes in the project's scale and design will be expensive. But – again within limits – it can vary the time of completion, pushing it through rapidly, or slowing down and taking it easy.

This makes it possible to define short- and long-run adjustment processes, corresponding respectively to short- and long-run fully adjusted positions.

Very roughly, the long-run position is one in which prices are such as to establish the uniform rate of profit required to provide the finance necessary to construct the capacity that will supply the expected growth of markets; the corresponding adjustment processes will tend to bring the growth rates of different markets into line with one another, and consequently also rates of profit, which in turn implies adjustment of benchmark prices.[1]

Building on this definition of the long run, a fully adjusted short-run position, then, is one in which investment spending, implementing the investment decisions already taken, is being carried out at a rate justified by the firms' *current* earnings and financial position. Such a fully adjusted position will imply a certain level of output and employment, and one project in short-run analysis consists of comparing such levels for different values of the parameters.

Besides comparisons of alternative short-run positions, short-run analysis must deal with adjustment processes – and here the multiplier is pre-eminent. Instead of comparing the fully adjusted levels of output, employment (and other variables), corresponding to two different levels of investment spending, we examine the sequence of effects resulting from a *change* from one level of investment spending to another. This sequence is examined within the framework of *given long-run conditions*; changes in those conditions may or may not affect the short-run adjustment process. But the problem of new factories coming into operation does not arise so long as those new factories are consistent with the given long-run balance of growing capacity and growing markets. Since the long-run position is defined as a balance between the *growth* of normal capacity with the *growth* of markets, the short run need not be – and has not been here – defined as a period in which capacity is fixed. Instead, the short run concerns the current percentage of capacity used, including the capacity to build and equip factories, while the long run concerns the planning for the construction and financing of new capacity to supply new markets. In precise terms, the short-run problem is to determine the ratio of actual output to normal capacity where both actual output and normal capacity are conceived as growing at their long-term rates. Hence we first require an adequate characterization of the economy's long-run position at a moment of time.[2, 3]

II Short Run Changes in a Long Run Setting

One sector produces means of production, the other the consumption good.[4] In each sector the price of a unit amount of output equals profits plus replacement and materials plus wages, where prices will be such that the ratio of profits to value of capital will be the same in the two sectors.

Besides prices and profits, the amount of output and its division between consumption and investment must also be shown. The output of consumption will be divided between the workers in the two sectors, and the output of means of production will go for replacement and growth in the two sectors. Thus we have:

$$p = (d+r)\ ap + (1+w)\ b \qquad q_A = (d+g)\ (aq_A + \alpha q_B) \qquad (1)$$
$$1 = (d+r)\ \alpha p + (1+w)\ \beta \qquad q_B = (1+c)\ (bq_A + \beta q_B) \qquad (2)$$

Here d stands for the rate of depreciation, assumed to be constant and the same in both sectors, r is the rate of profits, w the net real wage (expressed as a percentage of subsistence), and p the price ratio – the price of capital goods in terms of consumer goods. The Roman letters (a, b) give the input requirements of capital goods and labor, respectively, in the capital goods sector, while the Greek letters α, β state the same requirements for consumer goods. (Note that b and β are the consumer goods required at the socially desired subsistence level to support the labor needed during the production period.)

Turning to the equations on the right side, g is the rate of growth, c is the level of per capita consumption, and q_A and q_B are the respective sizes of the two industries.

Eliminating p from the equations on the right-hand side of the price equations gives r as a function of w; eliminating w gives p as a function of r.

Letting $\omega = 1 + w$, $R = d + r$, we write the first:

$$\frac{\alpha b}{a \beta} = \frac{(1/\beta - \omega) \cdot (1/a - R)}{\omega R}, \qquad (3)$$

a hyperbola bending inward or outward, according as $\alpha/\beta \gtrless a/b$, and the second:

$$p = \frac{b}{R \alpha b + \beta \cdot (1 - Ra)}, \qquad (4)$$

a rise in R can lead to a rise or fall in p, depending on $\alpha/\beta \gtrless a/b$.

Defining $q = q_A/q_B$, $C = 1+c$, $G = d+g$, and then eliminating q we have:

$$\frac{\alpha b}{a \beta} = \frac{(1/\beta - C)\ (1/a - G)}{CG}, \qquad (5)$$

the exact counterpart of the ωR trade-off. But the relationship between q and G does not echo that between p and R. It follows from the first quantity equation alone:

$$q = \frac{\alpha G}{1 - Ga} i \qquad (6)$$

a rise in G will always lead to an expansion of the capital goods sector.

For simplicity we can assume that all and only wages are spent on consumption, from which it follows that the rate of growth equals the rate of profit. Of course, we should allow both for worker saving and capitalist consumption, but neither seriously affects the working of the system.

Hence,

$$\omega = C. \qquad (7)$$

Now we are in a position to see the consequences of the preceding discussion of long-run/short-run distinction. The short run is a moment of historical time; at the point when the period begins, therefore, there will exist a well-defined level of productive capacity in each sector. This calls for careful consideration. Presently existing capacity was constructed because it was expected that it would be used at a planned normal rate, in certain expected market conditions, as regards prices, sales, etc., and that by so using it certain results in the way of market growth and profits would be achieved. In other words, existing capacity both embodies the expectations of market conditions and the goals of those who built it. This makes it possible to give an *instrumental interpretation* of the actual system existing at any moment of time.[5]

Both the goals and the specific conditions are given, embodied in the existing plant and equipment. Thus we can solve for the behavior patterns that would achieve the goals, given the expected conditions – the expectations held at the time the capacity was built. These behavior patterns – outputs, prices, growth and profits – then, are inherent in the existing system. They are the ones which are implied by the goals and expecations held by those who planned and built the capacity that exists today.

Even though these values are inherent in the system, it may be asked whether they are relevant to short-run effective demand questions. For this they would surely have to be centers of gravity, or at least starting points for current operations. But capacity constructed in earlier periods may have been based on mistaken or incomplete information about technology or markets. If current information is better, then surely current behaviour would be based on it; inherent or embodied values would then simply be 'bygones', having no practical significance.

This confuses two very different matters. Up-to-date or superior information is indeed relevant, but to the current planning of *future* investment projects. It is no use in running current operations. What good is it to know that you could have built a better plant? Or catered to a more reliable or wealthier market? The plant and the marketing system at hand make up the current operation that will produce current revenue. There isn't anything else; the information about what might have been is largely beside the point.

The construction of the present system engendered commitments, obligations and expectations. Business borrowed or issued shares, promising to pay a certain rate of interest and/or raising expectations of dividends or capital gains. Banks and households made loans and investments, planning their revenues and expenditures accordingly. Worker households located near factories in the expectation of jobs and incomes. Retail merchants placed their outlets in what they regarded as appropriate neighborhoods, and banks financed them, both decisions being based on expectations of certain levels of income and employment. Examples can be drawn from virtually any sphere of economic activity. The anticipated values inherent in existing plant and equipment are also written into formal contracts, or form the basis of practical work-life decisions for households and firms in all parts of the economy. They are necessarily the starting point for current operations.

To derive these values we must start from the given capacity levels in the two sectors. Call these q_A and q_B , respectively.

The ratio $q = q_A/q_B$ will therefore be determined. This requires that the new capacity coming on the line during the short period be balanced, so that q will remain constant. But from (6) this means that G is determined; hence C follows from (5). Since we have assumed that all and only wages are consumed, ω is determined by (7) and R follows from (3) which determines p in (4). Thus, at whatever moment of historical time (within the capitalist era) the short period in question begins, it always has a well-defined long-period setting. Note that in this setting the long-run equilibrium real wage is determined in relation to the capacity sizes of the sectors. To change the real wage, relative capacity sizes will have to be changed, which requires investment.

Moreover, this setting is centered on a basic relationship whose short-period counterpart will prove to be the 'multiplier' mechanism. Multiply the price equations by the quantities and the quantity equations by the prices. Both sides of the means of production equations in (1) now equal Pq_A; both sides of means of consumption equal q_B. When $\omega = C$, we know that $R = G$. Hence, cancelling 'a' terms in the first and β terms in the second , we have:

$$\omega b q_A = G a p q_B$$

$$C b q_A = R a p q_B.$$

(8)

Numerically, of course, these are equivalent forms of the sectoral balance condition, but it will pay to look closely at the interpretation of each. The first states that the investment goods paid as wages (whose *value* equals the wage bill) in the investment goods sector, must equal the net growth or capital accumulation in the consumer goods sector. The second states the value of consumption goods spending by workers in the investment goods sector equals the profit earned in the consumer goods sector.

Together, these two interpretations of the balancing condition make it

Figure 5.1

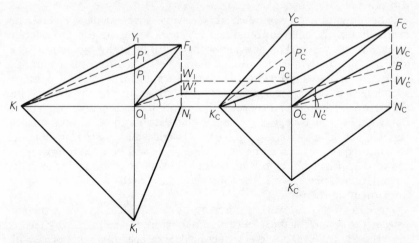

possible to express these equations in a diagram of long-run equilibrium, with uniform wage and profit rates in both sectors (see Figure 5.1). Employment in each sector, N_I and N_C is measured in manpower along the horizontal axis from the origin to the right; capital invested for each sector, K_I and K_C is measured in money value from the origin to the left along the same axis. The vertical axis reading upward in each case measures output in money value, Y_I and Y_C, and reading down from the origin it measures capital again.

The sectors are drawn with consumer goods assumed labor intensive and capital goods capital intensive. The slopes of the lines $K_I - Y_I$ and $K_C - Y_C$ give the respective output–capital ratios, those of the lines $K_I - N_I$ and $K_C - N_C$ the capital–labor ratios, and those of $O_I - F_I$ and $O_C - F_C$ are the labor productivities. Angles $W_IO_IN_I$ and $W_CO_CN_C$ represent the wage rates, equal in both sectors, and angles $P_IK_IO_I$ and $P_CK_CO_C$ are the profit rates, also equal. Lines F_IP_I and W_IO_I are parallel, as are F_CP_C and W_CO_C. Hence, O_IP_I and O_CP_C are the respective amounts of profit in the sectors. If all, and only, this profit is invested, then the two sectors will grow uniformly.

The balance between the sectors is shown by line W_IP_C, which expresses the fact that profit in the consumer goods sector equals the wage bill in investment goods.

The long-run equilibrium setting, therefore, consists of the outputs, prices and profits which are implied by an instrumental analysis based on the existing levels of capacity in the two sectors. This is a notional equilibrium, not an actual one, but it is not fanciful, either, for it is the position implied by the goals and expectations which underlay the construction of the presently existing plant and equipment. Hence the long-run prices can be used to value output and aggregate the capital stock; the long-run real wage will be the full employment real wage, and so on. But in actual fact, the current situation of the economy may be very different. The current situation, of course, is the economy's short-run position.

It is important to see what this means. Investment spending, for example, may be delayed. But the delay need not invite the cancellation of investment plans. The new factory will still be built, and another one after it. But the whole time horizon will be shifted into the future. Of course, delaying a project may sometimes mean a greater burst of spending than otherwise at some later date, in an attempt finally to bring the new plant into operation according to the initial schedule. But this is likely to be the exception. Usually the date of inauguration will be variable within some range. Similarly, a boom which shifts plans forward will not require less spending later; new plans will be moved forward – the whole horizon shifts forward or back, but the long run still means the formulation of plans, while the short run concerns the actual spending on implementing them.

The case of the real wage is different, but the short-run level of the real wage is also defined by the pattern of actual, current spending, as this results from the current level of aggregate demand. Such spending takes place both in the market for goods and in the market for labor. Depending on the level of capacity utilization and the degree of price flexibility, money prices may be bid up, stay constant or fall, and the same is true for money wages. The short-run level of the real wage, then, can be defined as the deviation from its long-run position which results from the relative movement of money wages and money prices consequent on the state of effective demand in the labor and product markets, respectively. Since there is no *a priori* reason to expect that the proportionate changes in money wages and prices will be the same, the real wage is likely to vary in the short run with changes in effective demand. It is plausible that changes in effective demand will pressure money wages and prices in the same direction. But notice that the real wage can either *rise or fall* when money wages and prices are moving in the same direction, *whichever the direction*.

III   Utilization Functions

The theory of effective demand concerns the causes and consequences of the varying utilization of existing productive capacity.

Presently existing plant and equipment was constructed – and financed – in the expectation of a normal pattern of usage, reflecting both the expected variance of normal demand, and the socially accepted patterns of living. In particular, most factories will run a full-scale first shift, a light second, and a skeleton third, mostly for maintenance, repairs, and clean-up. The plant size will be chosen so that normal demand in the initial years can be met by effective operation of the first shift; as the market grows the second shift can be run more intensively, until new factories are ready. In the event of an unexpected, or cyclical, drop in current demand, the second shift can be laid off, and if the drop is severe the first shift can be cut back. Alternatively, suppose there is an unexpectedly strong boom in sales; the first shift will work flat out, the second will be beefed up; if necessary the third shift can move – at least for a time – from maintenance and repairs to production. In short, the possibility of varying utilization – and therefore employment – is *built-in*; it is an essential part of industrial design.

The advantages are evident from the point of view of the firm and from that of business as a whole. For a firm, its future sales depend on overall prosperity, on the growth of its particular market, and on its competitive position vis-à-vis other firms. All of these must be regarded not only as uncertain, but as liable to fluctuate in the winds of chance. When a new market opens up, it must be able, at relatively short notice, to increase its output, to capture part of the action. When the market stagnates for what look like short-term reasons, it does not want to go on stockpiling indefinitely, running up carrying costs. On the other hand, investment in long-lasting plant and equipment requires reliability in the stream of earnings over time. Otherwise financing will not be secure. Firms cannot cut price and dump with every dip in the sales curve; that will just 'spoil the market'. Adjustments in outputs and employment provide the required safety valve.

Plant and equipment, of course, cannot be operated without a labor force. So factories must be located where a pool of potential workers exists; when output is increased new workers will be drawn in; when sales fall off, workers will be laid off and supported by their families or by state welfare. If the swings are wide or long lasting, however, this can create social tension.

Each plant will be able to run at greater than normal capacity, but this does not imply that *all together* could, for that would entail a large pool of surplus labor in normal conditions. The labor supply must be adequate for all plants to operate at normal capacity, and business would not wish to locate where there existed no surplus labor at all; we can therefore presume that some short-run surplus labor is available, but to say anything more would require a long-run analysis.

So, in normal circumstances there will be three kinds of unemployment. Let N_F represent the fully participating labor force (all the workers who want to work given the kinds of jobs available) and the operative wage structure, N_C the level of normal capacity employment, and N_a the actual labor demanded, while N represents the level of actual employment. Then in normal conditions $N_F > N_C \geqslant N_a > N$ where $N_F - N_C$ represents structural unemployment – there are not enough places in the assembly line when it is running at normal capacity to employ all persons willing to work or capable of being drawn in. This is Marx's 'reserve army'. $N_C - N_a$ represents Keynes' 'involuntary unemployment', where the actual demand for labor is less than the demand at normal capacity operation, indicating that sales are slower than required for 'normal' plant operation. Note that this does *not* imply that sales are slower than 'expected', for the current short period. They may be running *exactly* as expected at this time. They are lower *only* in relation to the expected average level of sales over the lifetime of the plant, and they may well fall within the variance foreseen when the plant was built. Finally $N_a - N$ represents unfilled vacancies, a measure of frictional unemployment due to job search by workers and personnel screening by companies. Our concern here will chiefly be with Keynesian unemployment, $N_C - N_a$.

In an industrial system, employment reflects the degree to which capacity is utilized. Demand in excess of engineering capacity cannot be met, nor will it lead to the employment of more labor; demand in excess of normal capacity can only be met by adding another shift. Employment as well as output, therefore, is constrained by capacity. No more men can be employed than there are places on the assembly line; jobs reflect the equipment installed in factories. Jobs will be offered as demand increases up to capacity; workers will be laid off as demand falls below capacity. Output will increase or decrease to meet demand as employment is varied. So there will be a definite functional relationship between employment and output,[6] assuming that the level of output is uniquely correlated with the level of employment, that is, with the degree of capacity utilization, regardless, for example, of whether utilization reached that level by increasing or decreasing. When employment increases output will increase.[7]

Utilization functions can be defined for each plant and aggregated to show the correspondence between output and employment for the whole society. What is the shape of the resulting function? There are three possibilities: constant, increasing, and diminishing returns to the utilization of capacity. Tradition would have it that successive doses of additional labor applied to fixed equipment will bring declining increments of output. But this belief is based on a misunderstanding. The argument for diminishing marginal returns depends on successive doses of employment being applied to *efficiently utilized* equipment. Each time labor was added, the use and perhaps also the nature of the equipment changed; only its amount as capital remained constant. Different levels of employment might be engaged in very different types of labor. Each level of employment, therefore, represented the 'best practice' technique for that amount of labor applied to the *given amount of capital*, which, however, will generally be embodied in very different concrete forms at different points in the function. That such a function cannot be constructed has been demonstrated in the recent 'capital theory' controversies; but this in no way affects the very different concept of a utilization function (Nell, 1980b, Part II). However, for the same reason, the traditional arguments for diminishing returns have no weight either. Why should returns diminish when the plant is being run more nearly at the rate for which it was designed? Surely one might expect returns to be higher, and maintenance costs per unit lower, at the rate of output for which the engineers planned. And this is what some evidence seems to suggest. In any case, a conventional short-term production function shows alternative positions of fully adjusted equilibrium. Capital is embodied in the best choice technique, labor is organized efficiently, and so on. Hence, the system cannot move from one level of employment to another, for to do so would require reorganizing and perhaps rebuilding the capital stock. By contrast, a utilization function shows alternative levels of employment when a *given* industrial system is run more or less intensively, according to capitalist principles. So there is no difficulty describing movement from one level of activity to another. It is precisely the appropriate concept for analyzing short-run changes in activity.

Firms adjust employment to sales, then, producing output to maintain their inventory at a reasonable level, in the light of storage space and carrying costs. Now consider a change in the level of business receipts, say an increase. Firms will increase employment, paying out more in wages. They will also increase their purchases of materials, replacement parts, and energy from other businesses. In other words, increasing their output requires increased outlay on variable costs. But, so long as this increase lies within the normal range, there is no reason to suppose they will have to pay higher wage rates or higher prices. There will *not*, however, be any change in their fixed obligations. (To increase their spending firms have to draw on working capital. To operate at normal capacity they must have suitable lines of credit, in proportion to their expected net worth. But this is part of their long-run calculation, even though interest on working capital rises with the level of activity.) Debt servicing and management salaries are the same. Earnings, however, rise. But these earnings are not passed on. Indeed, their amount will not be easy to determine at once. For while a change in the level of sales can be ascertained quickly from order books and delivery reports – making possible a relatively quick adjustment of output and employment – the effect on earnings cannot be finally determined until both the consequences of working the equipment harder have become apparent, and the rate and average time lag of payments have been determined – for payment is never immediate. Moreover, replacement costs may very well differ from historical costs. Inventory must be taken, storage costs assessed; sales commissions, packaging and handling, and overheads must be allocated. At some point, usually for the annual shareholders meeting, an audit will take place, estimates of all these various costs will be evaluated, and an earnings statement prepared. At this point a dividend will be declared. But it is unlikely that this dividend will bear any strong or direct relationship to the change in sales. A far more important factor in determining the size of the dividend will be the firms' need for finance in order to carry out its future new investment plans. In short, profits, being the value of the surplus generated in production, are a *withdrawal*, or leakage, from circulation. Wages and materials costs are passed along, as one would expect from the concept of 'variable costs'. But interest costs, dividends and other fixed costs are not. Hence the multiplier, which should equal the inverse of the marginal withdrawal rate, will be set by *the ratio of variable costs to business sales receipts*, as will be shown in the next section.

A superficially similar point is sometimes expressed by claiming that the propensity to save out of profits is greater than the propensity to save out of wages, or, in extreme form, that the former is unity and the latter zero. This is misleading in several ways. Saving (refraining from consumption) is performed by households. But except for dividends and some top management salaries, profit income never *reaches* households. The point is not that profit income is paid to households and then saved; it is never paid out at all. Nor is this a 'market failure' or an 'imperfection'. It is how the business system works.

This requires both recalculating and reinterpreting the multiplier. This must be done with some care. We will develop both a diagrammatic and an analytical account of the multiplier.

IV   The Multiplier

The basic principles can be illustrated most easily by concentrating on the constant returns case. First, the functional correspondence between employment and output must be drawn (Figure 5.2).

Below a certain level, one would expect output to turn negative, indicating that workers use up more in the value of materials, energy, and user cost than they produce. However, this section of the utilization function can be ignored so long as the wage is always positive. For workers will not take employment in a capitalist system unless they are paid wages, which, having no assets to speak of, they must spend at once to support their families. Hence employment generates positive spending on consumption goods, which in turn generates further employment. So long as the wage line lies above the output line, employment at such levels would generate demand in excess of output. Conversely, the costs of such employment would exceed the returns from it. Either way, the range of values below N_O is infeasible. So N_O becomes the effective origin.

The slope of the wage line is shallower than that of the output line, reflecting the fact that the working force in a factory system as a whole

Figure 5.2

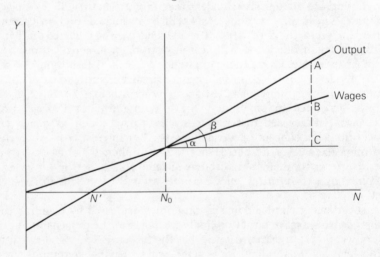

produces more than is needed to sustain and reproduce itself, given the life-style of the working class. Thus the ratio between the angles β and α, β/α, or between the corresponding line segments, AC/BC, gives the short-run rate of exploitation, or, more accurately, the ratio of total output to wage cost, or the markup over wages.

The real wage bill here is represented by a straight line, indicating that the real wage rate is constant in the short run for different possible levels of employment. A change in the real wage would thus be shown as a change in the angle α. (Yet surely, according to traditional thinking, if employment is below capacity, the unemployed workers will drive the wage down? This argument is defective. Unemployment will be accompanied by excess capacity, so, if prices are flexible, they will tend to fall. Hence the real wage may be unaffected, or, if prices fall further than money wages, it could even rise. But in the short run neither prices nor money wages are likely to be flexible. Employers may be unwilling to interrupt the cycle of production to dismiss workers in order to replace them with cheaper ones, and frequent price changes can spoil the market, cf Nell, 1988a.

In any case, it is very easy to show changes in the real wage: the slope (angle) of the wage line changes. It is important to remember that this may happen as a result either of changes in money wages or of changes in consumption goods prices. In either case the change is likely to be the result of interaction between a number of factors, and so should be derived precisely, rather than assumed. Hence for the basic analysis, it is best to begin on the assumption of a given real wage, reflecting current prices and the established money wage.

Investment *spending* can now be shown (see Figure 5.3). As argued above, investment *decisions* are taken by firms in the light of their long-run prospects – for new markets, developing new products, in the anticipation of growth of demand in existing markets, moving their

Figure 5.3

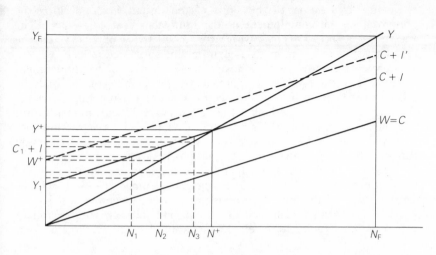

present products into new regions or classes of the population, or, in the case of capital goods, persuading new categories of business to adopt improved or new capital equipment. But current investment spending depends upon how rapidly businesses feel they should implement, carry through or complete the projects they have decided upon. This will depend partly upon their ability to finance investment spending, and partly upon their confidence that the time is now ripe to bring these projects into operation. Assume for simplicity then, that investment spending is determined independently of the current level of employment and output.[8] Aggregate demand will then be the sum of investment spending plus consumption spending (neglecting government spending and consumption by the capitalist class at this time). The intersection of aggregate demand and the employment or utilization function then gives the short-run equilibrium output and employment as percentages of capacity output and employment. Equilibrium output is Y^+, and W^+ is the corresponding total wage bill. The difference, $Y^+ - W^+$, then, is profit, P; so the division of the vertical line rising from N^+ to the output line gives the distribution of income between wages and profits, and also between consumption and investment. Other things being equal, then, the lower is the productivity of labor, the higher will be the level of employment, for a given real wage and level of investment.

Consider an upward shift in investment (the dotted line $C + I'$). Employment and output both increase, by a multiple of the increase in investment. Profits increase by the exact amount of the additional investment. 'Workers spend what they get; capitalists get what they spend'. The point of this aphorism is that the direction of causality is different in the wage–consumption and profit–investment relationships. Wages are the source of consumption spending: workers have no income-yielding assets, so cannot sustain a spending stream unless they receive wage income. By contrast, capitalists, owning the means of production, are in a position to initiate spending, which then generates the profits to underwrite it. The multiplier depends exclusively on the slope of the real wage line in relation to the slope of the output function; it is the reciprocal of the complement of the unit labor cost $1/(1 - \omega n)$.[9] The multiplier reflects the real wage, the productivity of labor, and the characteristics of the property system in this simplified model.

Suppose, for some reason, business offered a level of employment different from the equilibrium. Can we say, on the basis of this analysis, what would happen? In orthodox theory, dynamics is notoriously tricky, requiring special assumptions, which often prove difficult to justify. But here none are necessary. The assumptions needed for a rudimentary dynamic analysis have already been incorporated into the utilization function. Employers adjust their current production to their current sales, keeping inventory stocks constant. If the employment offered is below equilibrium, say at N_1, then the aggregate demand, $C_1 + I$, will be greater than Y_1, the output corresponding to N_1. Inventory will be run down, and additional plant and equipment, idle initially, will be brought into operation, leading to the employment of more workers. Employment will rise to N_2, but at this level of employment the wage bill, and so consumption spending, is now greater. Hence, aggregate demand now equals $C_2 + I > Y_2$. Again, inventory will be run down and more idle plant and equipment will be brought into operation, with employment rising to N_3 and aggregate demand to $C_3 + I > Y_3$ and so on until the equilibrium point is reached. Starting from an increment of investment, the resulting change in output is given by the wage times the amount of additional employment caused by the increase in investment; the second term by the wage times the first term, and so on. Hence, the additional consumption each time is the fraction of investment spending that goes to wages, which will be the wage rate times the amount of employment generated by the investment spending. Employment per unit output, $\Delta N / \Delta Y$, is the reciprocal of the productivity of labor, the slope of $Y = f(N)$.

So, remembering that the economy is divided into two sectors, the multiplier sequence will be:

$$\Delta C_1 = \omega n_I \, \Delta I$$

$$\Delta C_2 = \omega n_C \, \Delta C_1 = \omega n_I \omega n_C \, \Delta I \tag{9}$$

$$\Delta C_3 = \omega n_C \, \Delta C_2 = \omega n_I (\omega n_C)^2 \, \Delta I, \text{ etc.}$$

Hence:

$$\Delta C = \frac{\omega n_I}{1 - \omega n_C} \, \Delta I \text{ and } \Delta Y = \Delta I + \Delta C = \left(1 + \frac{\omega n_I}{1 - \omega n_C}\right) \Delta I. \tag{10}$$

Notice that the effects of the multiplier are concentrated in the consumer goods sector after the initial round of spending. It is there that employment and output increase.

Consider a change in investment spending. This can be represented in a two-sector diagram (see Figure 5.4). Initially gross investment demand is at capacity and, with the given real wage, employment in consumer goods is N_C and output Y_C, both also at capacity. Now let investment demand shift down to Y'_I so that equilibrium employment falls from N_I to N'_I. This reduces the wage bill in investment goods from W_I to W'_I and consequently lowers profit, output, and employment in consumer goods. But the decline in employment in investment goods depends only on the labor coefficient there (i.e. the slope of the Y_I function), whereas the decline in employment in consumer goods depends both on the productivity of labor in consumer goods and on the real wage. The higher the productivity of labor, given the real wage, the smaller will be the decline in consumer goods employment for a given fall in investment demand. Given the productivity of labor, the higher the real wage, the larger the decline in employment. If investment goods is capital intensive and has, therefore, the higher productivity of labor, then, especially in high wage economies, fluctuations in investment demand may cause greater changes in employment in consumer goods than in the investment sector itself.

Figure 5.4

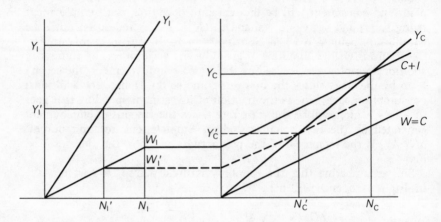

Rewrite the formula.

$$\omega n_I \Delta I = (1 - \omega n_C)\Delta C. \tag{11}$$

The left-hand side is the additional consumption goods demand resulting from additional employment in the investment goods sector; the right-hand side is the additional sales of consumption goods *minus* the additional sales of consumption goods to workers in the consumer goods sector itself. The right-hand side therefore represents additional profit in the consumer sector. This is a dynamic form of equation (8), the 'balancing condition' for expanded reproduction, interpreted in the second of the two ways discussed earlier.

In this formulation the multiplier no longer depends on anyone's 'psychological propensity' to consume. The multiplier here is based upon structural and institutional features of capitalism. It depends first and foremost on the level of real wages, which reflects the division of income between pay and profits, or, more generally, between variable costs and the markup. It further depends on the labor coefficients in the sectors and, in more complex versions, on the degree of technical dependence between them and upon the welfare policy of the state.[10]

V The State and the Managerial Class
Now let's extend our basic formula to take into account some aspects of the role of the state, and also a more complex class structure. First, consider taxes. It clearly matters whether taxes fall on wages – a variable cost and therefore 'passed along' – or on profits – a leakage. To see this most starkly, consider the case of balanced budgets in a simple fully aggregated model:

State neutrality: taxes fall on wages. Let Y be output, N be employment, ω the wage rate, C consumption by households, I investment, E total expenditure, G government spending, t the tax rate, and P profits. Assume that ω I, and G are given, so there are six unknowns. The equations are:

$$Y = \chi N, \quad \chi > 0 \quad \text{output rises with employment} \tag{12}$$
$$C = (1 - t)\omega N \quad \text{household consumption equals}$$
$$\text{disposable income} \tag{13}$$
$$E = C + I + G \quad \text{total expenditure, by definition} \tag{14}$$
$$G = t\omega N \quad \text{government spending equals taxes} \tag{15}$$
$$Y = E \quad \text{output equals expenditure} \tag{16}$$
$$Y = \omega N + P \quad \text{output equals income} \tag{17}$$

Prices are assumed constant, and output is assumed to vary within a range below the level of full capacity utilization. Solve by substituting (12), (13) and (15) into (14), using (16). This yields:

$$Y = \chi N = \frac{I}{1 - \omega/\chi}, \text{ where } \frac{1}{1 - \omega/\chi} \text{ is the multiplier} \tag{18}$$

(Note that from (17); $P = I$)

These are exactly the expressions one would get if there were no state at all – i.e. if we crossed out equation (15) and rewrote (13) as: (13') $C = \omega N$. So the level of output and employment and the pre-tax distribution of income are the same as if there were no state.

Note that the fully aggregated assumption is equivalent to all government spending going on employment. If all taxes fall on wages, there is no worker saving and all government spending is on employment, the state is neutral. Clearly this is an extreme case. Now consider taxes on profits.

State non-neutrality: taxes fall on profits. Change the example now by rewriting (13) as: (13') $C = \omega N$, and (15) as: (15') $G = tP$, leaving all the rest unchanged. Solve by substituting (13') and (15') into (14) using (16) and (17). The result is:

$$Y = \chi N = \frac{I}{(1 - \omega/\chi)(1 - t)}, \tag{18'}$$

where $\dfrac{1}{(1 - \omega/\chi)(1 - t)}$ is the multiplier, and

$$\frac{dN}{dt} = \frac{I}{(\chi - \omega)(1 - t)^2} > 0.$$

The new multiplier is larger than in the previous case; hence a given amount of investment generates a higher level of employment. But even more significantly, an increase in t (matched by a rise in G, so that 15' is always satisfied), leads to an increase in employment and output. A rise in government activity, even when the budget is balanced, raises total output and employment, except in the extreme case above.

A full analysis of taxation and government spending is far beyond our scope here, but let's take up welfare spending and at the same time bring the relationship between the sectors into focus. Define:

n_r as the labor coefficient in investment goods
n_c as the labor coefficient in consumption goods
ω as the real wage, assumed to be wholly spent
u as the ratio $\dfrac{\omega - z}{\omega} > 0$, where z is the level of spending which can be sustained by an unemployed worker, financed by borrowing and the welfare state
a as the coefficient of replacement demand by the consumer goods sector for investment goods.

Let
$$x = u\omega n_C$$
$$y = u\omega n_r.$$

Then when effective demand varies due to a change in investment, ΔI:

$$\Delta C_1 = y\Delta I$$
$$\Delta C_2 = xy\Delta I + ay^2\Delta I = (x + ay)y\Delta I$$

$$\vdots$$

$$\Delta C_n = (x + ay)^{n-1} y\Delta I.$$

So the series will be:

$$y\Delta I[1 + (x + ay) + (x + ay)^2 + \cdots],$$

which gives,

$$\text{multiplier} = \frac{\Delta C}{\Delta I} = \frac{y}{1 - (x + ay)} = \frac{u\omega n_I}{1 - u\omega(n_C + an_I)}. \quad (19)$$

This formula shows sectoral coefficients explicitly together with the inter-sectoral relationship. The principal impact will take place in the consumer goods sector; the effect on employment in investment goods will be secondary. It also shows the effect of welfare and unemployment compensation. The higher z is, the lower will be u and so the lower the multiplier. This is intuitively obvious; the change in spending as a result of moving from employed to unemployed, or vice versa is not so great.

Formally, let m be the multiplier, and let A stand for ωn_I and B stand for $\omega(n_C + an_I)$. Then,

$$\frac{dm}{du} = \frac{A}{(1 - uB)^2} > 0.$$

Now suppose $z = 0$. Rewrite the formula and cross-multiply. We have:

$$\omega n_I \Delta I = [(1 - \omega(n_C + an_I))]\Delta C. \tag{20}$$

The left-hand side is the additional consumption goods demand resulting from additional employment in the investment goods sector; the right-hand side is the additional sales of consumer goods, *minus* the additional sales of consumer goods to workers in the consumer goods sector itself, *minus* the additional sales of consumer goods to workers newly employed in investment goods to produce additional replacements for consumer goods. In short, the equation reads:

the extra demand for consumer goods by investment goods workers = the extra supply of consumer goods (over and above the costs in consumer goods of producing this supply).

This is, therefore, a more complex form of the balancing condition for expanded reproduction.

Let's now extend the analysis to take account of the managerial class, and express the results in a simple diagram (see Figure 5.5). The spending of salaried managers must be separated from that of workers. Since they possess assets, and are not hired and fired as output and sales vary, their consumption will normally be constant in the short run. Hence it can be represented by a line lying a constant vertical distance above the one showing the consumption of workers. This, however, will not in reality be the wage line. The unemployed also consume – out of welfare, public and private. Such consumption will be at a maximum when employment

Figure 5.5

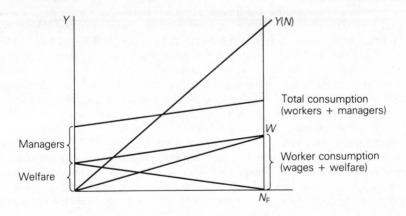

is at its minimum, and will normally be less than consumption based on the wage. It will decline in proportion to the increase in employment, so that total worker consumption (employed and unemployed) will be given by the sum of the rising wage and declining welfare bills, as shown in the diagram. This line has a shallower slope than the wage line. Total consumption has the same slope, but adds in the consumption of the managers.

The value of the multiplier will now depend on the state's welfare policy, as well as upon the real wage and the productivity of labor. Clearly a realistic theory will require still further extensions, but the principles upon which these should be based ought by now to be apparent.

VI The Markets for Funds

In conventional theory, households make savings decisions, based on their income and the interest rate, while businesses make investment decisions, based on their sales receipts and the interest rate. The *IS* curve is then defined as the locus of all combinations of income and the interest rate for which household saving equals business investment. This is then put together with the locus of all combinations of income and interest for which the supply and demand for money are equal, to determine overall macroeconomic equilibrium. The interest rate, then, functions as a neo-Classical 'price', helping to equate supply and demand, in two markets: for investible funds, and for money to hold.

But when the theory of effective demand is based firmly on Classical–Marxian foundations, no such markets exist. Withdrawals as well as injections are determined on the *business* side of the social accounts. Households are purely passive; they simply pass along their wage income as consumption expenditure. There are no savings, and no saving decisions, by households; so there is no market in which the rate of interest could play the role of a price.[11] 'The forces of productivity and thrift', in the neo-Classical sense, are not there. The funds to underwrite investment are generated by employment, since employment, because it produces a surplus over the real wage bill, creates the 'withdrawals' or 'leakages' required.

Not only is there no loanable funds market here, there is no supply and demand market for money either. When employment increases, businesses draw on their lines of credit, previously established to provide the working capital necessary to operate their productive capacity. Using this credit they pay the higher wage bill. The wage payments are deposited, then spent and redeposited as sales proceeds. Since the wage bill in the investment goods sector generates the profit in consumer goods, it provides the finance for that sector's purchases of investment goods, while the investment goods sector's own purchases of its products can be financed by borrowing against investment goods inventory. So bank deposits and hence 'the money supply' automatically increase as employment increases. Note that this is consistent with the banking system being fully 'loaned up' both at low levels and at high levels of activity. At low levels deposits are low, but so is the volume of loans.

Established lines of credit lie unused. But when they are drawn on, wage payments and consumption (and therefore bank deposits) rise. Loans and deposits rise and fall together *reflecting* changes in economic activity. The supply of money for transactions – current deposits – adapts to the demand for it, once we grant that the banking system will provide business with credit lines equal to the working capital required to operate existing productive capacity.[12]

Alternatively, suppose that banks will lend to businesses the amount required to finance their investment spending, against the security of the expected profits from the sale of their inventory. Business will then spend the proceeds of these loans on investment goods. That sector then deposits the receipts, repaying its advance from profit, and with the remainder hiring labor to replace its now depleted inventory. Its workers then spend on purchases of consumer goods. The spending of investment goods workers equals the profits of the consumer goods sector, enabling it to pay off the bank advance for its new investment. The profit in real terms, for both sectors, will be the new plant and equipment, paid off and in place. Besides investment goods workers, the consumer goods sector must sell to its own workers; but this can be accomplished simply by writing pay checks as claims against inventories of consumer goods. So, circulation can be financed either way. In practice, however, it will most likely be a mixture of both, depending on the preferences of businesses and banks for the different kinds of loans.

VII   The Employment Market

So far our argument has shown that in the short run changes in the real wage will cause corresponding changes in the same direction in employment, as a consequence of the spending of the changed wages. It is time to develop this idea more fully, elaborating it into a full-scale picture of the employment market. To make matters as simple as possible we will provisionally adopt the assumption, taken over from Marx, that the capital–labor ratios of the two sectors are the same. This makes it possible to simplify the multiplier expression, using 'n' for both n_I and n_C. The formula can then be rewritten to show the relationship between aggregate employment and real wages, for a given level of investment spending:

From (10) and having in mind that $\omega N = C = W$ we obtain

$$N = \frac{n}{1 - \omega n} I, \tag{21}$$

where n takes the place of n_C and n_I, and ω is the real wage.

This tells us the total employment, N, generated directly and indirectly by investment spending, I. Suppose we now take both n and I as fixed, and consider the effects of changing ω on N. Clearly

$$\frac{dN}{d\omega} = \frac{In^2}{(1 - \omega n)^2} > 0 \tag{22}$$

Increases in ω will *increase* employment, by stimulating activity in the consumer goods sector, and vice versa for decreases in ω. Moreover,

$$\frac{d^2N}{d\omega^2} = \frac{2\ I\ n^3}{(1\ -\ \omega n)^3} > 0. \tag{23}$$

That is, the higher ω is, the greater will be the impact on N of a given change in ω. The real wage–employment relation can therefore be represented on a simple diagram (Figure 5.6). There will be a positive

Figure 5.6

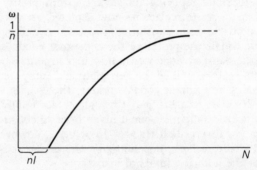

intercept, nI, when $\omega = 0$; as ω increases to its maximum, $1/n$, N tends to infinity. (Of course, this is not practically possible; N is constrained by the feasible capacity of existing plant and equipment.)

Next consider a simple labor supply function, showing the number of workers seeking jobs for each perceived level of the real wage. There is some evidence that this number will rise with the real wage, possibly just reflecting the fact that in boom times, when real wages are high, there are more opportunities; so that it is the rise in job openings, more than the rise in wages, that calls forth labor supply. For the sake of argument, however, let us accept the conventional positively sloped labor supply function, and add it to Figure 5.6 (see Figure 5.7a).

Clearly, for a given level of I, a unique equilibrium exists, (ω_e, N_e), which clears the labor market. (If the S curve were shallower, and had an intercept lying between the origin and nI, then two equilibria would exist.) The position of the demand for labor curve will shift in and out according to whether I is smaller or larger. Somewhat paradoxically, at first glance, a smaller I implies a higher ω_e and a higher N_e; a larger I, a lower ω_e and N_e. But, in fact, there is no paradox. If investment spending is, for example, higher, there will be more employment in the investment goods sector, and therefore a larger wage bill. But the labor force varies only slightly; when employment is larger in investment goods, less employment will be needed in the consumption goods sector to make up the total. Consequently less additional consumer spending is needed to generate the demand for employment; hence a lower real wage will be necessary in order to ensure that only the required amount of consumer

Figure 5.7a

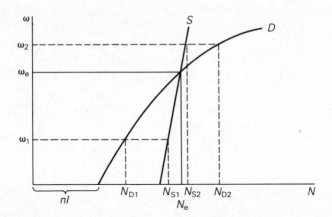

demand will be forthcoming. Hence, a higher demand for labor at every level of the real wage – an outward shift in the labor demand function – implies a *lower* equilibrium real wage, and, if the labor force supply function has a positive slope, a lower equilibrium level of employment. The labor market works just the reverse of the way neo-Classical theory assumes that most markets work.

Next, looking again at Figure 5.7a, consider a level, $\omega_1 < \omega_e$; demand for labor will be $N_{D1} < N_{S1}$. There will therefore be excess supply of labor, putting downward pressure on money wages. What happens to the real wage then depends on how prices move, assuming flexibility, for the sake of argument. But the likelihood is that prices would fall at the same rate or more slowly; excess supply in the labor market does not necessarily mean unwanted excess capacity. As argued earlier, businesses plan to carry some excess capacity and prefer to locate where there will be some excess labor. So there is no reason to suppose that the circumstances represented by ω_1 will put strong downward pressure on prices. The situation is likely either to be stable, prices falling at the same rate as money wages, or one in which the real wage drifts downwards, as money wages fall faster than prices. In the first case the excess supply of labor will remain constant; in the second, it will increase. Flexible wages and prices are not going to eliminate unemployment.

Now consider $\omega_2 > \omega_e$. This will require looking at another diagram (Figure 5.7b). The labor supply at ω_2 is only N_0; hence the *respending of wages*, creating additional employment, cannot take place. Thus the section of the labor demand curve lying beyond N_0 is inoperative. But there is nevertheless excess demand for labor. The wage required to generate employment equal to N_0 is $\overline{\omega}$; the actual wage is ω_2. There is therefore excess demand for labor equal to:

$$(\omega_2 - \overline{\omega})N_0 n_C = \Delta C_0 n_C; \qquad (24)$$

Figure 5.7b

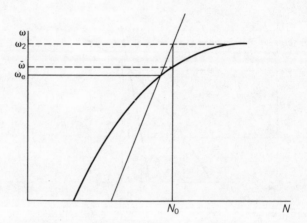

and of course the corresponding excess demand for consumption goods is:

$$(\omega_2 - \bar{\omega})N_0 = \Delta C_0. \tag{25}$$

The *proportional* excess demand for labor is therefore

$$\frac{\Delta C_0 n_C}{C_0 n_C} = \frac{\Delta C_0}{C_0},$$

which, of course, is equal to the proportional excess demand for consumption goods. Hence the *pressure* in the labor market is the same as the *pressure* in the consumer goods market. If the two markets respond to pressure in the same way, wages and prices will rise in the same proportion. So the real wage will remain unchanged, while money wages and prices rise in a general inflation. Too high a level of the real wage has no tendency to correct itself any more than too low a level. Upward flexibility of money wages and prices no more eliminates a labor shortage than downward flexibility cures unemployment.

An even more extreme contrast can be obtained by reconsidering the labor force participation function. In place of the preceding conventional idea, imagine a household determined to maintain a certain standard of living. At high wages, only the chief breadwinner will work, putting in a normal work week. At lower wages, the breadwinner will put in for overtime, then will add a part-time job. At still lower wages, other members of the family will enter the market, first for part-time, then for full-time work, and so on. In the extreme case the curve will be a rectangular hyperbola where proportional cuts in the real wages will just be matched by proportional increases in the hours of work offered (see Azarchs, 1987). Put this together with the wage-employment function

Figure 5.8 *Labor supply and demand*

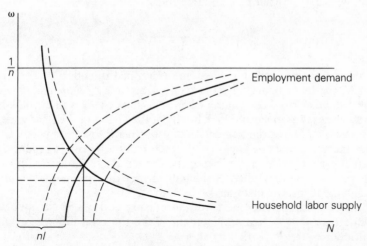

Note: The dotted lines represent shifts: the employment function shifts when investment spending changes, and the household labor supply shifts with changes in the normal standard of living. The labor demand curves differ in their intercepts along the horizontal axis, but they asymptotically approach the *same* limit on the vertical axis – that is, when $\omega = 1/n$, N tends to infinity, and this is true for all the curves, regardless of the level of I. The labor supply curves are asymptotic to both axes.

and we have the exact opposite of the conventional picture: a rising demand for labor, and a falling supply curve. Here a shift in the demand for employment implies perverse movements only in the wage. A shift outward, for example, would require the wage to fall, in order to force enough workers into the labor market. But, of course, an outward shift would, if anything, tend to drive wages up. As before, above the 'equilibrium' real wage the excess demand is not operative, since with no workers available to be employed, there will be no responding. But below the equilibrium the excess labor force surely exerts some downward pressure. Hence there will be tendencies for the market to move into disequilibrium.

So, there are two differences between the labor market and the normal neo-Classical conception of a market.[13] First, shift in the demand function, *ceteris paribus*, cause the equilibrium wage and, in some cases, employment levels to move *inversely*, and secondly, deviations from equilibrium, in either direction, have no tendency to self-correction. In the short run, therefore, there will be a tendency for deviations from equilibrium to persist or grow worse.

VIII *Real Wages and Productivity*
Our project so far has been to examine the short-run effective demand relationships between real wages, employment, productivity and

investment. These are summarized in the formula with which we have been working, written in simplified form:

$$N = \frac{n}{1 - \omega n} I. \tag{21}$$

First we took n and ω as fixed and examined the effect of changes in I on N, the traditional multiplier relationship in a new format. Then we took I and n as fixed and examined the effects of changes in ω on N. Now we shall treat I as given and look briefly at the effects of the joint variation of ω and n on N. For the foundation of modern anti-inflation policy is that wage increases must be kept equi-proportional to the rise in productivity. Such a wage increase, according to the conventional wisdom, will be the only possible 'neutral' change, the only change that will not affect prices, employment, profits or other key variables.

But, in fact, in the short run increasing real wages in step with productivity will *reduce employment*. Take the total differential of the multiplier equation, with I fixed:

$$dN = d\omega \frac{\delta N}{\delta \omega} + dn \frac{\delta N}{\delta n}, \tag{26}$$

where

$$\frac{\delta N}{\delta \omega} = \frac{In^2}{(1 - \omega n)^2} \text{ and } \frac{\delta N}{\delta n} = \frac{I}{(1 - \omega n)^2}.$$

Substituting and rearranging gives:

$$\frac{dN}{N} = \frac{1}{1 - \omega n} \left[\omega n \frac{d\omega}{\omega} + \frac{dn}{n} \right], \tag{27}$$

since, *ex hypothesi*,

$$\omega n < 1, \text{ and } \frac{d\omega}{\omega} = -\frac{dn}{n}; \text{ clearly } \frac{dN}{N} < 0.$$

In words, when the real wage is such that the value productivity of labor is positive (rate of exploitation positive) and real wages rise in step with increases in productivity, then the level of employment will steadily fall.

To be sure, this is over-simplified. At the very least the productivity changes in the different sectors should be distinguished. But the point should be clear: the productivity rule is not neutral in terms of its short-run effects on employment. Of course, these could be offset by an investment policy or by planned government spending. But most discussions of incomes policies have not recognized their short-run impact on employment, or the need to offset this through demand management policies.

IX Price Adjustment and the Multiplier

So far we have assumed that, when faced with demand changes, firms would adjust employment and output. But firms could, instead, alter their prices. In the modern economy the largest part of output is produced by giant firms with substantial market power, operating large-scale industrial processes with significant indivisibilities. Faced with increased demand, which they may fear to be temporary, while training and starting up costs may be large, such firms could reasonably choose to raise prices to ration demand. On the other hand, faced with a decline in sales they might also raise prices, to try to maintain their cash flow, in view of their financial and other commitments. Such options, of course, would not be open to firms in conventionally defined competitive conditions.

Now consider the diagram for the relation between the two sectors. The spending of the wage bill in the capital goods sector (Figure 5.9a) generates the profit in the consumer goods industries (Figure 5.9b). If we now assume that demand for investment goods rises (in 5.9a) and that, instead of increasing output, firms in that sector raise their prices just enough to absorb the increased demand, employment, output and the wage bill there will remain unchanged, but profit will be higher.

Let us consider this carefully. On our diagram such a price increase cannot be distinguished from a productivity increase. Both are represented by an upward swing in the slope of the productivity line, since every level of employment will produce a higher money value of output. Real output will be the same for each level of employment, but the value represented will be greater. Notice that this price change cannot be treated as a fall in the real wage. For that would require that all variables be expressed in real terms. But the demand for investment goods will be a money demand, fixed in money terms for the short period in question. Now let us examine how responding to a change in the level of demand by changing prices will affect the multiplier process.

Take first the case above, where a rise in investment demand is met by a rise in prices instead of output, even though additional capacity exists. Prices increase just enough to absorb the additional demand; hence

Figure 5.9

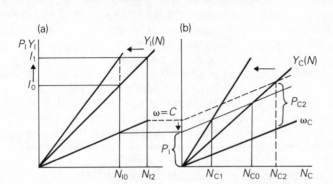

employment, output and the wage bill remain the same, but profit increases. But the relative price of capital goods has risen; to restore the terms of trade between the sectors, firms in consumer industries (Figure 5.9b) must raise their prices not just in the same proportion, but more or less than in proportion, according to the ratio of their capital/labor ratio to that in the capital goods sector. (For example, if consumer goods are relatively labor-intensive, as drawn here and explained in the fourth quadrant of Figure 5.1, their prices will rise less than in proportion. The point is to restore the original relation between the full capacity profit rates of the two sectors, for this is what their long-term borrowing is based on.) But such a price increase will have unfortunate short-term consequences for the consumer sector as a whole. As can be seen from Figure 5.9b, both employment and output there must fall, although they will continue to enjoy the same level of profit.

Raising prices in response to demand pressure, even when both sectors raise prices in the appropriate proportions, is *not* equivalent to lowering the money wage with prices and the demand for investment given in money terms. To see this we must first consider the difference between the results of reacting by raising prices and by raising output. Had output been increased, employment in the capital goods sector would have been proportionally larger, with a correspondingly larger wage bill and smaller profit. But by the same token profits and output and employment all would have been larger in the consumer goods sector. If, with this larger output, money wages were lowered and the relative prices adjusted, the resulting level of employment and profit in consumer goods would be lower than with the initial real wage, but higher than in the case where prices adjust. And, of course, both output and employment are higher in the capital goods sector. So raising prices in response to higher demand, with the money wage constant, is not the same as lowering the real wage. It is important, therefore, to specify effective demand relationships in monetary terms.

But the preceding argument establishes another, perhaps even more significant point, which can be extended to other contexts as well. The strategy of raising prices rather than output in the face of increased demand works, in the short run, to the benefit of firms in the capital goods sector at the expense of consumer goods firms and workers. This does not depend on the increase in demand being directed exclusively to the capital goods sector. If, say, demand for consumer goods rose due to government programs (which would have raised employment from N_{C0} to N_{C1} in Figure 5.10b), but consumer goods firms reacted by raising prices instead of producing more, with capital goods firms following suit in order to maintain their relative profitability, then a portion of the profit from the additional demand will be transferred to the capital goods sector. The price rise in the capital goods sector lowers the wage bill there, shifting the aggregate consumption demand down by a corresponding amount, and the resulting level of employment will be N_{C2} in Figure 5.10b and N_{I1} in Figure 5.10a. If consumer goods firms had increased output, keeping prices constant, they would have captured the entire

Figure 5.10

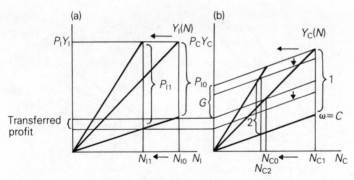

1 possible P_C, adjusting output

2 actual P_C after both sectors raise prices

additional profit from the increased demand (see the profit at employment level N_{C1}). But, of course, no individual firm could know this. To a price leader, for example, it might seem that the increased demand could turn out to be temporary or unreliable, so that raising prices would be easier than going to the trouble of hiring more workers and raising output. And if the market is oligopolistic, the rest would follow suit.

This is not the only possible scenario. Oligopolistic firms could practice 'target return' pricing, so that faced with a *decline* in demand they would increase prices, hoping thereby to maintain their cash flow. For each individual firm this would be reasonable, since each would appear to face a relatively inelastic demand curve. But, taking capital goods first, for the sector as a whole the total level of money demand will be fixed at the new, lower level. Hence the price increases will not succeed in maintaining revenue, but they will bring about a lower level of real output and employment. This can be seen in Figure 5.11. With lower employment, N_{I1} in Figure 5.11a, fixed revenue and a constant money wage, profits will be higher and the wage bill lower, in the capital sector. Consequently profits in the consumer sector will be lower than they would have been had capital goods firms adjusted to the lower demand without raising prices. Making it worse, consumer goods firms must increase their prices to maintain relative profitability, which will further reduce employment and output in the consumer sector, to N_{C2} in Figure 5.11b. Analogous results hold if the price increases originate in the consumer sector. The effect then is the same as if the real wage fell; currently realized profit is shifted from consumer goods to the capital goods sector.

So, in the short run, with a given money wage and a given (but changing) money level of investment spending, a policy of raising prices in response to demand changes tends to benefit the capital goods sector at the expense of workers and the firms in the consumer sector, regardless of the direction of the initial change in demand. Not surprisingly, a symmetrical

Figure 5.11

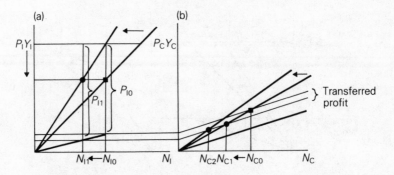

■ - after drop in demand, before price increase

● - after price increase, in capital goods

result can be established for price declines. If demand falls and prices are lowered, say, in the capital goods sector, then more items will be sold, so if the drop in price is equi-proportional to the decline in demand, employment will be maintained unchanged and consequently the wage bill will be the same, though profits will be less. Competitive pressures will force prices down in the consumer sector, too. So profits, employment and output will be higher in that sector. Total profit, in money terms, of course will be unchanged, but a larger portion will be realized in the consumer sector. So if prices are flexible downwards when investment demand falls, employment and output will actually increase, while realized profit will be shifted from the capital goods to the consumer goods sector. A rise in both profit and output in consumer goods could well trigger an increase in investment demand there, just as, in the case of price increases, a fall in activity could lead to a decline. Pricing behavior, in other words, could either exacerbate or dampen swings in ecnomic activity, not only directly through the effects on demand for consumer goods, but also indirectly through the induced effect on investment spending.

Thus the policy of raising prices tends to lead not only to inflation but also to slumping output and employment, while a policy of cutting price in response to demand declines would tend to prevent slumps from worsening. This corresponds to empirical findings: in the era of pre-corporate capitalism, before the rise of the great oligopolies, downturns showed up primarily in falling prices, with relatively insignificant drops in output. Since the 1920s, however, prices have fallen very little or not at all during downswings, in recent years even rising, while the fluctuations in output and employment have been considerable.

X Conclusions

We find that the Keynesian theory's lack of concern for real wages and distribution is a mistake; a Classical and Marxian framework in which distributional variables are central makes it possible to develop the multiplier on much sounder foundations, providing the basis for an analysis of employment and effective demand.[14] The argument shows that the job market does not function in the way orthodox theory supposes, and, in particular, that it has no self-correcting tendencies. Even worse, in modern economies where large corporations set prices, their likely pricing policies will lead to a combination of wage–price inflation and slumping output and employment. Stronger medicine than Keynes prescribed will be necessary.

Notes

1 Such a position satisfies the growth rate and profit rate equations below. It can be shown to be reached as the result of a sequence of adjustments of 'benchmark' prices, where such prices are defined as the ones which provide the profit necessary to finance the construction of new capacity to match the expected growth in demand. They equate *growth* of supply to *growth* of demand, rather than supply to demand (Nell, 1980c, 1988a, Part V).

2 The long-term position in practice can often be neglected. Suppose the long-term rate of growth is 4% per annum, and the relevant short period is one quarter. The error introduced by neglecting growth altogether is only 1%, far less than the margin of error in the statistics. But if the rate of growth were 12% and the relevant short period three quarters or a year, we would have a different story. In any case, theoretical concepts must be theoretically exact, however rough and ready their practical counterparts.

3 This argument clearly implies that the long run cannot be analyzed as a succession of short-period positions. Each short-period position is based on a specific long-run setting. Such long-run settings *develop historically*, which means they generally do not grow along a steady-state path. Moreover, such historical development may, from time to time, reflect influences from short-period phenomena. But the path of historical development is grounded on separate factors – the opening of new markets, the development of new products and new methods, together with the centralization of capital and the growth of professional management, the segmentation of the labor force, and the shifts in the structure of industry. Some of these are causes, some effects, and some are both. But none could easily be explained by looking at a succession of short-period employment and output equilibria. Secular analysis deals with separate questions; the same is true for the long-period setting in which short run is located. It, too, is concerned with the determination of different variables, answering different questions.

4 Why only two sectors? Why not n sectors? Because the *point* of a sectoral model is that the sectors are defined as producing an output the expenditure on which is underwritten by a particular category of income. Wage (and salary) income is chiefly directed to consumption goods, profits chiefly finance investment. Kalecki worked with a three-sectoral model in which fixed capitalist incomes underwrote luxury consumption: Lowe has developed a three-sectoral model in which one sector produces specialized capital goods for use only by the consumer goods sector (Kalecki, 1971; Lowe, 1976). The relationship between source and use provides a precise definition for the sectors. This specificity of definition is sacrificed for a spurious generality in the n-order inter-industry model.

5 By 'instrumental analysis' Lowe means an analysis which takes the macro goals as pre-selected, in given conditions, and finds the most appropriate route by which to reach that goal or set of goals, at acceptable cost. In *The Path of Economic Growth*, the goal is full employment, under various conditions, and the analysis determines the best path and examines the relative likelihood of different economic systems being able to follow that path. He contrasts such analysis with the traditional approach, which takes the patterns of behavior as given and tries to find whether or to what extent these behavior patterns will achieve certain goals. Thus the behavioral system may be free market relationships based on utility and profit maximization, and the goal, full employment equilibrium. The traditional analysis would then seek to determine whether and under what conditions free markets will achieve full employment.

6 This relation will be *independent* of the real wage, in the short run. The wage must be at least sufficient to support workers and their families for a given period of time. (If it were insufficient, in the long run the working class would die off or emigrate.) In return, workers do the jobs their employers set for them during the time for which they have contracted. The faster they work, the more raw materials they process into finished goods, and the greater will be the employer's potential profits. But the faster they work the harder the job. Workers will, therefore, resist speed-ups and job reorganization. To maintain work discipline and keep productivity high, employers design equipment to run at the highest speed consistent with minimum safety and accuracy in work, paying workers the minimum premium above subsistence necessary to induce them to accept the resulting working conditions. When sales fall off in the short run the plant cannot be redesigned, so parts will be shut down or run part-time, and workers on various shifts will be laid off until business picks up.

7 Remember, there is no substitution here. Techniques of production, job definitions, organizational structures, plant and equipment, and business location are all fixed. What varies is the degree to which the given production system is *utilized*. The correspondence between the utilization of plant and equipment and the amount of employment depends on the rigidity of job definitions. The precise tasks are specified, together with the sequencing and the pace of work on the assembly line, as well as use of the labor force to clean up the shop, make repairs, and so on.

8 The question of the determinants of investment is simply too large to enter into here. Nevertheless the present argument remains seriously incomplete until it is tackled. For first a discussion of investment *decisions* in relation to pricing and planned growth, and then an attempt to analyze investment *spending* in terms of current sales revenue, risk and the availability of finance in the capital market, see the respective articles in Nell (1988a) Parts IV and V. It is easy to allow for worker saving out of wage income; it merely reduces the slope of the expenditure line. The aggregate demand function will therefore cut the output function at a lower level of output and employment. Imports and income taxes also lower the slope of the worker consumption line.

9 Savings, taxes, imports and other influences are easily added. But the basis of the multiplier is the wage-labour system: employment adjusts until profit withdrawals equal investment injections.

10 Keynes, in a letter to Beveridge, 28 July 1936, presents the multiplier in this light, rather than, as in *The General Theory*, depending on a psychological propensity. 'Take the case of an increase in investment, say, the building of

additional houses. The men who are directly employed in building the houses will have a higher income than before. They will spend this income on consumption . . . except when there is full employment, there is an elasticity of supply in the consumption-goods industries, and . . ., if more men are employed in building houses, more men will also be employed in making things for the house-builders to consume. . . . The additional men employed in the consumption industries will themselves consume more, so that we have a whole series of repercussions' (Keynes, 1973, vol. XIV, pp. 57–8). Joan Robinson's account of the multiplier runs along these lines (1937, pp. 15–22). R. F. Kahn in his famous original article takes account of both inputs and the 'dole' (welfare support of unemployed), but mistakenly believes, first, that an increase in employment will yield an increase in realized profits in the short run, and, secondly, that there will be current spending out of these profits (see Kahn, 1931, pp. 11–12). This erroneous perception of the role of profits in the short run pervades the entire Keynesian literature. By contrast, Kalecki was always clear that investment expenditure (and capitalist consumption) determined realized profits, which, therefore, exercised no influence on current spending.

11   Garegnani (1978/9) argues strongly and convincingly that the chief role of the theory of liquidity preference in Keynes was to provide grounds for rejecting the neo-Classical conception of the interest rate as the price which equated savings and investment in the capital market. Yet, as he also argues, liquidity preference, dependent on a somewhat unsatisfactory concept of the speculative demand for money, is a weak platform on which to base so fundamental a position. But when the theory of effective demand is developed along Classical–Marxian lines, the basis for the neo-Classical conception is undercut. This leaves the question of the rate of interest open; for an approach to that subject, see Nell (1987b).

12   But how much working capital is required? This depends partly on the expected level of activity, but, of course, also on what businesses and banks expect prices to be. How much banks can afford safely to lend depends on what banks expect their deposits to be, which depends partly on expected activity, but also on expected prices and wage rates, since their deposits will be sales proceeds and deposits of wages and salaries. In a pure banking system, one not tied, or not strongly tied, to outside money, there is always pressure to lend, since that is how banks earn profits, but there is no evident barrier preventing the banking system from validating any reasonably well-grounded and widely held set of inflationary expectations.

13   The neo-Classical theory of the labor market has its own problems. The short-run demand curve for labor is normally interpreted as the first derivative of the Aggregate Production Function, '. . . showing diminishing marginal returns – as the capital stock is spread over more and more workers' (Branson, 1979, p. 96). The supply of labor is derived from the individual's work-leisure decision: '. . . a worker can allocate hours to work, thus earning real income . . . or to leisure' (p. 104). Then, '. . . we can sum all the individual labor-supply curves to get the aggregate labor supply curve for the whole economy' (p. 106). The labor demand curve considers additional workers joining an established workforce; it shows the demand for a *varying* number of workers, each working a *fixed* work day, as they join the established pattern. But the supply curve shows the supply by a *fixed* number of workers (all those over whom the aggregation took place) of a *varying* number of hours per day. The two curves are dimensionally inconsistent. Dennis Robertson once wrote to Keynes, 'Has "classical" theory, in *any*

sense, ever tried to apply the notion of *marginal* disutility in connection with the *numbers* of work people? It seems to me appropriate in connection with the amount of work done by an individual, but not in connection with numbers. . . .' (Keynes, 1973, vol. XIII, p. 500). Unfortunately, the answer to his question now, is 'yes, in most textbooks'.

14 For both neo-Classical and Marxist economics, higher level real wages should lead to lower investment spending. In the neo-Classical view, higher real wages imply lower annual earnings from investment projects, so a lower marginal efficiency of capital schedule, while at the same time, for any given level of employment, they imply a higher transactions demand for money, so a higher level of interest rates. Both effects tend to reduce investment. For Marxists the case is even simpler. Higher wages mean lower profits, which means lower investment, since there is less available to plough back. By contrast, the position here is that higher real wages are likely to stimulate investment, provided that higher money wages cannot simply be passed along in higher prices, and that the economy is closed, so that capital cannot simply flee. Higher wages tend to shift profits and activity to the consumer sector. If this presses against capacity then it is likely to stimulate a speed-up of investment plans, to bring new capacity on line sooner than previously intended.

6
The State and the Corporate Economy

Perhaps the most striking feature of the social organization of modern life is the extent to which it is arranged by means of hierarchical bureaucratic institutions. In every walk of life jobs are structured by rank in an ascending ladder. In business this is universal; a company's employees occupy jobs defined in a pyramidal table of organization. Academic employment is no different. Government service is equally structured. Even in those professions where a high degree of self-employment remains, the professional organizations themselves are constituted in a hierarchical fashion and sometimes – formally or informally – grade and rank their members. The primary motivation of an employee or even a self-employed professional is to climb the job ladder, to win a promotion. The pyramidal form of organization ensures that this will be a competitive process. But this phenomenon is not confined to the sphere of employment. Political organizations, consumer and environmental groups, and housing cooperatives are also constructed along similar lines, providing a chain of command running from the top down, with a competitive promotion structure. (Note that this is in no way inconsistent with the leadership being more or less democratically controlled by the membership.)

What has happened to the family firm? These hierarchies are mostly urban; where has the family farm gone? And where is the simple government of the nightwatchman state?

It may be that hierarchical organization promotes efficiency and is the best or only way to manage modern technology. Such is the popular wisdom. However, it is also a form of organization that provides great and detailed control over employees, and sets up strong incentives to exhibit loyalty in order to win promotion. Since promotions are competitive, there being more eligible candidates than places at every level, the system also divides the better to rule. Employees set at each other's throats are not likely to unite against the company. This is competition, but it is very different from the competition between small, family businesses.

Corporate Hierarchy and Economic Theory

The universal development of hierarchical bureaucracies is so much a part of the fabric of our lives that we tend to take it for granted. It seems so natural that we never ask how it developed or where it came from. How else could we organize ourselves to manage our complex technology and social problems? Yet, while there have always been bureaucracies, the modern forms of articulated hierarchy are the control system for competitively organized capitalist mass production. It is not technology *per se*, but its economic form, that calls for hierarchy.

It is commonplace to deplore the growth of bureaucracy. But the increasingly articulated forms of hierarchy are not the same thing. A bureaucracy can in principle expand by 'widening' or by 'deepening'. In the first case it expands its area of control, while leaving its top management unchanged, so the ratio of height to base falls. In the second, it respecifies and restructures its system of control, increasing the number of levels, so that the ratio of height to base rises. Of course, it could also grow in fixed proportions (or shrink, though that does not seem to happen), changing base and height in the same percentage. Expansion by widening is certainly an 'increase of bureaucracy', as is expansion in fixed proportions. But at least a substantial part of the modern-day increase of bureaucracy involves deepening – increasing the articulation of hierarchy.

It is important to be clear about the relations between hierarchy, bureaucracy and the activities being organized. First as regards *employment*. The width of an organization is measured by the amount, or sometimes the proportion, of a certain kind of employment it controls; its height will be given by the number of levels or ranks between the point of production and the point at which basic decisions are made. Height is therefore a measure of social distance or accessibility. (Obviously, informal as well as formal channels of communication must be considered, but these are also governed by strict social conventions.) Second, the same measures can be applied to the *products produced* or *activities performed* by the organization. This is necessary because the organization, say of sales and distribution, may be quite separate from that of production. Moreover, the *diversity* of products and activities controlled by the organization must be considered, in particular whether they form a linked pattern of stages of production. Third, the same measures can be applied to organizations controlling social activities and access to environmental resources which are not part of the economy as ordinarily understood. Trade unions are organized hierarchically; so are schools and universities, professional societies and private clubs. Large voluntary, charitable organizations and small, intense political parties both exhibit this same structure, and in none of these cases can it be plausibly argued that the structure is determined by the requirements of modern technology.

The deep organization

Broadly speaking, a wider organization means bringing together a larger number of people under one umbrella of control; it is promoting cooperation on a larger scale, a process of unification. It can eliminate duplication, bring about rationalization and standardization, permit greater quality control, better management of inventory, and so forth. Both accumulation and centralization of capital under the system of family firms consisted of widening the organization. Organizational deepening, by contrast, separates the point of production, the point of effective activity, from the point at which decisions are made. Deepening means introducing layers of authority between the points of decision and the agents who execute them; decisions flow down, information flows up, responsibility is fractured and personal contacts are replaced by impersonal rules and procedures. Deepening intensifies the alienation of workers from the understanding of, let alone control over, their everyday working lives. However, deepening also permits more precise control over the pace of work and makes it possible to coordinate widely divergent activities, for example, adjusting the pace of production to the rate of sales.

Of course, it may be objected that bosses are bosses. It does not matter whether they are protected by layers of subordinates and a multiplicity of rules and procedures. What finally counts is ownership of the means of production. But this is far too simplistic. First, even in worker-owned companies, the development of a modern managerial hierarchy can produce not only the sense but also the reality of worker alienation. The worker may be an owner in his capacity as a shareholder, but in his capacity as a worker, in the job, he takes orders from his immediate superior, he struggles for promotion and raises, and he is effectively shut out as a worker from any say in the decisions that concern his immediate working conditions, let alone over the general direction of the company.

Secondly, where there is direct contact between the point of effective activity and the point of decision – and where this contact involves give and take, where the workers are allowed some say – many studies have shown that productivity and the quality of work, as well as worker job satisfaction, are all considerably enhanced. Of course, it is not merely a matter of distance; the crucial element is give and take – workers must know that what they say is taken seriously. This is precisely what social distance, the introduction of intermediate layers of authority, makes difficult or prevents altogether. (It is in the interest, for example, of intermediate managers to appropriate good suggestions from below and present them as their own.)

Third, an important consequence of deepening is to create a ladder up which to climb to higher status and pay. Instead of a largely undifferentiated mass of common laborers, no doubt doing different jobs but all bearing the same status and similar pay, there is a highly structured system of rank and privilege, with different and ascending pay scales, creating competition among workers for promotion. Of course, there is normally a sharp distinction between the management level and lower ranks, but within both there is hierarchical organization.

Fourth, and most fundamental, what we have called deepening is the form that the division of labor/separation of function takes in the process of controlling a multi-dimensional activity. Under a system of craft production, even on a large scale, costs cannot easily be adapted to sales. A mass production process, on the other hand, is designed to do precisely this – but it will require the financing of massive production facilities, so that both production and sales will have to be managed with an eye to recovering capital costs. Mass production has to be coordinated with mass marketing and both must be integrated into a financial plan. To run the resulting system against the competition will require carefully defined divisions of responsibility, joined at the higher levels. Deepening, in other words, is the organizational response to the development of competitive mass production.

Considering how all-pervasive hierarchic bureaucratic organization has become, and how seriously it has altered, for example, the working of competition in the labor market, so that in large areas the chief form of competition is for promotion, it is both surprising and significant that neither neo-Classical theory nor standard Marxian theory presents an adequate account of this phenomenon. Let's examine this more closely.

The firm in neo-Classical theory
Neo-classical theory basically presents us with a picture of firms moving toward price and output equilibrium, hiring factors in response to factor prices, while households supply these factors, also in response to (expected) prices. Different market forms are distinguished – monopoly and monopsony, oligopoly, perfect and imperfect competition, and so forth – but the underlying forms of calculation are all the same – profit or utility maximization, consideration of marginal revenue and marginal cost, and the like. The 'firm' is treated as an integral decision-making unit. Nothing prepares us to consider the consequences of an investment decision for the firm's table of organization. Indeed, the consequences of investment decisions are not treated adequately at all in many, if not most, standard presentations.[1]

Nor does the labor market fare better. The picture there is of supply and demand for labor as functions of the (expected) real wage, in various market conditions, with the competition (of various degrees of 'perfection') being for jobs and workers, respectively, 'at the margin'. But as we have already seen, among the already employed, at both management and lower levels, besides this there exists an intense competition of a different form, namely for promotions and raises. This is simply ignored in most standard presentations, although it is believed by some experts to account at least in part for 'wage drift'. In extreme forms of neo-Classical theory, 'labor can hire capital just as easily as capital can hire labor'. The institutional features of the employment relationship are simply not there at all. Even in less extreme forms, the organizational aspects of the firm are missing. There is no account of the evolution of single proprietorships into corporations, of the implications of different forms of corporate organization (functional, multi-divisional), or of the way a company may structure its product cycle and relate its earnings to its investment plans. (These may be discussed in textbooks, but usually in a separate chapter from the one that presents the basic theory.) Within the framework of the theory there is no way to explain the systematic growth of large-scale, intricately hierarchical forms of organization. The question is excluded by the assumption that the firm can be treated, as far as all important calculations on prices, outputs, investment, finance and employment are concerned, as a *unitary* decision-making agent. Its internal structure need not be considered, or, if it is, the results of doing so will merely modify the standard model in acceptable ways.

The argument here, by contrast, is that the growth of hierarchical organization comes as the result of the shift from craft production to mass production, because of the need to coordinate financing, sales and production under conditions of market competition. So it both facilitates and is facilitated by the development of markets – and it leads to the result that markets come to work differently, which, in turn, has consequences for economic policy.

The Marxian analysis

The Marxian tradition is well aware of and tries to explain the tendencies to concentration and centralization of capital. Concentration refers to accumulation, the result of successful investment; centralization refers to take-overs and merging of already existing enterprises. Concentration results from the process of uneven development in accumulation, while centralization is the result of victory and defeat, or truce and treaty, in the competitive struggle between capitals. There is therefore the ground work for an account of the development of large-scale organization as an integrated consequence of capital accumulation. We are not stuck with a picture of a large number of small firms, speckled over with accidental monopolies and 'imperfections'.

However, this vision of growing concentration and centralization lacks any appreciation of the special problems that accompany the shift from craft to mass production. Unemployment in the Marxian system, for example, is explained by new technologies destroying old industries and skills, or by a general crisis. It is not seen as the normal result of adjusting the rate of production to the rate of sales, as in the Keynesian theory of effective demand. In this respect, Marxian economics remains close to the traditional theory, and so misses the significant changes that have taken place in the way capitalism works.

Moreover, it retains a strikingly simple picture of the class structure of modern society. The system divides into two classes. First, there are capitalists who are owners and top managers, and who reproduce themselves through a network of top families, providing exclusive access to the best schools, allowing for some recruitment of talent from the lower orders, co-opted through marriage, etc. Then there are workers, made up of the rest. Unlike capitalists, who own and manage the means of production, they own no significant amounts of property and are handicapped in access to education and training. Of course, both assets and handicaps vary in degree, so there is significant differentiation in the working class, and this differentiation tends to reproduce itself, though the proportions may vary over time – often with political consequences. The process of centralization will dispossess many capitalists, particularly the smaller and weaker ones, who will be thrown into the ranks of the proletariat, more than likely increasing the degree of class differentiation there. The result will be the relative swelling of an increasingly disunited proletariat, together with the formation of an increasingly concentrated and centralized capitalist class. The prospects for political stability, indeed for democracy itself, do not look bright in this picture.

Certainly there are strengths in this vision, which is intended in any case as a deliberate simplification, designed to highlight only the central features. The question is, has it captured the central features correctly? Here the problem arises over the relation between capital accumulation and the development of the forms of capitalist organization.

Capital accumulation

In the Marxian scheme accumulation is spurred by competition, which necessitates expansion and the reinvestment of profits, while centralization results from the defeat of competitors. Both are therefore related to competition, but neither is tied to changes in the internal organization of the firm. And what counts especially are those changes that occur as a consequence of the development of mass production.

Here, then, is a set of relationships that are missed in most accounts of Marxian theory. For, once we are out of the realm of traditional craft production, investment involves product design, plant location, and the development of facilities for marketing, as well as the financing and construction of factories. Capital accumulation means building up the firm's ability not simply – or even chiefly – to *produce* but, principally, to make money. To do this successfully in a competitive world, a firm must be able to predict and to control its sales. This means both adapting to its customers and adapting its customers to it, which means developing effective marketing. This in turn must be closely coordinated with production, and the development of both, over time, must be kept in line with the firm's financial position.

Such coordination of diverse activities requires a clear-cut chain of command. Competition is a form of limited warfare and like all warfare requires military organization. The important thing is to make the strategic moves effectively, so as to attain the objective at an acceptable cost. This makes loyalty and obedience the prime requirements in subordinates. The structure of control must therefore not only coordinate the diverse activities but do so in a way that ensures not only an effective chain of command but no defections to the enemy. A firm does not want its sales representatives or dealers going over to competitors and taking their customers with them. Nor does it want its skilled workers leaving.

It will be argued here that the development of 'job-ladder hierarchies' is the major corporate answer to this problem in the capitalist West. It is not the only possible answer - the Japanese have another – but it is an effective answer, and apparently well suited to American social traditions. However, it involves a strong interaction with the state, and it brings about important changes in the class structure. For one thing, it generates a large and influential intermediate formation, the professional middle classes, partly allied with and working for top management but also, in fact, employees and sharing the difficulties and dependency of the working class. Yet precisely because much of their work (especially in education, social work and the state bureaucracies) is devoted to aiding, policing and servicing the poor and the needy, the culture of this group takes a paternalistic and superior attitude toward the traditional working class. A second effect is even more important: the development of the self-perpetuating professional managerial system effectively brings about what we shall call the institutionalization of capital, and with this comes a fundamental change in the class structure.

Institutional ownership of capital

Prior to this development, social classes were classes of *families*; class structure was grounded in the relation of the kinship system to the means of production.[2] With the flowering of the corporate economy, however, effective ownership of capital shifts from families to an *institutional structure* of foundations, trust funds, investment banks, and mutual funds. Capitalist families remain as beneficiaries or as nominal owners of these funds, but increasingly they no longer exercise direct control over their placements. Moreover, in addition to income from assets, nuclear capitalist families also obtain income from employment, often from earnings in *two* careers, as women increase their participation in the work force. These careers will generally be more significant to the immediate family's life style and circle of friends than its ownership of capital.

Just as the basis of the capitalist class – effective ownership and control over the placement of capital – shifts to institutions, so does the basis of the working class. In the early capitalism of the nineteenth century the working class was composed of the *families* that owned neither capital nor land and had to sell their labor power to obtain a living. They did not enter a career, they took a job. With the growth of corporate and public sector job-ladder hierarchies, schools, the family, the courts and the welfare system become keyed to preparing people for vocations, for careers. Indeed, a new profession, vocational guidance counseling, emerged in the school/welfare state system. So class position then became a relation not so much between the kinship system and the means of production, where the significant differentiation was ownership or lack of it, as between the socialization system, predominantly run by the state, and the job-ladder hierarchies of the corporate system. Family origin still remained the chief determinant, at least in the United States, of where and how one entered the school system and other socialization programs. With schools supported by property taxes, the best schools will tend to be in the richest districts. But this is not necessary; a different way of financing schools could provide more nearly equal education. Nor does a child's (family-based) social status on entry into the school system, etc., necessarily have to determine his/her vocational potential on leaving, although, statistically, this is the predominant pattern.

The shift from a family base to a socialization system, and from jobs to careers, provides the system both with better chances for recruitment from below (together with a means of excluding the incompetent wealthy from exercising influence) and with much greater flexibility in adapting the supply of talent to the needs of business. In particular, as the requirements of management and sales become greater, the school system can turn out people qualified for low-level white-collar (and pink-collar) positions, whatever the changing mix of engineering, computer science, or clerical work. The class structure is neither as rigid nor as determinate as it appears in Marxian writings; it responds flexibly to the requirements of capital accumulation, while capital itself has moved largely outside the control of the traditional '60 Families' and is now managed institutionally. Moreover, what it is and how it changes depends in part on state policy.

So far, I have suggested, first, that the shift from craft to mass production tends to produce not only the growth of large corporate institutions, but also the growth of job-ladder hierarchies. Second, I have argued that the significance of this point has been largely missed in both the orthodox and the Marxian traditions of economic thinking – the orthodox try to integrate price theory with effective demand, while the Marxists have been slow to recognize the phenomenon. Of course, writers in both traditions have discussed these questions, and some aspects figure very prominently in Marxian analyses of monopoly capitalism. Both have noted the shift from the 'nightwatchman' to the interventionist state of today. But neither tradition has succeeded in integrating these changes adequately into its basic vision. (This is not to put the two traditions on a par, however. The Marxian tradition is far more aware of the growth and power of large corporations and their interaction with the state. Yet detailed studies comparable to the work of Chandler, 1977, or Williamson, 1975, for instance, still remain to be done.)

The result is that orthodox theory (in both monetarist and Keynesian formulations) misconstrues the relationship of the state to private capital, misses altogether the changes in the working of markets, and consequently fails to understand the changing impact of state policy measures as markets develop. Marxian theory, by contrast, is largely aware of these changes, though its analysis of them is not as detailed as that of some post-Keynesians, but it misses the implications for class analysis. First, a closer look at hierarchy.

The Causes and Consequences
of Hierarchy

Control and firm size

The normal processes of competition alone will tend over time to produce a highly skewed size distribution of firms, approximately log-normal in a simple model. Other factors can be expected to help this along, and, in any case, the fact that size confers power (both socio-political and purely economic) will ensure that the process of centralization of capital will always be driven by strong forces. This in no way denies the presence of inhibiting factors. Not the least of these is the fact that large firms are in continual competition with each other, both along the market, competing for sales, and across the market, buying from and selling to each other. Moreover, too great a concentration of power in one firm or cartel, achieved too suddenly, may provoke a united front of opposition among otherwise diverse and scattered competitors, customers and suppliers.

An essential part of the firm's strategy is the attainment of some measure of control over the development of the market. This requires developing a marketing system, with a sales force, a distribution network and suitable advertising and promotion. These in turn must be coordinated with product design, production and handling of inventory. Moreover, the development and rate of expansion of the marketing system requires investment. This investment must be coordinated with that in the expansion of productive capacity – and in product design and development – and all such capital spending, of course, must be kept in line with the firm's financial position.

As a result, the large firm must coordinate quite diverse activities, even when it produces only a single line of products for a well-defined market. Coordination becomes all the more important as the firm develops production and plans its pricing strategies in line with the product cycle; it is particularly crucial when it tries to develop by-products from the wastes generated by its industrial processes.

Nor is this coordination simply a question of 'efficiency'. A business is in a continual struggle with competitors, suppliers, its own employees and its customers. The name of the game is making money, and in every transaction there is the ever-present feature that a higher or lower price benefits one party at the expense of the other. To control costs, to ensure revenue, every transaction must be controlled or monitored. There is potential danger at every point. Thus it is not merely a matter of proper coordination and ensuring the swift and effective mobilization of resources when the time is ripe for a market move or an investment project. It is also making certain that routines and regular procedures are strictly observed, so that no unexpected delays, costs or losses of revenue are incurred. The firm is in continuous operation and must be continuously controlled. Of course, there will be a margin of error that will be figured into the planning and coordination. But a delay or a production error – or a miscalculation of the market, as in the case of Ford's famous disaster with the Edsel – outside this margin may result in a victory for the competition. Nor is it desirable suddenly to lose key personnel, whether skilled workers or managers, to competitors.

The systems of control that have actually evolved to meet these problems reflect the cultural and social conditions of different capitalist countries. But the dominant theme is the development of the managerial hierarchy. The staffing of this hierarchy takes place through a process of recruitment from below, though not always from within the firm. Managers, therefore, look forward to a lifetime career, rising by promotion from their entry level, which is determined by their qualifications, normally obtained from the educational system. Promotions and raises depend on the quality of their work and their loyalty to the company, as judged by their relevant superiors. Management is thus self-perpetuating and permanent. It is also effectively segregated from ownership by the institution of the board of directors. Superficially, this last might seem to be a means by which owners control management, since the management must report to it. But in practice it is usually the other way around. The board meets rarely, and the directors normally have only a limited direct knowledge of the actual workings of the company. They are not, therefore, in a position to do more than deal in generalities. These may be very important, since they will involve general strategy and long-term plans, but once again management is in command of the details, and usually has control of enough proxies to elect a compliant board.

Professional management
However, this traditional conclusion must be modified in the light of the changes discussed earlier that have taken place in the holding of capitalist wealth. Large financial holdings are now managed professionally; moreover, to escape taxes and for other reasons, they are normally institutionalized, for example, in foundations, with the former owners as beneficiaries or trustees. When this happens, the former owner loses the power to determine the disposition of the wealth, in return for some kind of assured income, usually in conjunction with tax relief. Even where this has not happened, wealth-owners of any size have normally handed over control of a large part of their assets to professional money managers. When they have not done so, they have become professionals themselves.[3]

Nor is this at all surprising. In the complexity of modern money and capital markets, amateurs are not likely to last long. (The random walk hypothesis is not a counter-example. On the contrary, it is a sophisticated technique for use in planning the management of funds.) Moreover, amateurs who in fact do well are likely to cease being amateurs. But the managers of large funds are in a position to bargain for representation on boards, a position from which they can learn something. Being professionals, they will choose professional representatives, knowledgeable about the business world and on a par with management itself. Moreover, the financial interests so represented will normally manage portfolios containing holdings in many companies and will often move to take control. Boards, therefore, become places where representatives of competing and overlapping interests can meet and work out compromises and common policies.

Boards have always been places where interlocking directorates could iron out difficulties. But the fact that there is no longer a significant capitalist *class*, meaning a class of heads of families who both own and operate or manage either capital goods or capital funds, implies that today directors no longer represent *families* or wealthy individuals, except very indirectly. Since capital is becoming fully institutionalized throughout its entire circuit, those directors who represent financial wealth now represent *institutions* – pension funds, foundations, trusts or trust departments of banks, mutual funds, even universities. These institutions are run on the hierarchical principles just discussed. Top management has the ultimate responsibility (although it will report to trustees, or whatever) and will judge its own success or failure in terms of capital accumulation. The set of all such top managers, of both industrial and financial enterprises, interlocked through various boards of directors and trustees, together with the top management of state bureaucracies, constitutes the 'class' representing the interests of capital. But this is not a class of families, nor are such positions inherited, since they are reached by rising through promotions rather than assumed as a prerogative of ownership. (The children of top managers may sink back into the upper reaches of the professional middle class, or even 'return to the land' and become small farmers.) Top management is recruited from a broad pool, not including blue-collar workers, farmers and lower-level white collar, but drawing on almost the entire professional middle class.

The labor process
Complementing the development of hierarchical professional management is a parallel development of the labor process. Production must be controlled and predictable; otherwise planning rests on no reliable base. To this end, as many jobs as possible are progressively broken down into the simplest movements, repeated over and over, so many times per minute or hour. A production or assembly line, or some other mechanical force *over which workers have no control*, sets the pace of work automatically. Failure to keep up with it will bring penalties and eventually dismissal. By the same token, no one can work faster. Workers have no control, can exercise no initiative, and find their work maddeningly boring and trivial.

Nevertheless, this applies only to machine operators on a production line. Many processes cannot be arranged in line; many tasks cannot be broken down into successive motions that can be specialized. Even where the main part of production can be so treated, the same factory will also require a very large number of jobs of a different sort – for example, cleaning, sweeping, and disposing of garbage and waste products, cleaning and repairing machinery, spot checking and quality control, line supervision, watchmen and guards, handling, packaging, and shipping both products and materials, etc. A factory is not only a production system, it is also a social system, and these various jobs will come to acquire different status rankings – sometimes because they involve exercising authority or taking responsibility, but also because they may involve cleaner or more desirable working conditions. In any case, management can use this variety to its own advantage. By attaching higher pay to the more desirable jobs, and filling them by promotion from the ranks of the less desirable, it creates a job-ladder hierarchy. Promotion and higher pay are the possible rewards of loyalty and good behavior, just as dismissals and layoffs are the punishments for rocking the boat.

So we have a system of sticks and carrots, in which sycophancy will be rewarded while those who stand up for principles are likely to find themselves back on the street. Yet there is good evidence that a more agreeable organization of work, in which tasks are allocated by the workers themselves, who supervise themselves and organize their own division of labor, would greatly raise the productivity of labor, both on average and at the extensive margin.[4]

This result is of little interest to corporate business, however, for a very good reason. It depends on worker *satisfaction*; workers work harder because they enjoy their work, and can control its pace and quality. Hence, in the event of a labor conflict, without striking they could hurt the company through a slow-down. This sort of productivity is unwanted, for dependence on it in planning would simply make the company more vulnerable in labor disputes. As family firms turn into corporations, craft work is displaced by the fixed-productivity systems of mass production.

Very much the same obtains in office work. Jobs are mechanized, trivialized, and made routine in pursuit of control and efficiency. Promotion systems develop that often have little grounding in the imperatives of practical organization but are useful in encouraging 'company loyalty' and competition among employees. The upper levels of white-collar work shade over into the lower ranks of management. Blue-collar work in turn shades into white collar; many supervisory blue-collar jobs involve extensive record-keeping and writing of reports. Also the pay hierarchies overlap. Top-flight skilled operatives or construction workers (carpenters, plumbers) earn more than most office workers, more even than middle-level managers and professionals. The categories are not neat. Although the central cases are clearly distinguishable and contain large numbers,[5] there is a large area of overlapping, at least equally mixed when it comes to the children. The children of farmers and workers have often ended up in the white-collar middle class and small numbers of them have moved from the bottom to the top (much more rarely, but occasionally, even the reverse movement has occurred). The obvious reason for this is that, as capital has accumulated, the need for white-collar workers and managerial staff has grown relative to employment in factories – for reasons already indicated. This illustrates a crucial fact: the class structure of modern capitalism is fluid, for good reason – namely, that the proportions in which the system requires labor of various kinds change over time with capital accumulation. Further, this fluidity and the way it is administered contribute to the differentiation and fractioning of the working class.

The role of the state

The state is the chief agency making this fluidity possible. Through its growth and development it also contributes to the need for such fluidity. As to the first point, the state has progressively taken over functions of education and socialization as the extended family declined in importance. This can only intensify with the present-day disintegration of the nuclear family. The educational system certifies persons as qualified at various levels for entry into employment. It is a 'screening system', but much more importantly it also *shapes* people, both positively and negatively, providing some people with skills and others with a determinate and usually irremediable lack of them. It provides information, but also disinformation. It generates incentives for some, while fixing others more or less permanently in a state of apathy and ignorance. Ideally, for the smooth working of the system, the proportions should roughly correspond to the relative requirements for managerial and worker-level employment. Of course, this is an over-simplification; nevertheless, any gross disproportion is bound to cause problems in the labor market.

Besides socializing people to fit the categories of employment, the state also contributes to the development of managerial and vocational hierarchies. The growth of large powerful firms requires government regulation to prevent dangerous defects in products and to prevent dangerous labor conflict. The concentration of industrial processes in geographical space requires policing the effects on the environment. None of this can be effectively carried out unless the state is represented by a bureaucratic management capable of meeting private managers on equal terms. Hence the growth of professional management in private industry must be paralleled by a similar professionalization in public employment.

Finally, in a craft economy based on family firms, the state could play the role of nightwatchman, because its spending would just exactly offset the impact of its taxes, or taxes plus borrowing, so that state activity simply displaced an equivalent amount of private, the rationale being that the state performed certain functions that private business could not handle or could not do as well. With the development of a corporate mass production economy, however, the state *has* to adopt an interventionist stance. When output and employment are variable in the short run, the state budget will not normally be neutral; so its impact, positive or negative, will have to be taken into account.

The state must therefore perform a number of functions necessary to keep the system working properly. In this sense it acts for the system as a whole, making it work more smoothly, ironing out inequities, mediating conflicts, presiding over collective bargaining, regulating industry, both with regard to exercise of market power and with respect to the environment. It provides for national defense and promotes a favorable international climate for business. And so on. Liberal political theorists have fastened on this apparently universal aspect of the operations of the state as showing that it acts as the representative of the general will (or will of all?), and, while recognizing that the state is differentially responsive to the needs of the various social classes – usually responding more to money and organization than to mere numbers – they have argued the case for pluralism. Such theories claim that a capitalist democracy responds to public pressures, no matter where they come from. Any group or social class, once it organizes, can make itself heard and felt. Obviously, some groups, especially big business, are better placed. But they don't win all the time or get all they want when they do win. The system works by consensus and compromise and has an inherent tendency to move to the middle.

Business and politics

This view overlooks a fundamental aspect of the way the state works in a capitalist system. Regardless of its policy *objectives*, the state's policy *instruments* must be consistent with the regular process of capital accumulation. For, if that process is disrupted, the economy will experience shocks that both are a *multiple* of that disruption and are transmitted throughout its entire range. The state, committed to the defense of property and to orderly judicial processes, cannot (short of revolution) *take over* capital accumulation and the management of existing capital. Hence, it must cooperate with those who currently manage capital. To achieve its objectives, therefore, the state must bargain: basically, it can either bribe capital with subsidies, contracts, easy credit, protection from foreign competition, etc., or it can threaten it with taxes, regulations, investigations into compliance with the law, anti-trust suits, and so on. But neither bribes nor threats will work satisfactorily unless a long-term *modus vivendi* can be reached. For, while businesses can be induced or forced to cooperate in the short term, if the climate of investment created by state policy is not attractive, capital will leave the country and/or retreat into liquidity. The result will be a slump.

So, if the state is to encourage full employment, it must, on the whole, stimulate private investment, for example by tax credits or accelerated write-offs. It cannot, except in special areas, engage in investment itself, because although that would have the required short-run multiplier effects, the completed project, run by the state, would then be in competition with private capital. Of course, as in World War II, it could build factories and then sell them off at bargain rates to the private sector. And it can bail out private capital by nationalizing failing industries at attractive rates of compensation, as in the United Kingdom, pre-Thatcher. This can also be of considerable benefit to private capital, since the nationalized industries can then provide basic industrial products – coal, electricity, etc. – to industry at low rates subsidized by taxpayers or by household rate-payers.

Similarly, to combat inflation the state must persuade business not to raise prices. Managers are anxious to show a good current performance in their own profit centers; raising prices may be sensible policy for this end, although it may erode the market in the longer term. Jawboning and wage–price guidelines may help keep this under control. Holding down wages obviously helps, but it may lead to conflicts with the labor

movement. Imposing controls requires extensive and professional moni-
toring; it is certainly not impossible, but it would require a large
bureaucracy with powers to commandeer and inspect the books of at least
the 2,000 or so largest corporations, thereby tearing off the veil of
corporate secrecy. What might we then find? This is not the road to
cooperation between private business and the state.

Moreover, given the way democratic political processes are financed in
most advanced capitalist countries, business is exceptionally well placed
to influence the political system in its favor.

This is well known and superficial, however. To go deeper, we need to
consider some of the organizational features inherent in developing state
policy. First, if the state is to influence or regulate an area of business, say
transportation or mining, it must establish an appropriate bureaucracy
staffed with qualified personnel. But these will have to be drawn from
within the industry itself or from the same training centers that prepare
people for careers in that industry. Professionals in the field may well find
it to their advantage, in securing promotion, to have experience both in
private industry and in government. There will therefore tend to emerge
a consensus among professionals, allowing for differences in emphasis but
not including policy views that would lead to devaluing existing capital
or preventing further accumulation in that sphere. Either would inhibit
the field for professional advancement as, on a personal level, would
advocacy of such policies. Nuclear engineers are not likely to be among
the first to recommend phasing out nuclear power. Defense industries do
not oppose the arms race, nor do their workers.

Second, the same applies to other groups organizing to influence or put
pressure either on business or on the state. Labor unions, public interest
groups and political organizations must form themselves into an effective,
self-reproducing force in order to engage in a permanent struggle to
achieve and maintain their goals. Hence they must be able to make
effective day-to-day decisions and know that these will be carried out, and
they must be able on a regular basis to recruit replacements for their
leadership. There is therefore almost irresistible pressure to adopt the
same form of hierarchical organization, with a regular internal promotion
system, that their opponents have. To the extent that they do not do this,
as with the New Left organizations of the 1960s, they are likely to
fractionate and die off, as the original leaders become tired or discouraged
or move on to different arenas. But to the extent that they do, of course,
they lose their anti-bureaucratic character and sacrifice any hopes of
realizing participatory democracy.

Hierarchy, State Policy and
Class Structure

A confirmed pluralist will surely complain that this picture is overdrawn.
Governments of democratic capitalist states have in the past and will
in the future launch massive programs of social reform aimed at

redistributing income and, less energetically perhaps, wealth. Progressive governments have committed themselves to guaranteeing full employment through interventionist policies and extensive regulation of business, even to massive socialization. They have been and will be strenuously opposed by business, but they have succeeded, some would claim spectacularly, in many countries (notably Scandinavia), and there is no reason to suppose such a program could not succeed, at least in part, in the United States. (Some have argued that between the wars there was a substantial redistribution in the United States, but this claim is open to serious question.[6])

There is no claim here that progressive policies cannot succeed; they work very well. The difficulty lies in getting them accepted. A popular coalition may be forming around environmental issues, and this might be extended to economic reform. Private capital might be persuaded that such policies were in their long-term interest, but the obstacles may be greater than often believed. We shall return to this point repeatedly in later chapters. Before we can consider it properly we have to examine the ways in which the state and private capital interact in both developing and supporting the system of hierarchy.

First, we have to sketch the forces that determine the relative pay of different jobs. Only the barest outline can be given here, but it will be enough to help us see some of the ways the state and the private system interact, and how this interaction leads to significant changes in the nature of the class structure.

How pay scales are set

Many, probably most, studies of income distribution among workers start by considering workers, their education, skills and other 'human capital', their preferences, and the size and age structure of their families, and then try to determine what pay such skills and preferences could reasonably command, and how breadwinners would use it supporting their families.

This approaches the problem from the wrong direction. It implicitly (and, in neo-Classical marginal productivity theory, explicitly) assumes that workers are paid in proportion to their specific ability and willingness to contribute productively. Thus incomes are rewards for productive contributions, and both the average level and the distribution of incomes reflect the degree and the variance of worker productivity. However, this is not the whole story. Besides labor's ability and skill, labor's preferences must be taken into account. If workers will not exert themselves, their potential productivity will never be realized; but, to call forth the requisite effort, it may be necessary to pay certain workers special differentials. In other words, besides the amount of wages, there is also a question of the relative pay of different groups. Workers' attitudes are conditioned by social norms concerning fairness in pay, and industrial peace and good morale cannot be realized unless these are respected.

The picture, then, is one of employers directly and nevertheless automatically responding to worker abilities, modified by worker preferences. In short, what workers get, while it may not be what they deserve, nevertheless depends on what they are and what they do.

However, in fact that is not how pay scales are set. When the table of organization is made up, within broad limits nobody knows or cares about the characteristics or preferences of workers, as studies of 'deskilling' and job satisfaction show only too clearly. The only preferences that are taken into account, normally, are those of top management, and even those may be disregarded if they cannot be accommodated. Of course, worker characteristics do set constraining limits on the possibilities of organization, but the determinants of the table of organization involve quite different considerations. And pay scales follow the table of organization. In other words, pay goes with the *job*, not with the worker. To understand how pay is established we must first study the structure of jobs, not the characteristics of workers.

But this is a highly complex matter. Jobs are not defined by what has to be done to produce goods and services in some technical sense. Rather, they are defined by the way the technical problem is broken down and arranged for the purposes of bureaucratic control and oversight. An integral part of the definition of a job is its position in the hierarchy of control. For any job it must be clear to whom the job-holder reports, from whom he or she takes orders, and whom he or she commands. With position in the chain of command and responsibility goes status, and relative status in turn must be marked by relative pay. In short, pay goes with the job, not with the worker, as can readily be seen when workers in a plant are transferred from one job to another. Normally, unless they have seniority or are protected by a union contract, their pay will change though their abilities have not.

Nor can it be argued that the skills required for jobs are so exactly defined and the process of hiring so careful that the income paid corresponds to the particular job-holder's productive ability. On the contrary, it is precisely the claim of modern management to have defined jobs so that almost anyone with an adequate education can master them. Jobs have been profoundly and progressively 'deskilled' across a wide range of both industrial and office work. Any person of average intelligence with a high school education should be able to perform adequately, following on-the-job training, in over half of the jobs in the American economy. Yet these jobs differ widely in status, rank and pay. Clearly the pay differentials don't reflect differences in workers' measured productive abilities.[7]

Pay differentials

How then is relative pay determined, and how susceptible is it to influence from policy or social pressure?

To repeat what we have already argued, allowing for over-simplifications business organization is almost completely undemocratic. It is hierarchic, rigidly defining a chain of command along military lines. Superiors command subordinates, information passes up, orders pass down. There is a distinction between officers and troops, management and workers, with foremen playing the role of non-commissioned officers. R&D is staff; the rest of management is line. An officer enters at a low level, and the object of a career is to rise through promotion. Higher ranks carry larger responsibilities and higher status; *therefore*, higher pay. Pay symbolizes status, but also makes possible the *consumption appropriate to that status*. This is the point to be examined more closely.

Let us begin with the distinction between labor and management. Workers are not promoted to management jobs, but, as they accumulate seniority, workers *are* promoted, for jobs are graded and high-grade jobs are reserved for high-seniority workers. However, the grading of a job may bear little relation to the actual work content. A high-grade job need not require more skill or experience than a low-grade one, nor will it necessarily carry greater responsibility. The purpose is to permit workers as well as managers to look forward to promotions and pay raises during their careers with the company. This provides an incentive for good behavior and company loyalty – keep on the good side of the bosses and get your promotion. On the management side of the class divide, exactly the same holds true. Again, higher-level jobs need not necessarily involve greater skill or experience. Of course, they often do, and often the work requires judgment and maturity (just as the job of foreman – non-commissioned officer – requires the ability to handle responsibility). But the complexity of the hierarchy and the standards for promotion cannot be explained by the skills and experience required by the work.[8]

It is not relevant for our purposes to examine all the influences that combine to create the job structure. It is enough to have established that it is not simply determined by technology or worker productivity. The important point is that one's position or level in the organization is a matter of status, and this is marked by pay and reflected in one's pattern of consumption. Precisely because many job levels are *not* distinguished by skill requirements or by the range of real responsibility, they must be distinguished by pay and status to make promotions to them function as an incentive. The pay differentials must be great enough to make possible clear distinctions in status, as these appear in socially recognized consumption patterns.[9]

Now consider a normally functioning corporate economy. An elaborate hierarchy of jobs has been established both for labor and for management. Each family has one chief breadwinner, whose pay determines the family income.[10] Employees of both kinds normally enter at the bottom and work their way up. The system of promotions and raises helps to develop company loyalty and keeps employees docile and on their good behavior. Pay differentials are closely attuned to the society's distinctions of status and to the costs of consumption goods. If this is the nature of the system, what are the implications for government policy?

Redistributive policies
Consider mandated money pay changes first, such as minimum wages. These can be strongly resisted by businesses, since they interfere with company policies designed to maintain control while providing employees

with suitable career incentives. Hence the changes required by law would be immediately supplemented by other changes – in job design, upgrading or downgrading certain positions, bonus plans, etc. – whose purpose would be to undo the effects of the legally required changes. To prevent this, it would be necessary for the government to encourage companies to channel their efforts more usefully – redesigning jobs to raise productivity, for instance. However, business will try to maintain the differentials and, as a result, an increase in the minimum wage will create pressure to push the entire pay scale up.

Now consider government attempts to influence the income distribution through taxation. Here again companies can adopt offsetting policies, by planning their pay structure so as to achieve a certain *after-tax* set of income differentials. Unexpected taxes can be offset with end-of-year bonuses, and so on. For higher management, flexibility can be provided through stock-option plans.

The government can exercise a more effective influence through its own pay structure. Government employment is an alternative to private; hence the government can bid up wages or salaries for specific grades of labor that it feels are underpaid. Moreover, the government can refuse to do business with companies of whose pay structures or employment policies it disapproves. These tactics can be quite effective, but they can bring about only marginal changes since they must be targeted at any time on specific injustices.

Business, then, will be both able and strongly motivated to resist government attempts to alter the structure of pay differentials. Interestingly, in the craft economy it would be given some automatic help in this by the price mechanism itself.

Suppose that a change in the tax laws raises the after-tax income of lower-level workers while correspondingly reducing the after-tax earnings of top management. Suppose also that initially both the businesses producing lower-income consumption goods and those producing high-status consumption goods were fully adjusted to the current income distribution and were operating at their normal capacities. As a result of the redistribution of income we can expect increased spending on low-status goods and lower spending on high-status goods. Producers of low-status goods will have difficulty increasing production, since they will be pressing against capacity. Their costs will go up as they strain their facilities, and the unmet demand will bid up prices. Their gross profits will therefore rise, and if they believe the change in their demand is permanent they will invest and expand their facilities. By contrast, the producers of high-status goods will experience sluggish sales and diminished revenues, a situation that often leads to layoffs and competitive price-cutting as businesses fight over what is left of the market. Eventually the least efficient businesses will leave the sector, and firms will close out older and higher-cost plants. Hence in the craft economy we can expect price increases for the low-status goods, coupled with price cuts for high-status goods. These price adjustments then tend, temporarily, to reverse the effects of the government's redistribution, until business has adjusted capacity by making the appropriate investments.

The rising salary bill

A set of forces may arise in a corporate industrial system, however, that may lead to strong pressures to reduce differentials and that also help to explain the pressures on management in both the private and public sectors. These forces arise directly from the market developments we have been discussing. As businesses grow larger in relation to competitors, they will seek to establish control over their markets, investing in a sales division. This in turn requires specialized and professional management both to ensure perpetuity and to carry out planning and coordination. The hierarchical system requires pay differentials along the scale of rank. Now consider what happens when there is regular technical progress in the factory. Let us suppose that this is a function of gross investment. As investment increases, what has to be managed and sold increases; hence, assuming a given plan of organization, employment in management and sales must increase in the same proportion. But, according to standard collective-bargaining practices (the basis of shop-floor consensus), blue-collar wages must rise in proportion with worker productivity. Then if differentials are to be preserved, sales and management pay must also rise in this proportion. Hence the total salary bill for office work will rise in the proportion $(1 + g)(1 + t)$, where g is the rate of growth of capital and t is the rate of technical progress of production.

In other words, the salary bill for management, sales and office work has an inherent tendency to rise faster than wage costs as capital is accumulated. There are two obvious responses to this. One is to allow differentials to erode. But that may lead to tension and dissatisfaction, and tends to defeat the point of the system. The other is to improve management methods, reorganize and put pressure on manager and staff to carry the extra work. The most important development has been the introduction of technical progress into management and office work – computers, data retrieval and information systems, word-processing and the like. Yet the total impact of this has been an increase in the complexity of management, since it has required the development of entire new divisions in companies to handle the new systems. The same pressures apply now to these new managerial levels.

This analysis can be applied to explain the rising costs of the state. The size of the state must grow in keeping with the size of the private sector. So state employment must grow at the rate of capital accumulation. But state employees must be paid in line with their status; hence their pay must move to maintain their differential – whatever it might be – with respect to the pay of blue-collar workers. Consequently, the costs of the state will rise at the rate $(1 + g)(1 + t)$.

The impact of monetary policy

Under a regime of small competitive firms, functioning in the context of a craft economy, a restrictive monetary policy will lead to cut-backs in current investment spending. The higher short-term interest rates (for working capital and to finance inventory) cut into current earnings, and the higher long-term rates raise the costs of the investment projects – the more so if there is any hope that the policy will be eased in the future. The increased interest costs cannot easily be passed along as price increases, since no one firm can be sure just how much its rivals have been affected so will not know whether they would follow suit if it raised. Eventually this could be worked out through informal consultations, etc., and the industry might come to agree on a suitable increase, but in the meantime capital spending will have to be cut back. A restrictive monetary policy will therefore lead to a fall in the prices of capital goods, which will show up eventually as lower costs in the production of consumer goods. So a policy of monetary restriction and high interest rates will be anti-inflationary.

In corporate mass production, especially when markets have matured, however, things work very differently. Large businesses with extensive marketing and distributional arrangements have 'tied' customers, whose demand for the product is relatively inelastic. Long-range price policy is set so as to balance the rate of growth of capacity with the rate of growth of demand. This requires establishing a balanced plan of investment in both marketing and plant and equipment, so that when the new plant is complete marketing and distributional arrangements will also be ready. This means keeping them both on track, once a plan is established. When a restrictive monetary policy is imposed, current earnings will be squeezed through the rise in the cost of working capital, etc., and the long-term costs of financing the project will also be higher. But in these circumstances companies do not need to worry about competitors following suit; the price can be raised to pass along the higher costs. Of course, this will make the development of the new market that much more difficult. So if the higher interest cost is expected to be permanent, there will be some cut-back in the size of the project. If the policy is believed to be temporary, then the price increase will affect only the *existing* market and will simply generate extra earnings to offset the higher costs, though possibly at the price of alienating part of the market. In other words, when markets have matured, restrictive monetary policy, by raising interest rates, tends to generate corresponding price increases, accompanied sometimes by some cut-backs in investment.

This is not the end of the story, however. In the modern economy there are both mature and competitive market areas. Restrictive monetary policy squeezes the earnings of both areas; the mature giants raise prices to protect their earnings – and this *further* squeezes the competitive area, since it buys many industrial products from the giants. Thus investment will be much more severely hit in the competitive areas. Costs will go up all around, so there will have to be further price hikes to pass along the increases in prices of industrial inputs. The effect of creating a slump in competitive areas is to reduce their demand for the products of the giants. With sales revenue down, for essentially short-term reasons, mature firms will be tempted again to raise prices in order to keep earnings high enough to maintain their investment schedule. Thus the effect is to create an inflationary spiral in the midst of a recession while squeezing the competitive areas of the economy.

Class structure implications

Finally, let's turn to the implications of this argument for the theory of class structure in modern capitalism. It is common in both Marxian and neo-Ricardian economic analysis to work with a two-class model. Workers receive wages, capital obtains profits. Wages and profits function differently in the economy. In the short run, wages underwrite consumption, profits finance investment. The sources and uses of the two are different, and in simple models the causal relationships run in opposite directions: changes in wages cause changes in consumption; changes in investment cause changes in profits. In the long run, the wage rate and the rate of profit are inversely related in a manner that parallels the inverse relationship between consumption and growth. These simple relationships seem to exhibit something at least of the inner structure of capitalism. Admittedly, such models greatly over-simplify the categories of both income and expenditure, but it is at least arguable that the relationships they embody are the dominant ones.

The step from such economic models to social-class analysis is as treacherous as it is simple. Recipients of wage-type income are identified as the working class; recipients of profits – owners of capital – constitute the capitalist class. Just as there are two kinds of income, inversely related, so there are two classes, standing also in an antagonistic relationship, such that what one gains the other loses.

In a world of small firms, run by owner-operators and staffed by propertyless hired hands, this picture may have some validity. But *when technology has developed and markets have matured, even though the economic (income/expenditure) categories may still be related in the same way, the social–political categories of class are not.*

The most obvious change, of course, comes with the development of sales divisions and professional management as markets mature. This gives rise to the category of white-collar work. From an income/ expenditure or wage/profit point of view, these payments are not all that different from wages. True, they are not exactly variable costs – but then neither is some blue-collar work. Top-management salaries are no doubt fixed costs, but a large part of management and sales will be affected by booms and slumps, provided they are prolonged. From a socio-political point of view, however, the rise of white-collar work does make a significant difference. It is *not* that a new class has arisen – a professional–managerial class, located somehow 'between capital and labor'. Although this is a seductive simplification, and it contains an important element of truth, it misses a major point.

This is that the nature of class itself has been changed through the institutionalization of capital. The prerogatives of capital – hiring and firing, deciding on production and prices, determining the direction and pattern of investment – once exercised by owner-operators and passed along to their children, are now in the hands of professional managers and committees. Place in the kinship structure no longer confers the right to exercise these powers; that right must be attained through promotion, as a result of working in the organizations of private business and the state. An owner-operator could not be hired or fired; but he could hire or fire anyone else in the organization. In most modern corporations *no one occupies such a position*. Directors can hire and fire top managers, but, on the other hand, top management exercises considerable influence over the selection of directors. Major moves are not dictated by a single interest but emerge out of the consensus established through bargaining processes and committee work. While directors often represent large ownership interests, these interests themselves are institutions, foundations, banks, funds, and the directors they appoint to companies in whom they have holdings are professional managers.

Since everyone is an employee, then, does that mean everyone is working class, in some sense or other? The suggestion is ridiculous, but it is (becoming) true that everyone is an employee. *The dimension along which the traditional class distinction was measured is disappearing.* There remains differentiation by wealth, but that is a matter of degree, as is the status that attaches to a job or occupation. Moreover, ranking by wealth, ranking by status, and ranking by power or influence may yield different orderings. Which expresses the 'true' hierarchy in the community? And where do we draw the line between capitalists and workers?

No such line can be drawn definitely, precisely because so many are drawable. Capital has become institutionalized; hence, all managers, and many below management – such as foremen – speak and act for capital. Workers are those who must do as bidden, who are exploited, and who are likely to be sacrificed in bad times. Blue-collar workers fit this, but so do white-collar and many managers, even top managers. Differentiation no longer runs along a single dimension.

Nor is this surprising, for it is precisely the genius of capitalism that it is capable of avoiding the trap of the proletarian/capitalist split. Capital has created its own institutional framework, in the professionally managed hiearchical corporation, and in so doing has largely freed itself from the kinship system and has provided itself with an effective arrangement for dividing, differentiating and controlling its ubiquitous employees. Capital accumulation and the accompanying market development have converted the class system into a corporate and bureaucratic hierarchy divided as much along professional and occupational lines as by wealth and class distinctions. Both kinds of differentiation – and others – are present; none is always dominant. In many respects the resulting system is flexible and capable of adapting, for example, to new technologies and new products, but it generates its own rigidities and costs, the full extent of which we are only now beginning to see. The institutionalization of capital creates a highly specialized bureaucratic system, the working of which is not adequately represented by most contemporary economic models. But its most profound effect is probably upon the working of the political system. That, however, is a story that must wait till later.

So to summarize. The development of bureaucracy is not something opposed to the 'market economy', as is often contended. It is part and parcel of the development of capital, in particular of the institutions by means of which capital can exercise the kind of control required for success in competitive conflicts, control over conditions both of production and of marketing, as required by the transition from a craft to a mass-production economy. But this institutionalization breaks the traditional relationship to the kinship system, particularly when it is extended to ownership and the financial circuit of capital. Moreover, the rationalization of the hierarchy requires the state to shift from a nightwatchman to an interventionist stance, and so to take over education, promote regulatory services, and act as an arbitrator in disputes, all of which leads to the development of counterpart bureaucracies on the part of the state itself. One major result of these processes is the systematic stripping away of the traditional functions of the kinship system, which in turn undermines the established basis for drawing class distinctions – a fact that itself contributes to the strength of the system, though it in no way reduces its repressiveness.

Notes

1 Standard presentations focus attention on the ranking of investment *projects*, each conceived of as independent entities, costing so much, and yielding a stream of returns over so many years. This may have made sense in the era of family firms/farms, but is wholly misleading when investment is planned and carried out by a modern corporation whose many projects interact, on both the cost and the revenue side. The calculations implied by the 'marginal efficiency of capital' formula are simply impossible. Consider a project's net earnings three years hence: both the costs and the revenues to the firm will depend not only on the investment now being considered but also on next year's and the year after's investment. But those investments, in turn, will depend partly on the success of the ones being considered now. Investment, in short, should be thought of as the growth of the firm, and this growth is organic development, not mechanical accretion. In particular, capital accumulation requires the extension and articulation of the system of professional management.

2 'Class' has to be understood as a relational term, holding between institutions that prepare people for their station in life and the institutions in which they later function as adults. A class society is one in which this relationship is regularly reproduced – adults functioning in certain roles establish families that prepare children for those same roles.

3 Of course owner-entrepreneurs and owner-financiers remain. It is arguable, further, that they are not merely vestigial appendages but integral parts of the economy's capacity for self-renewal. Large bureaucratic organizations become calcified and rigid as they age. Committees develop the art of consensus to such a level that nothing ever happens. The owner-entrepreneur introduces new ideas, new products and new processes, and this is an essential part of the 'transformational growth' on which the economy's prosperity ultimately rests. The new ideas of the entrepreneurs may be bought up by the giants

later; but their introduction and testing require an innovative spirit that is unlikely to be found in the corporate bureaucracy, unless a special effort is made to cultivate it – and perhaps not even then.

4 Hierarchy is an effective method of *control*. When tasks are to be performed with precision and exact timing, a hierarchical system provides an appropriate institutional format. But it provides no scope for self-expression; it stifles creativity. Moreover, because it channels competition into the fight for promotion, it encourages back-biting and in-fighting, a point well known to readers of modern novels. Since productivity depends to a great extent on morale, productivity is improved under a democratic organization of work, as the extensive literature on workers' control shows. However, there is a dilemma: if 'worker democracy' is mere window dressing, with real power remaining in the hands of management, the bloom soon fades, since the productivity is only wanted in the service of profit. Given an opportunity to increase productivity by giving up the pursuit of profit, business recoils. This supports our contention that the organization of work reflects not only the requirements of technology, etc., but also, and perhaps more important, the requirements of capital for maintaining control.

5 Over-simplifying, we have factory work and office work, on the one hand, and working and professional classes on the other. All factory workers are working class, but so are many – perhaps most – office workers, in the sense that their work is boring, routine, involves little or no responsibility, and its pace and quality are controlled either by automatic processes or by a higher authority. Some office workers and all top managers are professionals. Top managers are recruited from the professional class; they are not *qualitatively* distinct. Nor can top managers ensure that their children will follow in their footsteps. The ruling class consists of the set of *roles* or positions with the power to make the key decisions (though who *actually* makes them depends on who wins in the internal power struggles within that class). But this class is replenished by recruitment, not through the kinship system.

6 The main changes in the US income distribution in the first half of this century can be explained as adaptation to the changing tax laws (tax avoidance and tax evasion), as the result of the decline in farming and other forms of self-employment, and as the result of the changing age structure. When these factors are accounted for, the chief remaining changes occurred as the result of the two world wars, plus the Korean and Vietnam conflicts.

7 Perhaps the different marginal productive contributions should be associated with the *jobs*, where such contributions can be made by any qualified and willing worker holding the job. But what is the marginal productive contribution of a job? How is it to be measured? There are two approaches, a simple and a complex, to these questions.

Consider an assembly running at its normal operating rate. Then hire an additional worker. What will the worker do? If the design of the production process is unchanged, there will presumably be nothing for him/her to do, since it was already running efficiently. (Similarly, removing a worker will bring things to a halt, since the job is necessary.) Hence, to consider the marginal contributions we have to compare *alternative designs* of the production process, using different kinds of equipment and defining different jobs. This is far too complex an issue to examine here. However, an extended discussion in the professional journals arrived at the conclusion that the 'productive contribution' of labor (like that of capital) could not be satisfactorily defined independently of prices. Given the prices, such contributions could be defined; but prices are supposed to be determined by costs, especially labor costs, which supposedly reflect productive contributions. The argument is therefore circular, and another explanation of wages (profits) must be sought. For further discussion, see Nell, 1972, 1973, Garegnani, 1970.

8 This has an interesting corollary. The 'Peter Principle' – that workers/managers rise to their level of incompetence – is based on the assumption that higher-level jobs involve significantly higher (and different) degrees of skill and competence, so that promotion based on successful performance of lower-level jobs is fundamentally irrational. People are promoted out of what they do well, and are no longer promoted when they no longer do well. Hence most employees end up stuck in jobs they can only just manage, and no one is doing what he/she does best. The argument was first presented as a joke, but it obviously has teeth. However, it misses the mark in an important way: higher-level jobs do not necessarily involve greater or different skills – they may be 'higher' in nothing more than status and pay. There is more than a grain of truth in the Peter Principle, but it seriously overstates the case.

9 A model such as that of Mayer (1960) can be adapted to exhibit the functional relationship. With a well-defined span of control and pay differentials proportional to rank, the distribution of earned incomes will be a variant of the Pareto.

10 Of course, instead of the man working and the wife homemaking, both can share the housework, and the wife can take a job. This has been characteristic of the past decade and a half.

7
Transformational Growth and the Slowdown

Theorists tend to analyze what can be understood with the methods available, and, unfortunately, this may lead to concentrating on less important but more tractable questions at the expense of what really counts. This is not just another recital of the familiar complaint that economic theory is 'unrealistic'. In a certain sense any theory is necessarily unrealistic; theories have to leave out the inessentials and abstract from detail. The problem here is that what has been left out is neither inessential nor a detail. It is an absolutely fundamental aspect of the capitalist industrial system, namely, that to work properly the system must grow, and to grow it must continually transform itself through the introduction of new products and new processes, creating new life-styles, redistributing income and generating new markets. Let's explore this further.

The Nature of Transformational Growth

New products and new processes don't just spring up from nowhere, nor do they normally appear at random. They arise because a new principle has been developed and is being applied in a variety of contexts, generating new ways of doing things. It is usual at this point in economic discussion to launch into a panegyric on the 'entrepreneur', the one who actually makes the application of the new principle and markets it (in another context, the 'pusher'). But our purpose here is different; we shall take the entrepreneur for granted – and instead ask how the new ways of doing things arise.

By a 'new principle' is meant a new way of accomplishing some general social purpose, like the provision of power – steam, or the internal combustion engine, or electricity – or facilitating communications or transport. The basic social purposes, of course, are the provisioning of the population with food, clothing, shelter, transport, education, and so on. New principles will usually be formulated initially in quite general terms, so that how and where one is to be applied may, in the early stages, be quite unclear. Experiments will be tried in many different areas, wherever the new principle seems to offer a prospect for improvement. So, as its uses are explored, both new products and new processes will become available. Indeed, the distinction itself is not always valid – many new processes depend on the use of new products; and many new products, in turn, are only made possible by new processes. The tractor was a new product, but it made new farming processes possible; petroleum cracking was a new process, which created petrochemicals and plastics. By generating both new products and new processes, a new principle thereby displaces both labor and resources from a variety of older ways of doing things.

However, the new products and processes do not simply displace older ways of doing things. Think of the impact of the automobile on American culture and the American way of life. When transport was by horse and buggy, or by foot, the farmer went to town once a week, the worker lived within walking distance of the factory. No longer. From drive-in movies to carhops to drive-in banking to commercial strips to suburbs and freeways, the social landscape and with it the mores of everything from courtship to commerce have been radically transformed, and not always for the better. In other words, the application of a new principle tends to generate an interlocked set of new products and processes, which create new activities and new social patterns, which in turn combine to create new *ways of living*, new forms of social life. For the original principle applied to a social objective or function – transportation, in the case of the automobile, power supply and light, in the case of electricity – which itself was deeply interlocked with other social objectives or functions, so that when the mode of achieving one is radically changed, what is done with the others must be adapted in various ways to take advantage of the opportunities created by the improvements.

The result is the development of many new industries, and the expansion and modification of many old ones, to supply the needs of both the new industries and the new ways of living. With the development of the tractor, capable not only of pulling heavy loads but of running machinery off the engine's power drive, farming becomes mechanized. Not only is the horse displaced, the skills of the mechanic displace those of the harness-maker, the groom, and the wheelwright and carriage-maker. The character of rural life changes.

Transformational growth tends to be expansive. The more new products and new processes change the system, wiping out old ways of working, rendering old factories and skills worthless, the more they create new opportunities and new jobs. Everything destroyed has to be replaced and, since what will replace it will be new, the means of production for these new products and processes will at least have to be retooled and redesigned. Blacksmith shops and bicycle shops are re-equipped to repair motor vehicles. So investment will be stimulated. New jobs will require new skills, so there will have to be training programs. Training programs in turn require teachers. The new factories and jobs will have to be located appropriately, and this will lead to a construction boom. Roads will have to be built to service the new factories and suburbs; shopping centers will spring up. Construction and road building require earth-moving equipment; this will draw again on the principles of the internal combustion engine, and will in its turn generate factories and jobs. All these changes are echoed in the income distribution, bringing new groups into prosperity, displacing others, and generating new market patterns.

A warning, however: in the absence of specific governmental planning, there is no reason to expect that the expansion generated by the investment to meet the demand for new products and process will just offset or reabsorb the displaced labor and resources resulting from the introduction of these new products and processes. Even if the old dogs can be taught new tricks, it will usually be cheaper to hire new workers. In any case, neither the timing nor the location of the expansion need necessarily coincide with those of the displacement. Why should new jobs come on line at the same time and in the same places that older workers with now obsolete skills are being forced out? The traditional reply, of course, will be that the price mechanism will ensure it. There will be cheap labor and supplies at the point of displacement; being cheap, they will quickly be snatched up by the expanding new sectors. But the traditional theory is simple-minded: the labor, etc., due to displacement may be available cheaply, but investment in new products and processes must be guided by long-term considerations, not by momentary advantages. The displaced labor and equipment will usually not be suitable, and cheapness is no bargain if quality is missing.

Finally, a general observation: transformational growth is not random; it normally proceeds in a certain *direction*. In the early stages of capitalism the basic provisioning for social existence was still carried out within the household or domestic economy, by the methods of the traditional crafts. The family household was the unit that raised and socialized the new generation. The pattern of control over these activities was defined by the kinship system, which determined the inheritance of property and therefore of the power to make decisions about investment, location, production, employment and training. The system of inheritance has traditionally been that of male primogeniture, embedded in a patriarchy, with various local modification.

Growth in nineteenth-century America began from a largely rural and small-town system of family farms and family firms operating traditional crafts, expanding extensively, by adding new regions, and gradually transformed this into modern corporate industry and corporate farming, operating large-scale scientific industrial methods, marketing on a mass basis, and controlled by a professional career management. A kinship-based class and property system has been (partially) transformed into an educational-and-career based income hierarchy. (Class and property, of course, provide a head-start in education and career.) Activities and control were shifted from the kinship-oriented domestic economy to the bureaucratically controlled industrial system, creating new markets in the process. It is this pattern of development that has created the long-term pressure for technological change and investment.

These developments could be expected to change the nature of rural and small-town life, and to enlarge the cities and the manufacturing sector at the expense of the former. And this has indeed been the pattern of the past century. But at a certain point a new pattern began to become evident:

just as crafts gave way to industrial mass production, so the latter is giving way to automated and computerized systems of production. The industrial economy substitutes massive sources of power and economies of scale for the skills of the craftsman; the computerized economy substitutes accumulated information and control of complex operations for the energy and scale economies of the industrial system. In the first movement, factory work expands at the expense of agriculture and the crafts; in the second, office and white-collar work expands at the expense of manufacturing. In the first, classes are transformed into hierarchies and the nightwatchman state turns into the welfare state; in the second, capital is insitutionalized and sets out to dominate the state. Schematically, the craft economy gives way to modern industry, as capital develops an appropriate technology, and this in turn yields to the information economy, as capital develops appropriate controls and institutional forms. This will be examined in more detail later.

Transformational Growth and Industrial Capitalism

So 'transformational growth', in the industrial era, means just what the words imply: it is growth that transforms the economy, changes its structure – meaning the relative sizes of its sectors (agriculture, manufacturing, services) – and, as a result and then as an interacting cause, the distribution of income and the urban–rural relationship, together with the nature of work, of household life, and so on. This is the kind of growth the US experienced during the 1920s, during the war and for twenty years after the war.

However, it is not the only kind of growth. There can also be growth that is simply a straightforward 'swelling-up', with no new products or processes. Indeed, this is the kind of growth most commonly studied by economic theorists of whatever school, since it is the most tractable, given the currently popular methods of analysis. It is growth in which everything becomes larger in absolute size, but nothing changes in proportions: there is more income, but the income is distributed in the same way between wages, rents and profits and between categories of households; there are more goods of every kind, but they are produced and consumed in the same proportions, and so on. Steady growth need *not* mean that income per capita, or per unit land, remains the same; if it did, it would be relatively simple and uninteresting, a special case of growth that proceeds by accretion, adding new regions or territories, as happened in the nineteenth century before the closing of the frontier. But under steady growth, a rise in per capita income cannot lead to changes either in distribution or in the composition of output. (To be fair, many economic theorists study hypothetical growing systems of this sort only as extreme cases, in order to see reality by contrast, as it were.)

One thing is clear: industrial capitalism is a system that works very well when it is in the throes of transformational growth. Not that it is any more likely to be fair or just – but it will deliver the goods. With new products and new processes coming on line, generating new ways of life and creating new markets, employment will be high, productivity and real wages will be growing, profits will be high and capital will be accumulating rapidly, while prices will tend to be stable as cost-cutting will tend to offset increases due to high demand. A high level of investment spending means a boom in the investment goods sector; with high employment and high wages in capital goods, the consumer goods sector will also prosper. And the effects will be cumulative (as spelled out earlier in Chapter 5).

Transformational growth, then, tends to encourage a boom. What about steady growth? We can rule out 'growth by accretion' as irrelevant after the closing of the frontier. But what about other forms of steady growth? Can the capitalist system sustain a high level of investment while expanding steadily in the same proportions, without new products and new processes?

The answer, we shall argue, is *no*. A capitalist industrial system, being inherently dynamic, has two and only two long-run options – transformational growth or stagnation, the latter eventually leading to deterioration and decline. These two choices tend to alternate, giving rise to the appearance of 'long waves' in economic life.

Let's consider why steady growth must end in stagnation. Basically there are four reasons, one concerning investment, one consumption, one saving, and finally one to do with natural resources and the environment. All are concerned with the failure of a process of steady growth to generate new markets and steadily growing demand. Each of them helps to explain why steady growth must sink into decline after a time, and each therefore also shows another way in which transformational growth would offset such influences, and thus promote or prolong expansion.

The first point, affecting investment spending, arises from the normal system of 'writing off' fixed capital. A new plant or new equipment is expected to pay for itself within a few years. Common rules of thumb in various industries in the postwar era have ranged between three and five years, and even faster write-offs became common in the inflationary 1970s. But the effective operating lifetime of plant and equipment is much longer, perhaps ten times as long or more if carefully maintained. A major reason for the short pay-back period, of course, is fear of technological developments that would render the equipment obsolete; another is a shift in consumer tastes, or in marketing arrangements, that would require redesigning the product, and so rebuilding the plant. When such innovations or changes in consumption patterns occur (often the result of innovation in household technology), firms have little choice but to scrap their plant and equipment and replace them with the new or more suitable kind – otherwise they will lose out to competitors. However, when neither new products nor new processes are being introduced, there is no reason to scrap and rebuild at the end of the pay-off period. The accumulated funds can be stashed in the money market, where they will earn interest, while the plant, now fully amortized, can be run at a tidy profit. So the firm's capital will now be earning the usual operating profit plus the interest on the amortization fund. Even if a new plant would be superior, in the sense that it would earn more operating profit for the same investment, it might nevertheless not pay to build it, if it would not earn more than the old operating profit *plus* interest.[1]

So when innovation is sluggish or non-existent, expecially following a period of high activity, there will be a falling off of investment, creating stagnation and unemployment in the capital goods industries, and a slackening in the growth of productivity, which will be reflected in slower growth of real wages. Both effects will tend to create a slump in consumer goods, and so set off a cumulative downswing. None of this will provide any incentive to firms to scrap their paid-up plant and equipment and replace it. Quite the contrary; if unemployment rises and a slump develops, there is all the more reason to sit tight on money that is earning good interest, rather than risking those funds on new facilities, especially when existing ones are adequate, while the new ones would not be markedly superior.

An economic theorist could object that, while this may be true enough in practice, it is not an 'equilibrium' argument. It depends on the system first experiencing technical progress, with new products and processes being added, and *then* shifting to steady growth with no innovation. For it is the expectation of technical innovations that leads to the practice of writing-off investment quickly. It would therefore be no argument against the possibility of a system experiencing *only* steady growth.[2]

This may be true enough. But a capitalist industrial system could never experience only steady growth – for three reasons we shall now examine. All of these are theoretically sound, in that each shows that a system in steady growth cannot continue in that state. Demand will tend to slump or shift and/or costs to change; both of these are reasons for writing off investment faster than the physical lifetime requires. So if any or all of our next three points are valid, our first point must be granted also.

Now let's turn to consumption. As income per capita or per household increases, the character of consumption changes. At low levels of income, households spend a higher percentage of income on necessities (food, clothing and shelter), but as income rises the spending on such items rises less than in proportion, and new items (for example, education, entertainment and travel) enter the budget. A relationship can be derived, called an Engel curve, which shows for each class of commodities the proportion of household income that will be spent on it at each level of income. The reasons for this are easy to see. The basic necessities have to be purchased in order to maintain a life-style that will permit the earning of an income and the raising of a family. These necessities fit together to make the life-style; a certain kind of house will have a certain size of kitchen, with only such-and-such equipment. This does not altogether determine, but it certainly limits and predisposes, the pattern of food purchases and resulting diet. When income rises, to change the diet would mean buying new kitchen equipment and learning new cooking skills, not just buying new or different foods. However, a new kitchen would very likely mean a new house – that is, a major domestic investment and a new life-style. And that could very well require a major change in social status. So long as social positions remain unchanged, a rise in income will lead only to minor changes in basic and established patterns of spending, and the additional income will go on new products or on non-basics like luxuries and entertainment. Adapting this to the aggregate, if the social structure is given, a rise in income will lead to greater *discretionary* spending.

We can go further. Given the distribution of income, for any category of consumer goods a critical or watershed level of income can be found above which the proportion of additional income spent on the good or service will decline. That is, if income is growing, spending will not grow in pace for those goods whose watershed level is at or below the current level of income. Such markets, e.g. consumer durables, are 'growth-saturated'. So long as the income distribution is fixed, they do not grow as fast as the economy as a whole; hence a point will be reached at which growth has to begin to decelerate, as more and more goods reach their watershed levels. And new products alone will not change this if the new products are merely improved versions of existing ones, enabling established activities to be performed a little better. A transformation is required that will change the income distribution so as to create new markets. (Besides the income distribution we should mention certain other major social parameters – the urban–rural division, the pattern of marriage and family formation, the degree of education and literacy, and so on. A change in the urban–rural division might bring a flood of new workers to the cities, creating new markets for urban consumer goods, acting in the same way that a major change in distribution would.)

Let's examine the consequences of Engel curves for steady growth more carefully. Suppose an economy were growing on a steady path; per capita incomes would be rising, but after a time, when income reached the critical level for some category of consumer goods, demand for them would grow more slowly than income. But won't demand for some other 'higher' goods or services increase, and so take up the slack? If it does, of course, a slump may be avoided, but steady growth will have been abandoned. Normally, however, such a change won't be automatic; uncertainty will surround the area of expansion. If the growth slowdown in the necessities is pronounced while the expansion in the 'higher' goods is still tentative, or if the contraction is in manufactured goods (with a strong multiplier) and the expansion in services (where the multiplier effect is weak), the result will be a tendency to slump. In any of these cases, change will occur and steady growth cannot be sustained.

How will firms in the slower-growing markets be affected? They will accumulate capital more slowly than others, so their shareholders will tend to fall behind. Of course they can try to diversify, but they may lack the expertise. Diversification is a long-term effort, requiring the building of new divisions, and changing the firm's management structure. Instead it might be better to try to develop new products within its own market, to try to persuade existing consumers to spend more by improving and amplifying existing goods or by providing various services along with them. Moreover, for any given firm there is always another possibility, namely to grow at the expense of its rivals. Even if a firm decides not to follow this route, it must make sure that it is well defended if someone else tries it. Hence firms must try to develop brand loyalty, which also requires product development. In short, the same factors that prevent steady growth from continuing also provide incentives to a form of technical progress and product innovation (even though progress of this sort is frequently more packaging than quality).

Next, not only consumption, but also saving tends to undermine steady growth. If the economy's proportions are to be maintained during expansion, then the relative wealth of the various social classes will have to stay fixed. If their relative wealth changes, then so will their income from wealth-holding. And if their relative income changes, then the pattern of aggregate consumption will change, since total consumption consists of the consumption demands of the different groups weighted by their incomes.

Now consider the accumulation of wealth by different social classes or groups. For simplicity take the case of two classes, a working class and capitalist managers, where the latter are much wealthier. For generality, assume that each class receives profit income, that is, interest on its savings. Let the rate of interest be the same, whichever class receives the income. The capitalist class receives managerial salaries, the working class receives wages – where, of course, salaries are higher than wages. Both classes save, but capitalists, being wealthier, save at a higher rate. They will therefore accumulate wealth more rapidly, with the results just outlined. Once again steady growth cannot be maintained.

Finally, of course, steady growth of the swelling-up kind cannot continue indefinitely, simply because an economy is based on finite resources in a limited space. Over time the initial resources will become exhausted or more difficult to obtain – the wells will run dry, the high-grade ores will be used up, the mines will get deeper and more dangerous, the soil will erode. And everything will get more crowded – more people, more products, more buildings, more roads, more cars, more garbage, more pollution; all in the same space. In the early stages, with plenty of space and plenty of resources, such problems could be neglected, but, as time passes and the economy grows, both shortages and disamenities accumulate, too. What's more, they interact: the cost of disposing of garbage is raised if it can't be burnt because of the already high level of air pollution. Nor can it be assumed that this interaction is simply additive; it may be, on occasion, *multiplicative*, which means that the disamenities and the costs of correcting them would then grow exponentially with increases in output. Thus a steady swelling-up of the economy will run into the classic Ricardian problems of diminishing returns from given resources and increasing costs in the use of limited space. If growth is to continue, there will have to be a shift to new products and new processes of production, drawing on different resources and making it possible to rearrange living patterns, so as to conserve on space.

So, capitalism has to grow in order to prosper. If it doesn't grow, the basic industries that produce capital goods will stagnate, and the stagnation will spread to the consumer goods sector. But we have just seen four reasons why growth cannot take place for long in a 'steady-state' or given pattern. Investment will tend to be postponed, consumption will change in composition as per capita incomes rise, distribution would tend to shift to the already wealthy, weakening consumer demand, which would tend to become saturated anyway. And Ricardian problems of diminishing returns to the use of limited space and resources would set in. The first and last are supply-side problems, although the first has demand implications. But the other two concern the failure of demand to grow adequately in steady-state conditions. So growth requires transformation, and the transformation has to ensure that markets will expand. Without transformative pressures, attempts to keep the economy growing – essential to full employment policy – will run into greater and greater difficulty. The economy will become progressively harder to manage.

The Transformation Draws to an End

Perhaps the most obvious source of transformational growth in the American economy in recent years has been the automobile, or more generally the internal combustion engine. And this has reached the end of the road. Or at least so the figures of Chapter 1 suggest. However, the problem in fact lies much deeper. As we shall see, the automobile has played a major role, but in a drama that encompasses far more than transportation. To grasp this we shall have to look at the changing nature of the system.

The falling off of consumer growth in the advanced countries, coupled with the rapid rise in the growth rate of world trade and especially with the emergence of fast-growing consumer markets in the NDCs, has created pressure for the export of both capital and jobs. In the past, profits from overseas were usually or at least frequently repatriated; now transnationals shift them to where taxes are least and invest them where growth is fastest. The effect tends to be stagnation and plant-closings at home and the development of dualism and dependency abroad, both of which are likely to undermine the ability of the respective states to provide growing and well-distributed provisioning for their expanding populations.

Nor will this trend be easily reversed. Indeed we shall argue that it poses major policy problems for the advanced countries. For the era of transformational growth seems to be ending in the advanced countries, with the consequences discussed earlier. It is not a matter of a 'shortage' of new inventions or new technology; in fact we are in an era of almost unprecedented technological innovation, coupled, paradoxically, with stagnation in investment. This is because many of these innovations tend to be labor displacing or market destroying, rather than expansionary. And instead of redistributing income to new groups of families, the innovations tend to concentrate it in the hands of corporations. This is not simply an accident of scientific development.

The reason lies deeper and concerns the direction of technological development. For the past century perhaps the chief impetus to growth has been the progressive invasion by industrial capital of the traditional province of the family. This is what has created the great consumer markets of the advanced West. Technology has certainly been important in this, but it has been technology organized by capital, technology in the service of capital.

As we have noted above, the creation of new consumer markets has largely taken place by destroying the traditional activities and organization of the family. The production system that directly supported everyday life, even as recently as a century ago, was largely organized through the household. More than half the population still worked the land, and another third lived in small towns. These households grew much of their own food, put up preserves every autumn, cooked whatever they ate, made their own bread, cookies, cakes, etc., mended their own clothes (and made many of them), made soaps and candles, grew or collected herbs for medicinal purposes, mended and often made furniture, and repaired and sometimes even built the houses they lived in. Of course, the basic consumer goods and most means of production were produced in factories, managed by capital, even then. Shoes and leather goods, for example, cloth, most basic clothing, patent medicines, building materials, staple foodstuffs, oil and kerosene, lamps, household furniture, stoves, kitchen utensils and all luxury goods, all were produced for profit and marketed on what was already becoming a national basis. But the household was not a 'final consumer'; the household produced. Indeed, members of the household were skilled in many serious crafts – sewing, wood-working, cooking and preserving, carpentry, herbal medicine, and many others. (Anyone who doubts this should consult the *Foxfire* books.) Besides craft work, many activities now routinely conducted outside the home went on within it. Birth and death and serious illness, for example, were largely handled in the family – with the assistance of outside specialists, to be sure, but the basic work was done in the home. Moreover, the family did much of the educating of the children and virtually all of caring for the aged and infirm.

Of course, not every family possessed all the skills or performed all these activities. Some households would specialize and exchange would take place, either barter within the framework of the extended family, or monetary exchange within the local community – perhaps more commonly, both. However, such local specialization and exchange still remained fundamentally within the sphere of the household. Even though money might change hands, the activities were neither industrial in their technology nor capitalist in their organization.

Much more could be said about the production activities of the premodern, non-urban household. It is important to realize the extent to which the circumstances of the everyday lives of our grandparents or great-grandparents were something they largely created themselves through the exercise of craft skills in the home. By contrast, we buy the circumstances of our lives in the shopping center and from the real estate developer, together with service contracts, should anything go wrong, as it certainly will. A glance over the very partial list of crafts, skills and activities mentioned above is enough to reveal a central, and often overlooked, feature of our economic development over the past century. Every one of these domestic crafts and household skills has been replaced by a major industry, dominated by one or more giant multinational firms. The household has been depleted, and has lost the power to control or shape its everyday circumstances (a loss actively resisted by the 'do-it-yourself' movement, and by the counter-culture), while the market has expanded. The growth of capital has taken place at the expense of the household.

Of course, it can be immediately protested that this is a distorted and perverse way of describing a well-known phenomenon – the freeing of both men and women from onerous toil. Progress, indeed, should be measured by the replacement of old-fashioned, even primitive, ways of doing things with modern, technologically superior mass production. We can buy bread cheaper than we could make it; perhaps homemade bread is better than the supermarkets', but the same could hardly be said about homemade clothes or furniture or soaps or cosmetics or medicines. (*Hand*made clothes or furniture – that is, made by skilled craftsmen – may be better than mass produced ones, but the modern crafts have themselves been transformed by industrial technology, and use its tools and materials.) The reasons for these developments are simple: the new products are frequently better, always cheaper, and moving production out of the household has provided a vast increase in leisure time.

There is no reason to deny this, and the only criticism of this view is that it is seriously incomplete. True, the new products are cheaper, frequently better, and their introduction lightens the burden of daily work. But this is not simply the onward march of progress; along with growth there is destruction. The preparation and processing of food, the manufacture of clothing, furniture, implements, soaps and cosmetics, medicine, birth and death, the care of the sick and the aged have all been moved out of the home. And traditional skills have been lost. Education, even day care, is now the province of the state. The market and the state between them have taken over most of the functions previously performed by the family. Small wonder, then, that the extended family has ceased to be a significant feature of modern life, and even the nuclear family shows signs of disintegration. Apart from the conceiving of children and caring for them while they are quite young, the family system is no longer the sole or even the central agency responsible for the reproduction of the material and social circumstances of everyday life. The development of the economy – and of the state – has been a process of taking over these functions, producing the goods and services required on an industrial scale, by new and more powerful processes, and then marketing them commercially, with the state providing the infrastructure to make this possible. That, for better or worse, has been the process of transformational growth.

And, evidently, it has come to an end. Given the distribution of income, and in the absence of a major attempt to create new incomes for the poor, there is nothing left to transform. The funeral business developed in the 1950s, nursing homes in the 1960s, the birthing business began before World War II, and had fully taken over by the end of the 1950s. The traditional crafts had long since perished, and the internal combustion engine drove people off the land and into the cities and suburbs. This last process went on during the 1950s, but slowed to a trickle by the late 1960s, and even reversed itself a few years during the 1970s. For the well-to-do and for the middle classes, probably for the top three-fifths of the income distribution, the transformation is more or less complete, and what we are now seeing is the slow disintegration of an institution – marriage, the family and kinship system – that no longer has social functions commensurate with its ideological and mythic status. We have arrived at what seems to be the end of one era, but the shape of the next is not yet clear.

Additional Factors in the Slowing of Growth

The postwar era began, as we saw, with a major act of redistributive demand creation, in the form of the G.I. Bill of Rights. A major new market for homes, automobiles and all consumer durables was established by the fact that 12 million ex-G.I.s were entitled to college tuition, federal and medical services – a program that was then given a further impetus following the Korean War. Unfortunately neither the Vietnam War nor the ill-fated War on Poverty carried on this tradition, and the markets established in the late 1940s and early 1950s, became saturated. During the 1970s the income share of the poorest fifth of the population actually deteriorated; distribution moved in favor of the better-off.

Two other factors should be mentioned. First, as mentioned earlier, pollutants may tend to interact multiplicatively in the environment, rather than additively. As growth takes place, both the impact of pollution and the cost of preventing it or cleaning it up may not only rise, but rise at an increasing rate. Thus the need to control pollution will probably tend to cause growth to slow down. New technologies might reduce the economy's impact on the environment, but so far the case is unproven.

Besides pollution, however, there is another reason for holding that the current pattern of growth will increasingly slow down. This is that energy supplies are either running out or becoming increasingly costly to obtain (and dangerous to the environment). Of course, we have recently been awash in oil, but that is due to a combination of special factors – Saudi Arabia's decision to pump until it can dominate OPEC, a worldwide slump, new producers coming on line, and so on. Even if it no longer makes headlines, however, there is an energy 'crisis', in the sense that cheap energy can no longer be taken for granted. Although that means that conservation and decentralized energy systems – solar power, wind generation and the 'soft' path – may be, or may shortly become, economically as well as socially preferable, they are none the less not so profitable, and in particular, they do not fit into the structure of the corporate business world. Centralized energy systems provide a measure of bureaucratic control, both over prices and over the volume, timing and mix of sales. Decentralized energy systems obviously do not, but, even worse for business, they could lead to the destruction of established markets. Co-generation, for example, according to some estimates, could actually lead to *reduced* demand from the grid. Even the limited conservation measures taken recently have caused stagnation in the demand for electricity. This cessation of growth has led to cancellation or postponement of investment in generating capacity – particularly in nuclear power, which has become extremely costly. So the slowdown in the growth of consumer energy demand causes loss of sales in capital goods. The very things that commend cheap locally produced energy to households – money saving, greater independence, simplicity – imply that it undermines the energy market.

The Information Economy

A chief cause of the slowdown of the 1970s is that one phase of transformational growth, the development of industrial mass production, is drawing to an end, while what appears to be the next phase, the setting up of the information economy, has hardly begun. Even at this stage, however, certain of its features have become clear, and these suggest that there will be problems in achieving the traditional goals of non-inflationary full employment with the tools of demand management.

For one thing, the cost structure of business in the new mold is going to be different, just as it changed with the shift from crafts to industry (see Table 7.1). In the craft economy, variable costs were low in relation to output, because a large part of the labor force was fixed. Hence fixed costs were high, but consisted of current rather than capital charges, and were set in real rather than monetary terms. In mass production, by contrast, variable costs are large, while fixed costs are amortized and are set in

Table 7.1 *The changing cost structure of business*

Type of economy	Variable	Costs Fixed	Nature
Craft	low	current	real
Industrial	high	capital	monetary
Information	low	capital	monetary

monetary form. The chief effect of the change to the information economy is to reduce, even in some cases (when automation is virtually total) to eliminate, variable costs. When variable costs are a high proportion of output, adjusting output to sales minimizes the pressure on profit margins. But when this cannot be done, there is a great temptation to cut prices to gain sales at the expense of competitors; yet if they follow suit everyone is worse off – a classic Prisoner's Dilemma. (Even worse, prices can be driven down very far indeed, as demand for manufactures tends to be inelastic.) Control over the market is therefore essential.

However, more than the market must be controlled. Corporate structures themselves require elaborate control, as does the financial system that sustains them. Most of all, the state must be controlled – or it will come to control capital. The Keynesian compromise, the standoff characteristic of the mass production era, in which the government plans and stimulates demand and leaves supply to the business world, no longer seems feasible. Supply problems require general coordination and demand needs detailed product planning; but even more important, when variable costs are low the multiplier, the cornerstone of demand management, will be much weaker. Government stimulation cannot be general and anonymous, a tide that raises all ships alike. It will have to be targeted, specific. And this means detailed planning, raising the crucial question, who will be in control of this process?

In the craft economy, consumption spending will tend to offset changes in investment, since, because of the cost structure, prices are more flexible than money wages. In the mass production system, by contrast, consumption and investment will move together. What can we expect in the information economy? Will prices be flexible, with employment and money wages stable? This is not at all likely. Low variable and high monetary capital costs suggest that prices will be programmed over the whole of the expected product cycle, and will be kept firm in the face of short-term fluctuations in sales. Moreover, labor costs as a whole are likely to be low relative to the other systems, so even if favorable distributional changes occurred, they would be a less effective stabilizer. But they are unlikely to occur.

All this is speculative; let's go back to the basic process of trans-formational growth – the transfer of functions from the domestic economy to industry and the market.

Public vs Private Goods

As we saw above, at low levels of income, households will chiefly be concerned with meeting basic material needs – food, clothing, shelter, transport. These will be largely private goods in the economist's sense, although some transport may be collective. As income increases, the household will increasingly try to introduce 'higher' – more distinctly human – levels of activity into its consumption pattern. For example, education, entertainment and communication, all of which are essentially collective, all rise as a percentage of household budgets at higher-income levels. We don't have to accept the interesting, though perhaps disputable, classifications of lower- and higher-level activities developed by psychologists (following Abraham Maslow) to see that here is a point of great importance: as income increases, the proportion of additional income spent on public (or collective) goods and services tends to rise. A good example is education: affluent families spend more in proportion to their income on education than do poor families, and, over time, education has risen as a proportion of the budget expenditures of all families.

Let's explore this further. By 'private goods' (or services) we mean something produced for consumption by a family or individual that can be bought and consumed without regard to whether anyone else is also concurrently consuming that object. Hamburgers, easy chairs, eye glasses, men's shirts, car washes and haircuts are all goods the consumption of which by any one consumer is wholly independent of the coordinated consumption of that good by others. There is, of course, a matter of scale of production; hamburgers and easy chairs, of course, would not be produced unless there were a large enough market. But the actual act of consumption does not have to be coordinated; I can eat a hamburger today even if nobody else does. However, for a seminar to take place everyone in the group has to turn up at the same room, having done the same reading. The telephone call won't be complete unless the party being called answers; more generally, no one would install a telephone unless they expected many others to do so at the same time. Of course, many ostensibly 'private' goods have a hidden public aspect. Automobiles are private – but they depend on highways that are public. Moreover, if everyone goes driving at once, there is a traffic jam; one party's successful consumption depends on others *not* acting at the same time.

The analysis of public goods, and of the public aspects of private goods (what economists call 'externalities'), is a complex and controversial topic. Economists define private goods by the exclusion principle – one person's consumption of a particular item precludes another's – and the payments principle – whoever pays for the good decides who shall consume it. When either or both of these are violated – you and I can both cross the bridge at the same time; if you pay your taxes and the bridge is built, I can take a free ride – the normal neo-Classical analysis of optimality will not hold. But our interest here is quite different; optimality is not the issue, so we are free to take a different perspective. Instead of non-exclusiveness, our interest turns on collective consuming – goods at least some of whose uses require, in principle, to be consumed publicly, that is, in an act or acts coordinated with at least some other agents. We have already seen that, as affluence increases, demand will tend to shift towards public goods. In addition, although the basic necessities are predominantly private, when they are consumed in abnormally large quantities (perhaps as the result of marketing) the result will usually be negative externalities – they become public goods. Think of overeating or excessive drinking, overdressing and creating a public spectacle, driving too fast, or building too large a house and spoiling the appearance of the neighborhood. Consumption of the necessaries of life confined within normal bounds can be treated as 'private' because it falls within the definition of the given style of life. But once it goes outside those bounds it generates public consequences. (Hence a theory that assumes 'non-satiation' must be rejected out of hand.) Let's examine the effects of a shift toward public goods further.

The production and consumption of public goods normally requires coordination by a public agency, usually the state. So the tendency (which we will document later) for the share of the state in GNP to rise all over the affluent world appears to be well grounded in the nature of things, and not easily reversible. However, it would be a mistake to think that private capital will readily accept this; indeed, its refusal to do so has had a profound impact on the character of our everyday lives.

For, in order to earn private profit on collective consumption, capital has to *privatize* the consumption of inherently public goods and services. This, of course, distorts the distribution of the public good, but it often affects the nature of the good as well. The commercialization of the media of communication is a good example. Television and radio are inherently public, raising problems of fair access and equal time for all points of view and subjects. But fair access and equal time are irrelevant to profit-making. Not so violence, glossy sex and trash. Worse, a distorted and manipulative picture of society is presented, partly the result of unconscious ideology, and partly in open deference to commercial sponsors. Copyrights and patents provide another example. Nothing is so obviously a public good as an idea or a work of art. Yet both have been reduced to the status of commodities, from the sale of which money is to be made. The effect, of course, is to exclude people who cannot afford the price from the benefits, and consequently to inhibit not only their consumption but also (especially in the case of education) their development. This, in turn, limits the possibilities for still others, who might have learned or profited from interacting with them. In short, privatizing public goods – limiting access to those who can pay fees – both distorts the goods themselves and limits the development of citizens.

This may be true, but why should it be a problem for capital? If the point is to explain the difficulties in re-establishing prosperity, why does it matter if privatization distorts? Because the process creates barriers both to the increase of productivity and to the development of markets. If education is limited, then so is the market for computers, for example. Privatization creates negative externalities.

It is none the less increasingly important. Indeed the Reagan–Thatcher program can be seen as, in part, an attempt to prevent the state from performing its regulatory functions, so that capital could act more freely in attempting to privatize public goods. With markets for normal goods maturing, capital must either move abroad or invade the domain of public goods if it is to sustain its rate of expansion. So we confront a clash between the system's need for profitable avenues of accumulation and its ability to provide a growing standard of living.

Work as a public good

Not only can we expect to witness increasing concern for public goods among the large and relatively affluent middle classes, there is one public good that may become particularly important, and perhaps dangerous to the interests of capital. With growing affluence people will increasingly fill their leisure hours (which may also increase) with satisfying and high-quality activities. But the bulk of their best waking hours are not leisure time – they are spent at work, and capital tends to organize work in ways that minimize the opportunities for creative or even responsible activity. Work is progressively deskilled and degraded, often morally as well as practically. At the same time, however, workers in their capacities as citizens and as consumers are becoming more educated and sophisticated. The result is therefore a rising demand for the restructuring of work – a demand for jobs to be made *meaningful*, to involve responsibility and to provide the opportunity to grow, to develop and exercise skills. As the society becomes more affluent, this demand can be expected to increase: more and better consumer goods simply cannot make up for a work week spent in boring, routine, unchallenging or sometimes morally question-able activity.[3]

But why shouldn't the modern corporation provide meaningful work? The rising demand for it surely makes sense, since the need for additional consumption goods on the part of the already prosperous middle classes cannot be urgent compared to their need to feel they are doing something responsible and useful during their working hours. Moreover, a sense of accomplishment in daily work would help develop loyalty to the company and the system. In fact, there are movements among management analysts to try to reduce employee alienation.

The trouble is, the corporation is a structure designed to serve the needs of *capital*. To this end it is organized to control work and to mobilize resources to meet competition. Providing opportunities for employee self-fulfillment is not one of capital's objectives. If it is done, it will be because doing so promotes one of capital's primary objectives sufficiently to be worthwhile. Yet the most basic aims of business are often considered distorted or perverted – no one respects a doctor whose aim is to make money rather than preserve or promote good health. But competition, which can become severe in times of stagnation, requires a focus on making money; those who fail to do so will be taken over or destroyed. In any event, the shift in consumption from private goods to goods and services with collective aspects, as per capita incomes increase, is going to prove an increasingly difficult problem for private enterprise systems.

Expansive vs introverted innovations

Yet this is not the main reason for introducing a discussion of private versus public goods. Innovations and technical developments affect the two quite differently, and these differences are important for understanding transformational growth. Very simply, an innovation in a private good may have only relatively narrow effects, whereas an innovation in a public good, or a good with a considerable range of public aspects, will have relatively widespread and wide-ranging effects. On the other hand, an innovation in a service, or in a good manufactured easily with relatively little manufactured input, will neither generate much employment nor provide much stimulus to the rest of the economy. Innovations have to create employment, and generate demand for manufactured components, to matter. Consequently goods have to be both public (or have public aspects) and be industrially manufactured to be capable of setting off a long-term boom in investment and employment. We've already discussed the multiplier relationships; let's look at the significance of the private/public distinction.

Consider an innovation in the design or nature of a private good. The new product, say an electric can opener, displaces an older product, the mechanical can opener, and thereby devalues the capital invested in the production of the older product, while generating investment in the production of the new. If the new product is cheaper than the good it displaces, the effect could be a reduction in total employment, and indeed in total activity, because the new product could perform the job well enough to reduce the total spending required to have the function performed to the degree wanted by households. An innovation may save on labor in two senses: it may require less labor to produce, and also less household labor to use. It may also require fewer total resources to produce, while still getting the job done. On the other hand the new product might be both better – performing the function faster or more accurately or to a higher degree – and more expensive, so generating more investment and (though not necessarily) more employment than it displaces. Of course, if the new good is cheaper it may appeal to a wider market, so the displacement effect could be swamped by the scale effect; this can be expected if the product is still in the expansive phase of development. However, if the good's development is already mature, so that it is already being marketed in all social classes, an innovation that simply cheapens the good will reduce activity. Ideally, this should be counted a benefit, since it means that labor and resources are now free to engage in the production of other things. But on the individual level, no company likes to see its revenue decline, while on the aggregate level less spending means less activity; in a demand-constrained economy, released resources will be *unemployed*, unless a new and specific demand for their use is created. What could and should be a social benefit tends to become a disaster if left to the mercy of the free market.

To shift from canned foods to frozen, from cotton shirts to polyester, or from gas stoves to electric, requires little reorganization of domestic life, and generates comparatively little net new investment. This will be true even when the new private good performs its function so much better that it justifies increased household spending on it. By contrast, to shift from the horse and buggy to the automobile, or from the written letter to the telegraph and telephone, will set up a pattern of 'linkage' and 'ripple' effects that will transform whole sectors of the economy, generating investment and employment all across the map.

'Linkage effects' refers to the impact of the development of a product on suppliers of inputs into its production, on the one hand, and on the users, on the other. A new product may require modifications of productive equipment or different refinement of materials. Users of a new product may need to invest in new space or in complementary goods that will make it easier to get the full benefit of the new product. New private goods also generate both kinds of linkage effects, but they are unlikely to involve such dramatic changes, since a new private good will be adopted only if it is either cheaper (in which case its backward linkage effects cannot even offset its displacement effects) or does the job so much better that it justifies an increase in cost. A new public good, however, will be adopted not simply because it is cheaper, or does the same thing better, but because it makes possible a new mode of life. Consequently it may not only be more expensive, but draw on completely different sources of supply, and set up forward linkages in all sorts of unexpected directions.

Even more important than linkage effects are what have been called ripple effects – the tendency of an innovation to set up new patterns of activity, which in turn require new investment, and often further new innovations. Thus the telephone brought about the reorganization of business offices, just as the Xerox and now the computer are doing. The internal combustion engine generated a whole set of new products, from tractors to cement mixers to earth-moving equipment, all of which opened new opportunities for the development of new forms of life – the automobile-based suburb, built around the need to drive to work and the shopping center. With public goods, or rather goods that have significant public characteristics, innovations, especially in transportation, education and communications, lead to changes in the patterns of social existence great enough to create new areas of prosperity and new markets, which may be sufficiently extensive to bring about a long-term investment boom in which the social order is rebuilt; however, this will require the active participation of the state. If the Keynesian compromise is no longer acceptable, a new formula will have to be found. But if the state itself is being cut back, transformational growth based on public goods is unlikely to take off.

So new public goods (in our sense) may have extensive (although perhaps unforeseeable) consequences; but their introduction and development will require expanded state intervention and regulation. There is another consideration, however. A new public goods sector may consist largely of services – as in education and communications. Even computers are to a large extent service-intensive. So they make comparatively small demands on the industrial sector, even though the innovations may lead to substantial changes in the activities of both businesses and households. If a new sector does not put heavy demands on industry, it will not generate much investment spending. Indeed, industry may find that it can supply the new goods required, e.g. in education, communications and computers, by adapting and retooling or converting present (underutilized) factories, rather than building new ones. (In Chapter 1 we saw how construction of factories had slumped.) Moreover, the products of the information industries help to make such conversions easier by streamlining operations and improving control and design. As a result, not much additional employment will be generated in the capital goods sector. Productivity there will tend to rise, but, as we noted before, a tendency of productivity to rise contributes to stagnation, and this is the more pronounced when such an increase occurs as the alternative to investment, as a means of expanding capacity.

In short, as the growth of demand leads progressively to a shift in the composition of demand in favor of a higher proportion of public goods, further demand increases can, paradoxically, be expected to intensify the forces leading to stagnation.

Conclusions

Let's recapitulate. We have argued first, that traditional tranformational growth, shifting activities out of the household, creating a new income distribution and new markets, has largely come to an end; second, that pollution, environmental questions and new decentralized technological opportunities create problems for capital and are unlikely to bring about an investment and employment boom; and, thirdly, that a new form of the system may be emerging, the information economy, with a different structure of costs and different behavior patterns. This fits with the natural evolution of consumption from private to collective, but it creates a dilemma for an economy organized around private capital. Although profit can be made by privatizing consumption, this distorts the nature of collective goods, usually at the expense of the general welfare. An important conflict may develop over the nature of work itself. Finally, transformational growth tends to be generated by innovations that affect public goods or the public aspects of goods (rather than simply cheapening private goods), because this is what will create long-term investment needs.

Notes

1   As an example, let the total capital be 100, of which 25 is operating capital and 75 fixed. Let the rate of interest be 10%, the old profit rate 10% and the new, 15%. Clearly the new profit rate is greater than the old and greater than what can be obtained from the money market. But, once the plant is paid off, the rate of return is

$$r = (10 + 7.5)/100 = 17.5\% > 15\%,$$

so the new plant will not be built.

2   The objection that, if steady growth were high enough, both plants could be operated cannot be sustained: whatever the rate of growth, new demand will be met with new capacity, and the point at issue concerns the use of depreciation funds to build replacement plant.

3   People will, finally, quit the system altogether, and try to make a living from small farming and craft work. During the 1970s millions of American adults tried this route for longer or shorter periods. A movement on such a scale begins to be a.threat to the system's ability to recruit, and it also presents a challenge to its legitimacy. But hard times have changed this movement; indeed, to do so may have been one important function of austerity. There are few jobs in rural America, and the market for crafts has stagnated. The result has been a large shift of drop-outs into the 'underground' economy – marijuana is now estimated to be the country's fourth largest cash crop. Nevertheless, though commercial, this represents a development of independent small business – 'working for myself' – and is consistent with the rejection of careers in the great bureaucratic hierarchies of the modern corporation or the modern state.

Appendix: Testing for Structural Change

Felix Jimenez has suggested a way to test the proposition that growth of demand substantially slowed down and changed in character in the late 1960s. The results, though preliminary, appear to confirm the claim.

The growth of domestic demand and structural change are the main factors determining the rate of growth of productivity, except at the end of the product cycle, when the pressure for transformation becomes crucial, that is, when all the linked markets begin their saturation period. This latter factor can be represented by the first difference of the rate of growth of real wages, since its acceleration invigorates the internal competition among capitalists. We can also break up the short-run and the long-run effects of the rate of growth of output (internal demand) on the rate of growth of productivity. Our productivity model for testing the long-run stagnation or de-industrialization of the US economy can be expressed as follows:

$$p = f(\bar{q}, q - \bar{q}, \Delta w, sc),$$

where $\bar{q}$ represents the long-run rate of growth of output or demand; $q - \bar{q}$ stands for its cyclical variations; Δw represents the speed-up of real wages; and sc represents the structural change variable.

The speed-up of real wages (consumer purchasing power) expresses the pressure of demand. The structural change variable stands for the relative degree of changes in product definition and design and in technical processes (its effect on the rate of growth of productivity would be insignificant in the case of a general saturation of the manufacturing markets). The long-run effect of growth of output accounts for endogenous technical progress of the sort that, ceteris paribus, all industries can afford. (This is what is called 'learning by using', where a given technical process is improved as a result of the long-run expansion of the corresponding markets.) Finally, the de-trended rate of growth of manufacturing demand stands for the temporal influence of economic cycles on productivity and, hence, on profits, given the markup pricing procedure.

By taking into consideration the twenty two-digits industries of the US manufacturing sector, we have estimated the following equation for the cycles 1951–59, 1959–66, 1966–73 and 1973–79:

$$p = f(q, sc).$$

Our proxy for structural change is a multiple of the net investment–value-added ratio. This ratio (I_i/V_i, where i stands for industry i of the manufacturing sector) should reflect the relative response of investment to pressures of a generalized demand expansion and/or competition. It shows the pressure that both demand and competition put on the corresponding industrial profits:

$$I_i/V_i = (I_i/S_i) [1 - (W_i/S_i)]^{-1}$$

where I is investment, V value-added, W total wages and S total profits in each industry i. In the case of a generalized market expansion, increases in the investment–value-added ratio could be associated with a constant share of wages. However, in the case of structural change, the ratio of wages to profits would necessarily have to change.

Now, the question is how to 'isolate' the structural change effect of investment. If productivity increases in all the industries at the same rate from peak to peak of the economic cycle (the rate corresponding to the growth of the manufacturing sector as a whole), the implicit process of technical improvement will not create any structural change, since the relative technical condition of each industry will be unchanged. We can therefore construct for each industry a theoretical level of productivity reached at the end of the cycle as follows:

$$\bar{p}^i_{t+1} = p^i_t (1 + r),$$

where r is the rate of growth of productivity of the manufacturing sector as a whole, t and $t + 1$ are the corresponding year-peaks of the economic cycle, and $\bar{p}^i$ and p^i are the theoretical and actual levels of productivity in industry i. At the end of the cycle the *actual* level of productivity in industry i is p^i_{t+1}. Therefore, the ratio $p^i_{t+1}/\bar{p}^i_{t+1}$ would express the relative technological position of industry i reached at the end of the cycle because of structural change generated by investment. As long as we want to isolate the effect of expenditures for new plant and equipment on the relative technical condition of each industry, the investment–value-added ratio in the initial peak of the cycle would have to be weighted by the above ratio of actual to theoretical level of productivity reached at the end of the cycle. Consequently, our proxy for 'structural change' would be

$$sc_i = (p_i/\bar{p}_i)_{t+1} \, (I_i/V_i)_t,$$

where:

> p is the actual level of productivity
> $\bar{p}$ is the theoretical level of productivity
> I is net investment in new plant and equipment
> V is value-added
> $t, t+1$ are the peaks of the economic cycles
> i industry, $i = 20, 21 \ldots 39$.

As may be seen from Table 7.2, the results provide strong confirmation of the hypothesis that this structural change variable had an important and positive influence on the rate of growth of productivity during the two cycles of the postwar period 1950–66. This influence practically disappeared during the cycles 1966–73 and 1973–79; the corresponding regressors are not statistically different from zero.

Next consider a time series analysis. Our estimated specification was:

$$p = f(\bar{q}, q - \bar{q}, \Delta w, ss),$$

where $\bar{q}$ is the long-term rate of growth of manufacturing output, estimated by five-year moving long-linear trend regressions and centered

Table 7.2 *Estimates of manufacturing productivity*
(cross-sectional analysis)

Cycle					
1951–59	(1)	$p = 1.454$	$+ 0.503q$	$+ 0.151sc$	$\bar{R}^2 = 0.61$
		(2.508)	(4.205)	(2.733)	SEE $= 1.07$
	(2)	$e = -1.454$	$+ 0.497q$	$- 0.151sc$	$\bar{R}^2 = 0.50$
		(−2.509)	(4.151)	(−2.733)	SEE $= 1.07$
1959–66	(3)	$p = 0.630$	$+ 0.369q$	$+ 0.249sc$	$\bar{R}^2 = 0.67$
		(1.106)	(4.515)	(4.197)	SEE $= 0.93$
	(4)	$e = -0.630$	$+ 0.631q$	$- 0.249sc$	$\bar{R}^2 = 0.79$
		(−1.106)	(7.719)	(−4.197)	SEE $= 0.93$
1966–73	(5)	$p = 1.557$	$+ 0.392q$	$+ 0.041sc$	$\bar{R}^2 = 0.59$
		(3.548)	(4.309)	(0.787)	SEE $= 0.83$
	(6)	$e = -1.557$	$+ 0.608q$	$- 0.041sc$	$\bar{R}^2 = 0.73$
		(−3.548)	(6.692)	(−0.787)	SEE $= 0.83$
1973–79	(7)	$p = 1.255$	$+ 0.477q$	$+ 0.030sc$	$\bar{R}^2 = 0.31$
		(1.668)	(3.199)	(−0.278)	SEE $= 1.26$
	(8)	$e = -1.255$	$+ 0.523q$	$- 0.030sc$	$\bar{R}^2 = 0.39$
		(−1.668)	(3.501)	(0.278)	SEE $= 1.26$

Notes: Figures in parentheses are t-values, with 17 degrees of freedom ($n = 20$ industries); SEE is the standard error of the regression.

Sources: *Business Statistics*, 1979, 1982; *Annual Survey of Manufactures*, various issues; *Census of Manufacturers*, various issues.

in the second. This procedure accurately reproduces the cycles and also corresponds to their average length.

We have to explain *ss*. In the cross-section analysis, structural change was proxied by *sc*, which reflects the relative technical condition reached by each industry at the end of each economic cycle. Consequently, this variable only gives a sectional picture of the manufacturing sector. However, in a longitudinal analysis, the structural change variable cannot be timeless any more. Accordingly, we have chosen to proxy the relative international position of the manufacturing sector. Hence, *ss* is the difference between the rate of growth of imports and exports of manufactured commodities during the period 1949–80.

The rationale can be found in the fact that technical change in the manufacturing sector is reflected in the relative position of the manufacturing sector vis-à-vis not only the non-manufacturing sectors, but also its international rivals. Systemic net-import penetration takes place when the capacity for seizing external markets (that is, technical advantage) is decreasing or stagnated. This would have happened in the American economy after 1966 when its period of structural change was exhausted.

What about the domestic situation of the manufacturing sector? Along with Kaldor, we argue that the rate of expansion of manufacturing markets determines the growth of the entire economic system. For this reason we have chosen a statistical procedure based on Chow's method for testing the presence of two different situations during the period 1949–80. the first, that is 1949–65, would be the era of transformational growth, and would therefore produce different regressors for our productivity model.

As may be seen from Table 7.3, all the results validate the hypotheses postulated so far. For the whole period 1949–80, only our variable *ss* is statistically non-significant, but it has the correct sign. Verdoorn's law is also confirmed. And the significance of the transformational pressure

Table 7.3   *Estimates of manufacturing productivity (time series analysis)*

1949–80	$p = 1.282$	$+ 0.574\bar{q}$	$+ 0.227 (q - \bar{q})$	$+ 0.302\Delta w$	$- 0.018ss$
	(2.481)	(4.116)	(3.840)	(2.037)	(−0.713)
	$\bar{R}^2 = 0.564$		SEE = 1.690	DW = 2.281	SSR = 77.115
1949–65	$p = 1.479$	$+ 0.541\bar{q}$	$+ 0.177 (q - \bar{q})$	$+ 0.140\Delta w$	$- 0.007ss$
	(2.049)	(3.365)	(2.315)	(0.775)	(0.269)
	$\bar{R}^2 = 0.553$		SEE = 1.591	DW = 2.652	SSR = 30.406
1966–80	$p = 2.116$	$+ 0.276\bar{q}$	$+ 0.331 (q - \bar{q})$	$+ 0.957\Delta w$	$- 0.128ss$
	(3.025)	(1.053)	(4.519)	(4.053)	(−2.808)
	$\bar{R}^2 = 0.747$		SEE = 1.313	DW = 1.467	SSR = 17.232

Notes: Figures in parentheses are *t*-values, SSR is the sum of squared residuals; SEE is the standard error of the regression; and DW is the statistic Durbin–Watson.

Sources: *Economic Report of the President*, 1985; *Handbook of Labor Statistics*, various issues; *US Commodity Exports and Imports as related to output*, various issues.

variable is remarkable. As expected, during the period 1949–65 the influence of Δw and ss on the rate of growth of productivity was statistically equal to zero. Pressure for transformation becomes irrelevant when the economy is itself in a transformational process. Furthermore, the technical advantages produced by this transformation had to neutralize the negative impact of increased imports by generating offsetting export increases. Finally, in the period 1966–80 the significant expected influence of Δw and ss on the pace of productivity provides a strong confirmation of our hypotheses related to the absence of transformational growth. Sluggish markets are also reflected in the long-run influence of the rate of growth of output; its coefficient decreases dramatically and becomes significant only at the level of 20 per cent.

As a final step we have estimated the F-statistic with 5 and 22 degrees of freedom for testing the equality of coefficients in our two linear regressions corresponding to the two sub-periods 1949–65 and 1966–80. The estimated value (2.723) is greater than the critical value (2.66), which substantiates the hypothesis that the period 1966–80 is structurally different from the previous period 1949–65.

PART III

Free Markets or Planned Prosperity?

In the 1970s both the US and the international capitalist system entered a period of crisis, which manifested itself in slower GNP growth, declining productivity growth, rising unemployment, unstable relations between national currencies, and frequent bouts of inflation. We have contended that the central complex of forces bringing about this crisis arose from the fact that a period of transformational growth has come to an end, while the next stage, if there is one, has barely begun – or even revealed its shape. In effect, the old frontier of accumulation has closed, and no new frontier has yet emerged. In these circumstances the normal tools of demand management don't work very well, and it may look as though the economy is suffering from a supply-side crisis. But it is not – the illusion results from trying to understand the corporate industrial system in terms appropriate to the family-based craft economy. Chapter 8 develops some of the economic implications of our discussion and extends it to the world economy. In particular, it explores the basic contrast beween demand-constrained and resource-constrained systems, relating prices and inflation and the balance of payments to the working of demand-constrained markets. Then we shall turn to an examination of why the business world has such affection for free market ideas and policies, and finally to the outline of a program for full employment and prosperity.

8
Inflation and the World Economy

Now we must try to consolidate our theory and connect it to the world of political problems and policy decisions. The traditional theory tells us nothing about the modern economy, although it yields very desirable conclusions from a conservative point of view. The theory of effective demand explains how the modern economy adjusts, but orthodox macroeconomics obscured the central differences between the working of the modern system and its predecessor. Now that we have clarified those differences, we must fill in the picture by showing how the system works in those respects that count for developing a program of full employment growth without serious inflation. Here a crucial point will be that, since the modern world is internationally interdependent, demand management and controls must be internationally coordinated. The economics of employment and inflation must be understood on a world scale. But first . we had better review some basics.

A Corporate Capitalist, Industrial Nation-State

The United States after World War II has to be seen as a capitalist, industrial nation, and its economy must be studied in that light. By calling it 'industrial' we characterize the way its output is produced (mass production rather than craft); by calling it 'corporate capitalist' (rather than family capitalist) we indicate not only that it is an economy organized for the appropriation of a surplus through a rate of profit (the point of terming it 'capitalist'), but that this organization takes the form of a meritocratic, hierarchical bureaucracy, independent of the kinship system. By now this may seem obvious, but it makes quite a difference to see things this way.

For example, to call the system 'capitalist' is to indicate that production is organized by private investment, with workers hired as wage labor, that is, on contracts that give them no say in the running of the system in which they work. All major decisions as to, say, the nature of the products, the method, scale and location of production, the layout of the plant, safety regulations and so on, are normally concentrated in the hands of management, regardless of how much these decisions affect workers or the community at large. Important veto powers and rights of representation and consultaton are lodged, not with workers or the community, but with banks and creditors. Of course, this situation can be modified by political action: laws can be passed, safeguards written into union contracts, regulatory bodies established, etc., and some of these measures may prove effective. But the system in its pure form puts the power of decision into the hands of those who put up the money. Their money, their choice. And they get to appropriate the rewards; whatever results from production is theirs, or, rather, belongs to the corporation they have formed.

An industrial system is one in which physical energy is harnessed, directed and delivered mechanically, as an assist for, or even replacement of, human labor in the processes of production. Industrial processes normally involve huge specialized equipment and facilities, with factories to house them and offices to keep records of their operation. By defining the work situation, these largely dictate the pace of work, the operations performed, the way workers interact with others on the job. An important implication of this is that a job cannot normally be said to exist unless and until there has been investment to create a factory or office in which the job can be located, providing the equipment for the worker to work with. Of course, just because a factory has been built doesn't mean it will be operated; there has to be adequate demand for the products. And if it isn't operated, there won't be any actual jobs, even though there are potential ones. Finally, productivity depends more on the qualities of the technology than on the characteristics of the labor force.

(These points may seem obvious, even banal, but they have a certain bite, nevertheless. They preclude the application of the normal supply-and-demand theory of wages and employment, for example, and the last point implies that the much-discussed slowdown in the growth of productivity is not likely to be due to changes in either the nature of work or the motivation of labor.)

Modern industrial technology requires raw materials and energy from all parts of the world; no national economy is self-sufficient any more. All are bound together by the technological interdependence of industrial processes. The various commodities produced for household consumption, for example, depend both on raw materials and energy, usually produced in the Third World, and on specialized capital equipment, which itself is produced in processes that depend on even more highly specialized and complex equipment that normally can only be produced and operated in the most advanced economies. These technological relationships can result in important patterns of economic dependency, which in turn may have political ramifications.

Effective Demand and Expansion

These points have a double significance. On the one hand, they are largely overlooked in mainstream economics, which continues to think about the economy in terms much more appropriate for the analysis of a largely commercial and agricultural system. Supply and demand, flexible prices that clear markets, diminishing returns, marginal costs and revenues, *et hoc genus omne*, all may make more or less sense in the simpler world of the past where agricultural products traded for textiles and handicrafts. (Even there, the identification of a market-clearing equilibrium with a social optimum is wholly unwarranted. Nor is it plausible to suppose that markets in such societies normally move towards equilibrium.) But these ideas have little or no place in the analysis of systems of giant corporations operating advanced industrial processes and marketing the products world-wide. Prices are planned and administered, markets (perhaps especially labor markets) don't clear, increasing or constant returns prevail, and marginalist notions, including the conventional idea of equilibrium, simply lack application.

There is a second point. To say that the system is capitalist and industrial implies that the system is not only dynamic, but in a profound sense unstable: if is not expanding, it will not merely stagnate but will tend to collapse. It cannot sit still, so to speak. Consider the industries that produce the sophisticated equipment used in the manufacture of all other products. Only if the system is expanding will these key heavy industries be operating at full blast. If they are operating at less than their capacity, they will not be employing their full complement of workers. Hence worker incomes will be down, and so therefore will be consumer spending. As a result, the consumer goods industries will not be operating at full blast either. Since both major sectors will be operating sluggishly, neither will wish to spend money on modernization and replacement. Hence the average age of factories and equipment will rise, productivity will sag, and so on.

In fact, the argument can be taken an important step further. Not only must a capitalist industrial system expand in order not to collapse, it must continually expand *in new directions*; capitalism has to innovate in order to sustain a regular expansion. The reason for this is not hard to see. Consider any important consumer market, say for automobiles or TV sets. When the product is first introduced it will be confined to the well-to-do classes. Then mass production will follow, the price will fall, cheaper versions will be designed, and production will expand. In this phase investment will be heavy, and the economy will be booming. But then everyone has a car or a TV; for a time expansion can be sustained by persuading the well-to-do and the middle classes to buy a second one. Eventually, however, the market becomes saturated, and sales fall to the level of replacements – which can be quite large. The point is, however, that the market is no longer growing. This brings a slump in investment, and the economy slides into recession.

The Idea of a 'Demand-Constrained' System

So demand is the key. But we will have to think about it carefully, for the point has proved so difficult and strange that even those who, like Keynes, first proposed it, have backed away from its full implications. To say that the system is 'demand-constrained', that is, that there is normally a shortage of demand, is to say that output is not constrained by the available resources, which clearly implies that they are not being fully utilized. So they are not 'scarce' in relation to effective demand. Not being scarce means they are not costly to use; they would just be idle otherwise. In economists' terms, being demand-constrained means that Say's Law – 'supply creates its own demand' – does not hold. No one can assume that whatever they produce will automatically be sold. Producers must compete with each other for the available customers; hence, incentives to efficiency will be strong, but markets, and particularly labor markets will not necessarily clear. In other words (and this is one of the points traditionally trained economists have found hard to accept), the very factor that creates the pressure for efficiency on the part of each agent entails that the overall system will be inefficient, because some available resources are not fully used.

To see the force of this point, consider an opposite kind of system, one that is supply-constrained, or, rather, resource-constrained. In such a system (procurement for the Defense Department, or a centrally planned economy) everything produced can easily be sold. Individual producers will therefore have incentives to overrun costs in order to turn out as much as possible. Since there is excess demand, as long as the output is passable it doesn't have to be good. The shortage of demand is what creates the competition for markets, thereby setting up powerful incentives for cost-cutting and the efficient use of resources. When demand is plentiful, then, quality will tend to deteriorate and costs will tend to rise, so that shortages will become chronic, for every individual producer. In the aggregate, however, the system will be efficient: no resources will be underutilized.

Notice the paradoxical contrast between whole and part: what is true for each and every individual unit is the *opposite* of what is true for the whole. In the first case, each unit is constrained by demand scarcity to cut costs and be efficient – but the system as a whole wastes resources and tends to generate surplus output or capacity. In the second case, each unit tends to overproduce wastefully – but the system as a whole uses resources efficiently and suffers from shortages. We will return to these paradoxes later.

In a demand-constrained system, costs must be cut, the product must be attractive and effective, and service must be prompt in order to compete for sales. Hence both products and processes of production will be designed to be maximally efficient, which means that functions will be separated and tasks will be divided, just as Adam Smith prescribed. But while division of labor and separation of function cut costs, they do not conserve scarce resources. 'The division of labor is limited by the extent of the market', said Smith; the implication is that there is enough labor to perform the separate jobs. If labor had to be conserved, then division of labor would not be called for; workers would each have to perform a number of functions. Exactly that happens in resource-constrained systems where the pressure of chronic shortages leads to product and process designs that systematically combine functions and multiply rather than subdivide tasks. A shortage economy develops the aerospace plane, the David gun, the space shuttle – systems, rather than products, which are designed to perform several functions simultaneously, and which have to be run by operatives who have mastered a number of distinct skills. Adam Smith's separation of function and division of labor are impossible. In a demand-constrained system, product and process design will tend towards simplicity, while jobs will tend to become repetitive and monotonous. In a shortage economy, product and process design will tend towards the baroque, while jobs will become excessively demanding.[1]

Bureaucracies are inherently resource-constrained systems in at least one respect: time and attention at the top are limited, hence projects will be tailored to conserve top management time, which means combining and coordinating different ventures. Bureaucracies also normally face political constraints; coordinating ventures and combining previously separate functions can help in forming coalitions in order to obtain support for projects. Thus there will normally be pressures for combining functions and multiplying tasks in project design.

When functions are combined and tasks multiplied, so that a project's complexity increases, scarce resources are conserved, but the impact of a breakdown is increased dramatically. For now a breakdown in any one function will mean a breakdown for all the rest; the combination has increased the costs and the output of the project arithmetically, but has raised the costs of a breakdown *geometrically*. If such breakdowns are a major cause of shortages and bottlenecks, then, as output rises, shortages can be expected to rise faster.

We saw in Chapter 5 (p. 95) that the characteristic operation of corporate capitalism could be expressed as $I/z < K/v$ (a shortage of aggregate demand), and that the pressure to cut costs and operate efficiently would lead to a tendency for z to rise, and v to fall, maintaining the tendency of effective demand to lie below capacity. The objective will be to minimize costs. Analogously, the characteristic operation of a planned economy can be expressed as $I/z > K/v$, which signifies excess demand in the aggregate, which will set up incentives that will lead z to fall, and v to rise, intensifying the condition of demand pressure. The objective will be to maximize output. (If anything, I will tend to fall in the first case, since there is already excess capacity, and to rise in the second, since there is a capacity shortage. But investment plans are too complicated and depend on too many other factors for us to draw conclusions about them from such simple premises. By contrast, cost-minimizing and output-maximizing behavior depend precisely on the factors under examination.)

(It may be worth noting that the relationships here are not so apparent when the multiplier is based on *saving* rather than profit. When there is scarcity of demand, there is pressure to cut costs, which raises the profit margin and reduces the multiplier, but there is no pressure to cut savings.

The present formulation reveals things the conventional one conceals.)

So the US economy normally functions as demand-constrained, although from 1941 to 1945, and perhaps again for a shorter time during the Korean and Vietnam wars, it operated as a 'supply-constrained' system so that output was limited, not by demand (i.e. what the market will absorb), but by capacity constraints, bottlenecks and shortages of raw materials. In World War II, whatever could be produced at once found a market, without difficulty, and efficiency considerations were not significant. There was no need to compete for sales, the war effort absorbed everything, and there were plenty of complaints about quality.

Finally, let's relate this point to our earlier distinction between two forms of capitalism. An industrial economy is demand constrained, but what about a craft economy? Is it supply-constrained? As we saw, in such a system output and employment do not vary much with changes in demand, in the short and medium term, since a high proportion of labor costs in family firms are fixed in real terms, whereas, for the same reasons, prices and productivity are variable. Moreover, these latter changes imply that variations in investment spending tend to be offset by variations in consumption spending, helping to keep aggregate demand stable. So the system will tend both to lie near and to move towards the point where aggregate demand and supply just balance. However, because of the volatility of both investment and the discretionary consumption of the well-to-do, there will always be the danger of demand shortage, and therefore competition and pressure for efficiency will be strong. In a sense, the craft economy has the best of both worlds – demand shortage plus an in-built tendency to move to full employment. (Nothing like this can be said about the emerging information economy, where the cost structure is different, and prices are likely to be inflexible relative to money wages.) But the ability to reap economies of scale is limited in a craft system. Now let's go on to examine the way prices work in a demand-based system.

Prices in a Demand-constrained System

Fixed prices, variable sales
In a modern industrial economy, prices are set by firms, not by customers, (although there are occasional auctions, which, as in the case of oil, sometimes assume importance). The first concern of a business firm is to ensure that it covers its costs, the second that its price will permit its market to develop. But if the market expands, then the firm must increase its productive capacity – otherwise its market share will fall. So the firm's prices must be such that the sale of its normal capacity output will generate the profit necessary to finance the investment required to keep up with the growth of the market.

But wait a minute, what has happened to supply and demand? Why won't competition force the prices down to the level of marginal costs, as the textbooks tell us? Remember, we are not in the world of agriculture and handicrafts; we are talking about a modern industrial capitalist system, in which agriculture and primary production serve the needs of urban industry – and the pricing system works accordingly. This does not mean that competition is unimportant or that it has been superseded. Far from it, but it takes on a different form. In particular, firms compete by improving and modifying their products, their production processes, and their selling techniques. They also compete in terms of price – but what is the use of capturing a market you cannot afford to supply? Prices have to remain high enough to generate the profits that will enable firms to finance the construction of the new factories and office that will be needed to service the new markets. To put the difference between this approach and that of the textbooks in a nutshell: in a capitalist industrial economy, prices are set to equate the *growth* of supply with the *growth* of demand, rather than equating the levels, as in the pre-industrial, pre-capitalist world. This means that prices are planned and administered over the lifetime of the investment.

The law of demand

From this perspective one of the oldest 'laws' of economics – that a rise in price will reduce demand, and a fall increase it – takes on a different meaning. According to the standard view, demand varies inversely with price because 'individuals' (either persons or households) will change their purchasing habits, and consume more of the cheaper goods and less of more expensive ones. The aggregate response is just the sum of these individual choices. From the present point of view, by contrast, the crucial factor in the reaction of demand to a change in price will be the distribution of household incomes. High-income households can afford high-priced goods. If sales of a good are to increase, the price must come down to put the product within reach of moderate- and low-income households. Thus larger sales are associated with lower price, because the income distribution is such that the high-income groups are small and the lower the level of income the larger the set of households, until very low levels are reached. (Note that larger sales also justify lower prices because they make it possible to take advantage of economies of scale in production.) Moreover, demand will normally be price-elastic, since the income distribution is pyramidal in shape, so that a successive lowering of prices will bring increasingly larger populations into the market. On this view, then, the 'law of demand' is not a matter of individuals making rational choices – though that could be involved – but is rather a reflection of the inequality in the distribution of income.

This way of thinking about demand ties it closely to investment, because each price level is implicitly associated with not one, but two distinct markets. There is first the established market, consisting of all those families and spending units who can afford the good at that price or higher, and then there is the new market, those who can just afford the good at that price. If these two markets are combined we have a conventional-looking demand curve, showing lower prices associated with larger total sales. But this would be a mistake, on two counts. First, we are not talking about an abstract 'reversible' functional relationship. The idea is that, as prices are successively lowered, new groups of consumers can be brought into the market; a later rise in price would not necessarily lose the same amount of trade. (The relationship between these two will depend on the *microeconomic* problem: how, why and with what consequences do consumers introduce new goods into their household budgets?) Second, the established market and the new market at each price should be kept separate; their ratio shows the growth of demand for that level of price, which will have to be matched by a corresponding growth in supply. If such an expansion of supply cannot be financed at that price, then price cannot be cut to that level. So we are not talking about a 'demand curve' at all; in fact, demand curves for manufactured goods in modern economies tend to be price-inelastic. What we have instead is a set of relationships between prices, investment, finance and income distribution.

Price competition
There is an important qualification, however. The preceding discussion really refers to *planned* prices, the benchmark prices that firms set as guides for their sales staff. What actually happens depends, of course, on people's tastes and information and prejudices – on the pattern of current demand, in short. So perhaps the textbooks have a point after all?

Not really. Consider what happens when current demand, at the benchmark price, is either below or above current capacity output. Suppose demand is above capacity. If this is because the market is now growing faster, demand will always be high, in which case a higher benchmark price is justified, but, if it is due merely to current special conditions, raising price might cut back the market's growth rate. Suppose demand is below capacity. Cutting price may attract more customers, but it also cuts into profits and hence into the ability to supply a larger market on a permanent basis. In either case it may very well not pay to change price.

All of this makes sense, but a textbook economist would object that it makes sense only for oligopolies or monopolies, or at any rate for markets with some kind of 'price leadership', because it doesn't concern the prices that are the outcome of competitive behavior. If firms are really in competition, they will try to take customers away from each other by cutting prices, especially when demand falls below capacity. And when demand is above capacity, competitive customers will bid up prices in their attempts to attract the available supply away from each other. This sounds plausible enough, but, for example, how much of a differential would be required to attract how many customers away from their normal suppliers? If the differential in proportion to the initial price is greater than the number of new customers in proportion to the initial sales, the price cut isn't worth making. But to attract *any* new customers a price cut will have to be of a certain size – or it won't even be noticed. Changing suppliers takes time and may cause trouble; a price differential may have to be fairly large to make it worth while, particularly in industries where firms go to some lengths to differentiate their products and to provide auxiliary services. This makes it easy to see why a small drop in demand below capacity might have no effect on price at all: if the demand shortfall in relation to capacity output is less than the ratio of the price cut required to attract demand to the initial price, then the price cut cannot possibly be worth while. Even a large collapse of demand may have little or no effect on price, because the price cut then required to reliably attract a large amount of demand away from competitors might push the price down dangerously near to, or below, the level of variable costs.

Primary products vs industrial goods

Broadly speaking, there are two cases. In manufacturing (including both capital goods and consumer goods), variable costs – materials, labor, energy – are a relatively large proportion of total costs, and the price cuts required to attract demand away from competitors are both sizeable and likely to invite retaliation. Hence price-cutting can quickly push prices down to the break-even point. It is not in general a desirable strategy; as a result prices can be expected to be relatively sticky downwards in the face of changes in demand. By contrast, in primary industries – mining, agriculture, petroleum – variable costs are a small proportion of total costs, the bulk of which consist of overheads and capital charges (or, in the case of family farming, the family subsistence for the year), while the price cut required to attract demand will be negligible, since product differentiation will be minimal. Price-cutting will therefore be an attractive, even a necessary, strategy when demand declines, and consequently in these areas prices will be responsive to changes in demand.

Next, consider price increases when demand outruns capacity. Producers of manufactured goods are generally trying to expand their markets over time, breaking into new geographical or social areas, and will be reluctant to snatch temporary profits at the risk of jeopardizing their long-term market growth. Again this contrasts with the situation of the primary producer. Primary products are generic: they may vary in quality, but, given quality, they are the same regardless of the particular producer. Hence a relatively small price differential between firms may bring about a sizeable shift in custom. Further, they are used as the basis of manufacturing, so the growth of demand for them depends on the growth of manufacturing as a whole. Since they are the most basic inputs of the system, the overall demand for them will be highly price-inelastic, that is, will depend very little on price. Thus, when current demand outruns current capacity, no potential new markets are thrown in jeopardy by price increases – and it will take very big price increases to reduce demand. Moreover, unlike manufacturing where capacity can be increased by building new factories, or in many cases simply by installing additional equipment in existing ones, primary productive capacity is limited by natural barriers that cannot normally be pushed back without technological innovation, in addition to investment. To increase the full capacity rate of production from farms and mines, either new methods of working or new supplies must be found. Hence excess demand may, at times, tend to push up primary prices very dramatically.

Notice also that this configuration provides an excellent basis for a cartel: the primary good is absolutely necessary; substitutes will be difficult and expensive; and overall demand is price-inelastic, being basically growth-determined. But any *particular* firm's demand will be quite elastic with respect to a difference between its price and that of a competitor, while supply requires heavy investment in overhead costs. Under these conditions price wars will be both tempting and disastrous; a cartel will be extremely useful.

In short, prices of primary products will tend to respond to changes in current demand, while those of manufactured goods will tend to be insensitive to such changes, particularly in the downward direction. This difference in the way these two large groups of goods react to changes in demand is the key to understanding the inflation–stagnation problems of the 1970s.

Cost-Shifting Inflation

Traditional theory recognizes two basic types of inflation – 'cost-push' and 'demand-pull'. The first results from a push by unionized workers, or by a cartel or a monopoly or oligopoly, raising money wages or some group of prices, thereby setting off a wage–price spiral. 'Demand-pull', by contrast, starts from excess demand, either in the aggregate or in some major sector, which bids up prices, leading to catch-up wage demands by workers and so to a wage–price spiral. Note how closely these two types of inflation are connected: the initiating wage increase of the 'cost-push' variety creates demand inflation in the second round, while the 'demand-pull' inflation that initially bids up prices causes a cost-push in the second round.

In the mainstream view there is an even deeper connection, however, which shows demand-pull to be the more basic. In the absence of general-ized demand pressure, a cost-push would be a temporary disequilibrium, leading to substitution and a new equilibrium. The reason a cost-push becomes inflation is that there is generalized excess demand, so nothing is available to serve as substitute. Nor is this surprising, for the traditional theory assumes that the system is resource-constrained.

It is a peculiar characteristic of virtually all orthodox discussions of inflation that they treat it as merely a costly reflection of excess demand, serving no function or purpose. It is treated as a disequilibrium pure and simple; once started, a wage–price spiral is assumed to go on forever, unless brought to a halt by policy or by some other exogenous force. Yet this is not how things are: inflations begin, accelerate, reach a peak and decline, gradually petering out. They have a natural shape, so to speak, or perhaps several. Social phenomena so ubiquitous and complex, appear-ing in so many varied guises, seldom turn out to be simply point-less.

Precisely because it is so varied, inflation may sometimes be what the orthodox theory says it is. But this is not likely. The reason for claiming that the orthodox view is implausible lies in the fact that it is grounded on the neo-Classical assumption that markets tend to reach an equilibrium that can be described in *real*, that is, barter, terms. However, relative prices are the only relevant ones; hence if one or another money price changes, equilibrium will be disturbed unless all the others change in the same proportion. Since the usual, though not the sophisticated, presentations of neo-Classical micro theory assume that markets are stable, that is, tend to return to equilibrium if 'disturbed', it is natural to assume that the disturbance caused by the rise of some money price or other will be corrected by all others rising in the same proportion. Otherwise the market system would not be 'stable' in the normal sense.

Such inflations can be called 'neutral': they do not affect income distribution or the proportions in which goods are produced and labor employed. Most inflations, and certainly those of the post-Vietnam era, are not neutral. They bring about significant changes in distribution, and sometimes in demand as well. Moreover, these changes can be seen as their *raison d'être*. Non-neutral inflations have been discussed in several quarters. Post-Keynesian critics of the mainstream hold that inflation arises from excessive wage demands imposed under imperfect market conditions, and will continue indefinitely, unless checked by policy. A related school contends that it is not excessive wages, but excessive claims overall – wages, salaries, profits, rents – that set off inflation. A neo-Keynesian view, however, sees inflation as a price rise, relative to money wages, due to excess demand, bringing about a rise in profits that will increase saving enough to offset the excess demand. This is a good example of a non-neutral inflation, but it is a variation on the theme of a demand inflation. The 1970s suffered from a decade of demand shortage. Let's instead consider a non-neutral cost inflation.

Suppose that the system is faced with a major cost increase, such as a huge jump in the price of a necessary import, like oil. How is this cost to be shared? Who will pay how much, and how will this be decided, on what grounds, and how long will it take to make the decision? (Notice that essentially the same questions arise when the cost increase is internal, such as a rise in the money wages of unionized labor or, a few years ago, in the price of steel.) In some economic systems such questions are decided by administrative fiat – sometimes reflecting a popular consensus, and sometimes not. In modern capitalist economies, however, it is the function of the market to provide the answers. The market is the arena in which economic power can be exercised: those with power can pass along the increased costs; those without must bear them. More precisely, costs increases can be passed along in proportion to the ability to raise prices by a certain amount in a given time. Let's examine this more closely, using a simple numerical example.

Suppose initially that the import bill and the wage bill are the same size, but are composed differently. Let's say that the price of imports (oil, no doubt) is $5 and the quantity 20; money wages (w) are $4, and the number of workers 25 (millions, perhaps – but the quantities are arbitrary). The markup factor is 2, and the output will be taken as fixed at 100 units. So we have, at the outset: 2 [\$5(20) + \$4(25)] = \$p (100); hence the price of output (p) will be \$4, and the real wage (w/p) will be \$4/\$4, or 1; and the price of oil in terms of both output and labor will be 5/4.

Now the price of oil doubles; corporations are well-placed in their markets and are able to defend their markup, but labor's position is weak – a large majority of the labor force is non-unionized, the government is conservative and hostile, and too aggressive a posture will lead to extensive automation and/or factory flight overseas. Hence labor can push up its money wages by only 50 per cent of the rise in the cost of living in any given period:

$$(\text{change in } w)/w = 1/2(\text{change in } p)/p.$$

These are the assumptions; now let's see what happens.

The easiest way is to write it out period by period, starting with period zero:

0: $2[\$5(20) + \$4(25)] = \$4(100)$
1: $2[\$10(20) + \$4(25)] = \$6(100)$; p goes from \$4 to \$6.
2: $2[\$10(20) + \$5(25)] = \$6.50(100)$; w goes from \$4 to \$5, half the previous period's increase in p, and, since the markup is held fixed, p now rises from \$6 to \$6.50.
3: $2[\$10(20) + \$5.21(25)] = \$6.61(100)$; here 0.21/5 = one-half of 0.5/6 and then, to maintain the markup, p rises to \$6.61. But now the increases will be very small; p has risen from \$6.50 to only \$6.61, and w will rise in proportion by only half as much.
4: $2[\$10(20) + \$5.254(25)] = \$6.627(100)$. Here p has only risen by about 2 cents; the inflationary impulse has petered out.

The effects are plain, however: the real wage (w /p.) has fallen from \$1 to \$5.25/\$6.63 = \$0.792, a drop of a little over one-fifth. Oil in terms of labor is now \$10/\$5.25, almost 2 to 1 instead of 5/4, and oil in terms of output is \$10/\$6.63. The burden falls more heavily on labor, but note that both ratios are better than the initial 10/4 ratio that prevailed before the inflation. This, however, may merely lead the oil producers to raise their price again, setting off another round of inflation. This process would then be repeated until oil producers achieved their desired price ratio of oil to output – assuming that they have the market power to keep raising prices, which they may very well not. As we saw, primary products are highly demand-sensitive and, for reasons we shall explain in a moment, a rise in import prices will tend to cause a recession, cutting demand. Now consider a different case.

Suppose that labor were stronger, strong enough to raise money wages each period in the same proportion that prices rose. Then we would have, starting from the same initial position:

1: $2[\$10(20) + \$4(25)] = \$6(100)$
2: $2[\$10(20) + \$6(25)] = \$7(100)$
3: $2[\$10(20) + \$7(25)] = \$7.50(100)$
4: $2[\$10(20) + \$7.50(25)] = \$7.75(100)$, and so on.

Notice that the inflation progressively slows down as the money wage and price level approach $8. When the ratio $10:8:8 = 5:4:4$ is established, the real initial relations between oil, labor and output will be restored, and the inflation will cease unless there is another increase in the oil price.

Inflation, then, serves a definite economic function: it determines who will bear the burden of a cost increase, and it does so by testing the market power of the various groups in the economy. Corporations will try to maintain their markup, workers will try to maintain their real wage (standard of living). If both are equally successful, no one will accept the burden, and the inflation will tend to restore the initial real price ratios, eliminating the problem if the cost increase were a once-for-all accident, but leading to perpetual motion if the initial cost increase is one that has to be accepted in real terms. On the other hand, if some parties are successful in passing along coast increases, while others are not or are less able to do so, then the burden will tend to be shifted to the weaker groups, and the inflation will gradually peter out, unless or until there is another cost shock.

Of course, we've looked at a very over-simplified picture, with only two groups, labor and corporations. Even here we've only considered two cases, where the parties are equal and where corporations are in the stronger position. But in some countries, at some points in time (Scandinavia in the 1960s, perhaps), labor might be in a stronger position, in which case the markup would drift down and the real wage rise, since money wages would rise faster than prices. The inflation would be relatively slow and there would be less likelihood of it leading to a further increase in import costs, since the price of oil (or other imports) in terms of output would not be so much affected by the inflation, and the price of oil in terms of domestic labor is not of any interest to oil producers.

A more realistic approach, however, must take into account the distinctions between different groups of workers – union vs non-union, salaried white-collar and office workers, state employees, middle management, and so on. Also, the power of small business over its markups is likely to be much less than that of the major corporations. Finally, the earnings of the financial system and the other recipients of interest income will be frozen during an inflation – at least during the early stages. In general, non-union workers, white-collar and state employees, and fixed-interest recipients (e.g. savings and loan institutions and other financial bodies) are unable to raise their money incomes, and tend to lose out in the race. Union workers and big business set the pace, some parts of small business can keep up, while others get squeezed. The distribution of earned incomes tends to widen, and the concentration of capital tends to increase.

Now think back to the previous section. There we said that the different reactions of primary and manufactured products to changes in demand would provide the key to understanding the inflations of the post war era. Demand for primary products is highly inelastic – unresponsive – to price changes, either up or down (but very responsive to changes in income or activity levels); hence when demand is strong (because of high activity), a cartel can enforce very great price increases. But demand changes don't affect the prices of manufactured products very much; if costs are increasing they will be passed along, as far as possible, even in the face of weak demand. Strong demand, on the other hand will not set off an inflation by raising manufacturing prices, although it might lead to increases in primary prices, which will then be passed along. But such an inflation will tend to peter out, eventually, particularly since rises in primary import prices tend to create slumps. Demand for primary goods is price-inelastic; hence a run-up of prices raises the import bill – a withdrawal. The inflation raises export prices, reducing sales, and so employment. These slumps bring inflation to a halt not by weakening the ability of corporations or unions to raise prices and wages – the orthodox explanation – but by preventing further increases in primary products, so that when the inflationary spiral runs down it will not be kicked off again. Of course, the danger recurs when recovery comes, but if in the meantime stockpiling of the relevant primary products has taken place, the expansion could proceed without creating the kind of demand pressure that would trigger primary price hikes. To understand this better, it will be necessary to examine the working of the international economy.

The International Capitalist Economic System

Once again it is important to remember that we are talking about an international *capitalist* system. Just as in the domestic economy, production and trade are organized by capital, which tends to move into those areas as channels that are the most profitable, and/or growing fastest. This has certain advantages; it means, for example, that technical innovations and new products will be developed rapidly (in the absence of cartels and oligopolistic restraints). However, it also means that depressed areas or countries are likely to become even more depressed, as capital flees to more advantageous sites. Capital is mobile and can shift freely from country to country – that is the basic meaning of the expression the 'Free World', which, propaganda apart, has nothing much to do with human liberty.

The organization of production by capital on an international scale is supposed to be governed by the principle of comparative advantage, which means that when each of several parties can perform all of the same tasks, but not equally well, then each should do what he (or she) is *relatively* best at – even if someone could do all of them better than anyone else.[2]

Now what has to be explained? Some countries are industrialized and produce highly sophisticated manufactured goods, while other countries import these goods, and pay for them with exports of primary goods, agricultural products and raw materials, including petroleum. This kind of specialization probably owes little or nothing to the doctrines of comparative advantage, but a good deal to the imperialism of the nineteenth century. Notice that exporters of primary goods are at the mercy of fluctuating prices, while exporters of manufactures can count on prices that stay fairly stable.

National economies, then, divide broadly into those that are industrialized and those that are not, with a new group emerging into prominence in the late 1960s – the newly industrializing countries (NICs). Within these three broad groups, however, there are wide diversities, and these differences lend some countries economic strength, and leave others weak. Such strengths and weaknesses usually show up as soundness or otherwise in a country's currency. This is a complicated matter that takes some explaining.

Prior to World War II the international economy operated on the Gold Standard. National currencies were tied to gold; a country's central bank had to back its currency with holdings of gold. If a nation imported more than it exported, it had to pay out gold, thereby losing reserves. So, in theory, the money supply would have to contract, raising interest rates, and leading to deflation. With falling prices the country's exports become more competitive, and the balance of payments will improve. Alternatively, a country that exports more than it imports will experience an inflow of gold, and so an expansion of its money supply, a fall of interest rates, and thus an inflation, which will injure its exports, tending to reduce its balance of payments surplus. Thus movements of gold were thought to provide an automatic adjustment mechanism that would correct imbalances, sometimes painfully, but without requiring government policy measures that would inhibit the working of free markets.

Needless to say things didn't work that way in practice. Indeed, even as a matter of theory the case is far from watertight. Loss of gold leads to contraction of the money supply, and so to a rise in interest rates – at a time when prices are falling, so *real* interest rates must become very high. Surely this will attract short-term capital and capital seeking investment in real estate – so gold will be attracted back. Exactly the converse holds in the case of the country into which gold is flowing because of a balance of payments surplus: with low interest rates and high prices, short-term capital will move out. We shall return to this point later.

For the moment, theoretical problems are a side issue. The Gold Standard didn't work for two quite different reasons. One was institutional: fractional reserve banking had broken the link between gold and the domestic currency, what we call today the 'money supply'. Inflows and outflows of gold did not any longer correlate with movements in the volume of the currency, and hence they did not exercise any direct effect on price levels. The second reason for the failure of the Gold Standard goes even deeper – to the heart of the matter, in fact. It is that another, very different mechanism in actual practice governed the international system.

A deficit in the balance of payments constitutes a 'leakage' from the stream of expenditures, exactly comparable to savings or to profits. It therefore leads to a curtailing of employment. To put it another way, expenditure on imports amounts to not spending on domestically produced goods; hence domestic sales are less by the amount of imports in excess of exports. With sales down, employment must be cut. Exactly the converse holds for a surplus on the balance of payments. Exports in excess of imports mean extra sales, and so additional employment. The inflow and outflow of gold really doesn't matter; if too much is being imported the country will sink into a slump, until incomes have fallen so much that imports will be curbed because people can't afford them. The system does correct itself, but only by moving into a recession.

Even worse, the move into recession can become cumulative, because, when the countries in deficit go into recession, the exports of the countries in surplus collapse. If initially these countries were operating at full employment, with the collapse of exports they will sink into a slump unless domestic investment or government spending picks up to fill the gap. If exports fall off, however, unused capacity will exist in export-oriented industries. Why invest when there is idle capacity available? So it is unlikely that domestic investment will increase. As for government spending, prior to the emergence of Keynesian ideas, it tended to move with the level of activity. If the economy was expanding, government spending would rise also, to provide the services and infrastructure needed by the economy. Hence it would not expand in a time of contraction. So neither investment nor government spending is likely to fill the gap when the exports of the surplus countries fall as the result of contraction in the deficit countries. As a result the surplus countries will now contract through a multiplier process, reducing their purchases from abroad, and lowering the export sales of the deficit countries still further, bringing on another round of contractions. In short, the free-market, Gold Standard international system had a built-in bias towards recession, which it revealed in full detail in the inter-war years.

The postwar system was set up at Bretton Woods just after the war, and was designed to eliminate the tendency to cumulative downswings by helping countries to manage their adjustments, providing them with loans to tide them over and with teams of experts to plan the necessary austerity measures. In other words, the principle that a balance of payments deficit must be eliminated by the contraction of income and employment remained intact; all that was changed was the way it worked. Deficit nations still had to take their medicine, but none of it should be allowed to spill onto the surplus nations, and moreover, the medicine should cure them. The austerity measure should be followed by expansion and growth. How was this thought to work?

First, and realistically, gold was replaced by a system of reserve currencies, which meant basically the dollar, with the pound sterling, and later the Deutschmark and the Swiss franc, as the chief reserves for certain countries. Gold itself was also used, but its price was fixed in dollars, and it was only exchanged between central banks. The dollar was the basic reserve for the system, which meant that everyone had to earn dollars, which they would then hold, i.e. never spend. In other words, they had to sell goods to the US for money that they would never use to buy US goods. In short, everyone had to deliver goods to the US as a form of tribute.

This put the US in a peculiar position. In order to supply dollars for use as reserves it had to run a deficit. But the reason the dollar was acceptable as a reserve was that it was the strongest currency – the currency of the country whose goods everyone wanted, which is to say the country least likely to be running a deficit. This problem was partially solved when the US took on the role of 'Free World' policeman, for then its trade and current account surplus could be offset by expenditures for military bases and various police actions and wars. This alone was not enough, however. The US had to invest abroad as well. In other words, the US, as the dominant power in the system, would supply capital to countries needing funds – helping them to industrialize in a capitalist way and suspending the system's tendencies to recession by offsetting current account deficits. However, export of capital means not investing at home, so US domestic growth tended to fall below the growth of world trade. But dollar reserves had to grow at the same rate as world trade; hence dollar holdings tended to rise in relation to dollar assets and dollar output. Moreover, a number of important countries, heavily involved in world trade, tended to grow faster than the US, particularly West Germany (but also Europe in general) and Japan (and other Far Eastern economies). Thus the very success of the system in providing reserves and promoting recovery and growth tended to undermine it. By the late 1960s the weakness of the dollar was already evident, and a dangerous run on it took place in the late 1970s.

Of course, the countries whose growth has helped to undermine and weaken the dollar are precisely countries whose balance of payments is normally in surplus. Hence their currencies cannot possibly replace the dollar as reserves, since they are normally in short supply. This complex of paradoxes has led to many proposals for an international fiat money, as Keynes, foreseeing just these problems, had originally proposed at Bretton Woods. An agreement to issue Special Drawing Rights (SDRs) was reached, but it amounted to no more than a drop in the proverbial bucket. What has saved the system since the run on the dollar has been the practice of keeping US interest rates above those prevailing in Europe, since this attracts short-term and speculative money to Wall Street.

The system therefore required the US to run a deficit on its overall balance of payments, though its current account ideally should be in surplus. For the rest of the world the system requires that their foreign accounts should be in balance. A current account deficit can be offset by a capital account surplus, and supplying such capital is the traditional role of the dominant power, but this cannot be a stable or permanent arrangement. The deficit must ultimately be eliminated. The object of the system is to promote free trade and the free movement of capital. Protectionist measures are therefore anathema. The way to deal with a deficit is to cut back on spending, so as to reduce imports, while promoting private capital ventures that will generate exports. Devaluation might help, but until the 1970s it was reserved for intransigent cases, since fixed and reliable exchange rates were thought to provide a better climate for the movement of capital. Devaluation cheapens exports and makes imports more costly; but if the economy is already producing at full capacity, exports cannot easily be increased. So cheapening them will, in the short run at any rate, merely lead to lower revenues. Imports of essential goods, e.g. inputs into exports or into basic domestic capital goods, will be price-inelastic, so making them more expensive will merely set off inflationary pressures. Inessential imports, e.g. of luxury goods, can be curbed, but the very rich may go on spending anyway. So the chief burden of adjustment falls on the luxury or inessential imports of the middle and working classes. If spending of this sort is large, then devaluation may work; if not, it is unlikely to help much. Greater flexibility in exchange rates has therefore not proved to be the panacea some had foreseen.

Inflation in less developed countries
Less developed countries that are both users and exporters of primary products are often caught in a bind. When demand in the advanced countries is high, primary product prices are pushed up, setting off a domestic cost-shifting inflation in these countries, as well as in the advanced world. But when demand collapses in the advanced countries, exports in these countries also collapse, and primary product prices fall. This brings the cost-shifting inflation to an end, but it also tends to create a balance of payments crisis, since both the quantities and prices of exports are now down. As a result the value of its currency will be forced down, either by policy or through the pressure of free/black markets. Manufactured imports thus become more expensive, but since these countries, being incompletely developed, normally import capital goods and intermediate products, the prices of domestic manufactures will be marked up, and a new round of inflation will be triggered.

Interest rates and exchange rates
The Reagan era inaugurated a new form of the international economy, one in which a strong dollar again became the chief reserve currency. But this time the strength of the dollar was shown not in a current account surplus, but in a *capital* account surplus, corresponding to a massive and growing current account deficit. But how has this been possible? Why did the forces of supply and demand not lead to a collapse of the dollar?

The official explanation was that the strength of the US economy attracted foreign capital, which bid the dollar up, causing US exports to fall. Thus the current account deficit simply reflected the vigor of the recovery. It is doubtful if the IMF would have accepted this argument for any other country running a similar deficit. In any case the investment figures showed the real weaknesses in the recovery. The real cause of the strength of the dollar was the high real interest rates in the US relative to the rest of the world, starting with the change in Federal Reserve policy

Table 8.1   *Real rates of interest*

	Consumer price inflation	Central bank rate	Government Bond yield	Real rates
USA				
1980–81	10.4	12.0	13.72	1.6, 3.32
1981–82	6.2	8.5	12.92	2.3, 6.72
1982–83	3.2	8.5	11.34	5.3, 8.14
West Germany				
1980–81	6.3	7.5	10.38	1.2, 4.08
1981–82	5.3	5.0	8.95	−0.3, 3.65
1982–83	3.3	4.0	7.89	0.7, 4.59
Italy				
1980–81	17.8	19.0	20.58	1.2, 2.78
1981–82	16.5	18.0	20.90	1.5, 4.40
1982–83	14.7	17.0	18.02	2.3, 3.32

Source: Compiled from *Statistical Abstract of the US*, 1986.

in the Fall of 1979. The dollar began to climb in 1981 as US real interest rates rose relative to the rest of the world. Some sample figures are shown in Table 8.1.

The official account had it wrong, but did correctly understand that the forces of supply and demand, arising out of current account trading, do not determine exchange rates – just as supply and demand (current sales) do not determine the prices of manufactured goods. In each case the determinants of exchange value centre on the rate of return to capital. In the case of foreign exchange, we have, for two countries, A and B:

$$\text{(real interest rate in A) [unit of A's currency]}$$
$$= e \text{ (real interest rate in B) [unit of B's currency]},$$

where e is the exchange rate between the two currencies. What this says is that if A's interest rate is higher than B's, the value of A's currency must rise relative to B's, until there is no advantage left to shifting loanable funds from country B to country A. The international rate of return of capital must be equalized (allowing for risk, etc. as always).

(One special feature is worth noting: if the nominal rate of interest in a country is raised sharply, pulling up the value of its currency – as happened with the dollar in 1979–80 – this reduces the cost of imports, and so reduces the rate of inflation. But this in turn further increases the real rate of interest, and thus gives a further boost to the value of the currency, reducing inflation again. There is a feedback cycle here – and it may work both ways.)

The implication of this should be evident. The price of pursuing an independent monetary policy is pressure on the foreign exchange rate; if a country tries to provide cheap money to support expansion at a time of general high interest rates and austerity, its currency will collapse. This could be acceptable – it would stimulate exports and tend to curb imports – but it could become a serious problem. The international dimension of monetary policy is none the less inescapable.

Conclusions

Here we have tried to examine the basic working principles of a capitalist industrial system of nation-states. Such an economy is demand-constrained, which is to say that employment depends upon sales, in two senses. First, factories and offices have to be built, which will only happen if sales are expected to grow enough to need the additional capacity; secondly, at any given time such capacity will be operated only to the extent that current sales are running at a pace requiring it. Demand-constrained operation gives rise to the multiplier adjustment process, which is the basic cause of varying unemployment. Prices of manufactures are set so as to keep supply growth in pace with demand, where prices can be assumed to affect the growth of both. A high price makes it possible to finance the construction of more factories and offices, but a low price makes it much easier for the sales force to expand into new markets. One result is that such prices are relatively insensitive to changes in current demand. Primary product prices, on the other hand, are governed by rather different considerations, and are sensitive to changes in current demand. This sets the stage for the kind of inflation we have seen in the postwar period. Such inflation can be seen as a way of determining, through the market, which parties will bear the burden of various kinds of cost increases impinging on the economy. In the 1970s these have largely been due to increases in the prices of oil and food – primary products. Finally, these effects have been played out, not in the context of a single nation, but in an international system governed by a foreign trade multiplier process, and based on an inherently problematical reserve currency system, which has shown signs of coming unstuck.

Clearly, in such a system there is plenty of scope for effective government intervention. Deficit spending, or spending financed by taxes on corporate earning and other 'withdrawals', will normally have a stimulative effect. But a comprehensive policy package will be needed to prevent inflation and international repercussions from undermining a government-managed move towards full employment. This means that we must confront the ideology of the free market head on, for we are now facing the need for extensive controls and world-scale policies.

Notes

1 Won't capitalist excess capacity disappear in a boom? Couldn't a centrally planned economy become demand-constrained in a slump? Things are not so simple; capitalist booms *produce* excess capacity and socialist slumps *preserve*

shortages. Each system tends to recreate its characteristic mode of operation at all points in its cycle. Cf. Nell (1988a).

2   Consider a writer and a typist: the writer can type, and the typist dreams of writing novels. Now the writer may also be a faster typist than the secretary, but he should nevertheless spend his time batting out his plots and making notes on scratch paper, and not waste his time typing up the finished copy, so long as he is, in fact, a better writer than he is a typist. And the typist should type, and leave the novels to her (his?) dreams, so long as she/he is better at typing than at writing novels. Applying this to countries, each should specialize at producing what it is relatively best at producing, regardless of the fact that some other country might do it even better, and trade for those items the production of which has been closed down to further the aim of specialization.

Appendix: The Paradox of Protection

Under plausible conditions, in the absence of retaliation, the imposition of a tariff can lead to an *increase* in imports! A diagram illustrates this quite easily. Plot income (= output) along the horizontal axis and imports and exports on the vertical. Starting from a positive point on the vertical axis, the export line rises with a slight positive slope. This indicates that a large part of exports do not depend on domestic activity, but that an increase in domestic sales and output will increase productivity, make it possible to spread costs better, improve sales efforts, etc., all of which will contribute to making the export drive more effective. Hence exports will rise somewhat with income. Next, at low levels of income there will be no imports, but, after a point, imports will increase markedly with income. So, from a positive point on the horizontal axis, the import line rises relatively steeply, cutting the export function at the level of income, Y_b, that balances the external budget. At lower levels of income there will be net exports, providing an expansionary stimulus; at higher, net imports, leading to contraction.

Now impose a percentage tariff, say 20 per cent of value; at each level of income the actual imports will be 20 per cent less than before. Thus the import line will swing down and to the right, as indicated by the dotted line, intersecting the export line at a higher level of income, Y_t, and a higher level of exports – and therefore of imports too: $M_t > M_b$.

Figure 8.1

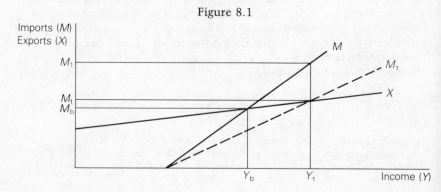

Looking at it another way, if the initial level of income were Y_t, imports in the absence of the tariff would be M_1. If income adjusted downwards to reach external balance, imports – the exports of foreigners – would fall to M_b. But, if balance were established by a tariff, foreigners' sales to the home country would fall *less*, to M_t. Hence it would be in the interest of foreigners, as well as to the benefit of the home country, to bring about adjustment through agreed upon tariff policies, rather than relying on contractions of income.

An agreed-upon tariff policy has the advantage over devaluation that it does not depend upon price-elasticities of imports and exports (the Marshall-Lerner condition), so long as there is *some* flexibility in imports. If all imports are rigidly connected to domestic output, as when they consist of inputs into production for which there are no domestic substitutes, a tariff may have little effect. But devaluation would be no help either. Moreover, devaluation normally needs to be accompanied by a policy-induced recession if it is to have a chance to work.

Such an agreed tariff policy would presuppose that all parties could control inflation and other problems without relying on policy-induced recessions. The point is that protection, by itself, is not contractionary. The argument, of course, depends on the assumption that the imposition of a tariff – a price change – would not greatly alter the composition of demand. If demand depends more on income than on prices, however, then there might well be a range of possible tariffs that could be effective policy instruments.

9

Government and the
Free-Market Consensus

There is only one thing which is free: prices. In our countries Adam
Smith needs Mussolini. Freedom of investment, freedom of prices,
free exchange rates: the freer the businesses, the more imprisoned are
the people. The prosperity of a few is everyone else's curse.

[*Galeano*, 1983]

An extreme statement, perhaps, and certainly more understandable in
relation to Latin America than to the United States. Yet it is worth
reflecting on a little. The claim is that free markets require some kinds
of social coercion, implying that the working of free markets, bringing
profitability to capital (belonging to the few), will normally endanger the
prosperity of the general public. By contrast, the traditional theory holds
that free markets will bring prosperity to all. Yet we have shown that this
theory applies only to a very special institutional context, a system of
family firms and family farms. Galeano's Latin America, with landless
peasants working haciendas and crowded barrios in the cities, hardly
qualifies – and neither does the contemporary USA. In both of these
cases, the free market becomes a free-for-all, a struggle in which the most
powerful, the best positioned and the luckiest make off with all the prizes.
It is easy to understand why the well-placed few applaud free markets.

Our concern, however, is not with the distributive aspects of free
markets, but with their ability to generate and sustain prosperity and full
employment. Once the free-for-all begins, there is no guarantee that
productive capacity will be regularly and fully utilized. In the traditional
system, full employment was ensured partly by the technological and
institutional fact that output and labor could not easily be varied in
response to changes in sales (whereas industrial systems are designed
precisely to do this) and partly by the fact that prices and money wages
respond flexibly to changes in sales. In the industrial system, outputs, and
therefore employment (instead of prices), are supposed to respond flexibly
to changes in demand, while prices must be set and maintained at levels
that will ensure the recovery of capital costs. Overall demand depends on
investment, and investment depends on the future. And what do we
know of the future? The future lies ahead, that much we can safely say
– but not much more. Investment will therefore be inherently volatile,

depending on business's views about future levels of sales, and the development of new markets.

Yet investment could be planned so as to maintain full employment, while developing the country's productive capacity in the socially most useful or most desirable directions. This would require government to undertake the overall direction of the economy, and to try to define a consensus on social priorities. (This would not be easy, but it is what a great deal of politics is about anyway.) And then it would mean making use of its powers of intervention, so as to move the economy in the directions indicated by the consensus.

Of course, no one can know in advance what such a consensus would be, but full employment is virtually certain to be part of it. So long as household income mainly derives from work, and social stigma attaches to unemployment, the availability of jobs will be a high priority. From the perspective of the economy as a whole, unemployment means lost output – if the economy's full capacity annual output is $3.5 trillion, 10 per cent unemployment means a roughly $350 billion loss. Worse, if the ratio of investment to income is 15 per cent, then about $52.5 billion represents capital stock that has not been built. Had it been built it would have produced a permanent addition to capacity income of $15–20 billion, on the assumption of a 2.5 to 3 ratio of new capital to output. Moreover, additions to capital normally incorporate the best new technology, so may raise output by raising productivity. Part of this additional output, in turn, would have been capital goods, which would have produced further additions to the streams of output, and so on. In other words, the loss of output is a permanent loss of growth potential.

Besides the loss to the economy as a whole, of course, there is the much more immediate loss suffered by the unemployed themselves. Losing a job, or just being laid off, means an immediate drop in family income – on average about 25 per cent – and a rise in insecurity – a rise in unemployment is correlated with a rise in child abuse, wife-beating, alcoholism, robbery and burglary, suicide, malnutrition and the incidence of deficiency diseases.

Full employment, the full use of the economy's capacity, then, must be a basic objective of any program that seeks prosperity for the populace as a whole. But it can only be achieved reliably through government intervention, and, as we have seen, this now seems to be very objectionable to a large part of the business community. We shall next consider some of the reasons commonly but invalidly advanced to justify this distaste, and then go on to examine critically the support for the broad consensus that presently exists on the supposed virtues of the free market.

The Campaign against Government

When we understand how a capitalist industrial system actually works, it is plain that the government budget can be used to bring about and maintain full employment. It should also be apparent that various kinds of regulations, including tax benefits and penalties, could be designed to inhibit and control inflation. But this is not the message that much of the business community wants to hear. Quite the contrary; they would like to see it demonstrated that the government cannot have any beneficial impact on the economy, that government budget deficits are dangerous, even ruinous, and that controls and intervention make everyone worse off. Fortunately, for those who hold such views, there is a theory that appears to uphold this position, and, moreover, can present its conclusions in sophisticated mathematics. However, to call on this theory is to present ideology in scientific drag, for it is the theory of another era, capitalist, but pre-industrial – the era of family firms and family farms, of the craft economy, in which output could be taken as fixed in the short and medium term, while prices reacted to changes in demand.

The inapplicability of the theory, however, has not prevented its widespread use and misuse. In the academic world, both the monetarists and the supply-siders have drawn on the traditional theory to try to demonstrate the ineffectiveness of government intervention, while the popular press is full of watered-down versions of the same arguments. Let's first consider the basic arguments, and then look at some examples.

The intersection of the supply and demand curves for the various goods in the economy determines their relative prices and absolute quantities. The equilibrium quantities of the various commodities can be added up in terms of the equilibrium prices, so the total output of the system can be determined just by summing up the individual markets. No need for Keynes here. When the money supply has been fixed by the central bank, the general price level can be found from the Quantity Equation. Employment and real wages will be settled by the supply and demand for labor, while the rate of interest will be set by the supply and demand for savings and investment. Such is the traditional theory and, as we have seen, there is something to be said for it as an account of a traditional craft economy. But that is not how it is being used today. Let's first look at a catalogue of free-market opinions, and then consider how the traditional theory is used to justify them.

Pillars of free-market wisdom
   Deficits: cause high interest rates
                          cause inflation
                          crowd out more worthwhile private activity

   National debt: burdens future generations unfairly
                          could bankrupt the country
                          will have to be repaid some day

   Government
      spending: is always unproductive
                          crowds out private activity
                          is too high, more thàn we can afford
                          goes largely on welfare cheats

Taxes: are very high on most people
                cause people to work less or less hard
                cause lower saving, and so lower growth

If supply and demand determine total output in the way just indicated, without any mention of government, then government activities can only be included in the system by 'crowding out' some private ones. The government does not produce, so it can only be supported by requisitioning privately produced goods and services, which therefore cannot be used as before. If this requisitioning is done by taxing incomes, then the burden falls on wages and salaries. Since the real wage is an incentive to supply labor, i.e. to put forth productive effort, the strength of this incentive will be reduced, so, in *addition* to the crowding-out, labor's effort will be less. If sales are taxed then business's supply of goods will be reduced. If the government's activities are financed by borrowing then interest rates will be driven up, and the demand by business for investible funds will be reduced (although, by the same token, the supply of savings will be increased).

Looking at the catalogue, then, we can see that the traditional theory can be used to support most of the opinions, and to make the others seem plausible, because, of course, if government spending has all these negative effects, it is more than we can afford, taxes are too high, and so on. Consider some examples:

Here is Richard A. Snelling, former Governor of Vermont, founder of the group Proposition One, which is dedicated to 'fighting the deficit', writing a piece called 'The Deficit's Clear and Present Danger' in the *New York Times*:

> The deficit must be erased, and quickly. We all have to limit what we spend and be prepared to pay for what we need . . . Otherwise the huge deficits will do us in . . . The strength and vitality of our economy rest foursquare on the funds that businesses and many millions of individual Americans put aside in bonds, bank accounts and other forms of savings . . . the Federal deficit competes with individuals and businesses for the money available to borrowers . . . as the deficit climbs, competition for the funds increases and the cost of borrowing – the interest rate – follows suit. As the interest rate starts to rise . . . economic growth grinds to a halt.
>
> (Snelling, 1984)

Nor is this an isolated instance. Martin Feldstein, Reagan's former Chairman of the Council of Economic Advisors, writing in *Time* (5 March 1984):

> The competition for money between the Government and private borrowers inevitably raises the level of inflation-adjusted or real interest rates . . . The principal reason for this increase has been the rise in the federal budget deficit. [He goes on to blame these high rates for the

strength of the dollar, because they have attracted foreign capital, and the high dollar, in turn, has brought about the foreign trade deficit (about which more later).]

It could hardly be clearer: savings determines the pool of funds for growth; the government competes for funds, and drives up interest rates, causing growth to slow down. This very common view is totally incorrect for an industrial corporate economy. Interest rates are not affected by government deficits; the belief that they are derives from the traditional theory, which is not applicable to a capitalist industrial system. To repeat: savings is not a fixed pool, and it is not primarily fed by households; business saving is actually much larger. The more activity there is, the more profits there will be and so the larger will be the contribution of business to the pool of savings. And more activity means more employment, so household incomes will be up and there will be more household savings, too. Government deficit spending – and government spending that is financed by taxes on corporate retentions – boosts economic activity by increasing sales, so raising employment and business earnings. So savings goes up and there is no need for interest rates to rise. The central point, however, which can't be emphasized too strongly, is that it is investment that determines growth in a modern industrial economy, not savings.

And remember our earlier look at the facts? There were huge deficits in the Civil War, in World War I, and largest of all in World War II. There were *no* effects on interest rates, none at all. Moreover, in the 1970s interest rates and the deficit moved contrary to one another.

Since we have quoted Feldstein in *Time*, it might be worth quoting his own *Economic Report of the President* (February 1985), which states (p. 105): '. . . the extent of upward pressure on real interest rates and on the dollar through this channel [expanded federal budget deficits] is uncertain, and numerous studies have failed to uncover significant effects.' (The credit for this has to go to the staff; Feldstein didn't sign the Report.)

Another popular analysis, this time a prominent investor letter, *Capital Gains* (New York, Winter 1984), sees 'an inflationary tidal wave . . . rushing toward us'. In a special report they 'look at the hidden economic upheaval that created the coming inflation wave: total federal indebtedness. The national debt.' Their argument is simple:

> The larger the national debt, the more money must be created by the Fed. The more money that is created, the faster inflation will rise. *In other words, inflation is the direct result of deficit spending. AND DEFICITS ARE INCREASING EVERY YEAR.* [Italics and caps in original]

There follows a long discussion of how the total debt has risen over the years. There is no mention of the correlative growth of government assets. There is no discussion of different concepts of the budget, nor is the deficit considered in relation to GNP, nor total debt related to total capital. The deficit could be financed by the Fed increasing the money supply, but it doesn't have to be. Even if it were, the effect would not be inflationary. The money supply increases in response to the increase in economic activity, or GNP. The two rise together, first because the deficit itself calls forth the additional money, then because the money multiplier only works if there is demand for additional bank loans. But if there is such demand, it means that the money so borrowed is being spent – so GNP is rising. As long as the two keep pace, there's no inflation. If GNP rises to the full capacity level, so that all factories are working full blast, then additional demand *would* drive up prices. But that's a different story; it's the extra demand, not the extra money that makes the difference. Deficits *don't*, by themselves, cause inflation. (By contrast, OPEC oil price increases do.)

Supply-siders take the view that it is not the deficit that matters so much as the government spending. They agree that there is little evidence to show that deficits by themselves inflict costs on the economy. As Paul Craig Roberts, cited earlier, has claimed, government spending pre-empts private, regardless of the method of finance. Moreover, supply-siders do not regard the pool of savings as fixed; it can be increased, for example, by improving the incentives to work and to save by cutting taxes. Thus a tax cut with given government spending would result in a deficit at first, but the improved incentives could eventually lead to enough additional work and saving that aggregate supply would rise enough to provide off-setting additional tax receipts, even at the reduced tax rates. (Yet if a tax cut would provide such strong incentives as to raise output enough to generate offsetting tax receipts, surely a general wage increase would likewise raise output enough to pay for itself! So why aren't supply-siders advocating higher wages for everyone?)

The supply-side position assumes that government spending, by comparison to private, is inherently unproductive or wasteful, that taxes are heavy and a drag on people's willingness to put forth economic effort, and, finally, that the level of output in the modern economy is limited by the ability to supply – whatever can be produced will eventually find a market – 'supply creates its own demand'. It should be clear by now that all of these ideas are false when applied to a capitalist industrial system.

What about the foreign trade deficit? Maybe the interaction between the two deficits explains why some of the terrible consequences of federal borrowing and spending have not shown up yet. Here is *Fortune* magazine:

> Foreigners have spared the U.S. the pain of financing the deficit for the past couple of years by shipping enough capital into the country to satisfy much of the government's appetite for cash. But that happy arrangement cannot continue indefinitely; the rest of the world simply doesn't have enough wealth to keep sending the U.S. $100 billion to $150 billion year after year. When the foreign capital finally ebbs, the government will have to finance its outlays by commandeering more domestic savings or by printing money. Either action would devastate

investment, the first by crowding business out of the credit market and the second by creating a new wave of inflation. (4 March 1985, p. 104)

This passage draws its conclusions, not from observation but from the traditional theory. Why is so much foreign capital pouring into the US? According to the laws of supply and demand, this foreign capital must be foreign savings, attracted to the US by high interest rates or high profit opportunities. But this is not so. If the US is buying more abroad than it is selling, then someone has to finance its purchases. Foreigners *have* to lend to the US if they are going to sell to the US. But they don't have to lend their savings – they lend their currency. It's a matter of liquidity; it would be absurd to think that, by increasing their sales to the US, foreigners would have to reduce their savings. Indeed, the additional sales to the US probably mean an increase in their savings, because the stimulus of net exports has raised their GNP. But, from the point of view of national accounts, the automatic and necessary corollary of a current account deficit is a capital account surplus. The reason \$100–150 billion a year is pouring into the USA is that it is buying about that much more abroad than it is earning.

It is true that, besides the funds to finance the trade deficit, long-term funds are also flowing in at an unprecedented rate, while US direct investment overseas has fallen off markedly. (And this is undoubtedly due to high US interest rates, compared to the rest of the world.) For the first time foreigners are investing more in the US than the US is there. But the order of magnitude of these flows of funds is still quite small: in 1983 foreigners invested a little over \$11 billion in the US, and the US sent a bit under \$5 billion in long-term money abroad. A net transfer of about \$6 billion, then; not much of a contribution towards financing the deficit, although these figures rose quite a lot in 1984. However, the inflow of foreign capital is still largely due to the trade deficit, which in turn results from the combination of the high dollar with the declining competitiveness of US manufacturing.

As for the *Fortune* argument, what can they mean by saying that the rest of the world doesn't 'have enough wealth to keep sending the U.S. \$100 billion to \$150 billion year after year'? As long as the US runs a deficit of that magnitude with the rest of the world, year after year, they will have just that amount.

The rest of the paragraph repeats what we have seen over and over again – the government will have to either 'commandeer' private savings, which are assumed (without argument) to be fixed in amount, or print money. Once again, the underlying theory is supply and demand, i.e. it is supposed that we live in an economic system in which output and employment are fixed, as in the nineteenth-century craft economy. Even *Fortune* magazine should know that we have long since left that century and that kind of economy behind. But they go on:

The only way to get the deficit down and keep it down is to solve the underlying problem by halting the inexorable growth of government spending. Those rising deficits [projected in coming years] . . . reflect the simple, chilling fact that the federal budget is growing faster than the economy . . . federal spending is still rising faster than GNP.

The first sentence just isn't true: taxes could be increased; or the government could start charging for its services. Nevertheless, government spending *has* been growing faster then GNP for many years, in all advanced countries. The important questions, then, which *Fortune* does not ask, is why? As we saw earlier, this reflects something significant about modern industrial societies, namely, that as they develop they become more complex and interdependent, and therefore require more regulation, and both more, and more expensive, public services. Private enterprise rests on public support. A business requires laws protecting property and enforcing contracts, needs a well-managed currency, an educated public, a system of roads, bridges, harbors, water and sewage, and so on. As the industrial economy grows, the cost of these public supports seems to grow more rapidly.

But *Fortune*'s real message does come through: the government must be cut back. That is the centerpiece of the new conservative revival – to free private capital and private enterprise from government restraints, enabling them to move about to take advantage of profitable opportunities world-wide. So it is not deficits, in fact, that are the real problem: it is the government and its role in the economy.

Here, then, we have the real issue, the clash between two approaches to the economy, one in which capital and money-making are given the freest hand possible, the other in which the needs and concern of the people are paramount – Ronald Reagan as against Franklin Roosevelt, Margaret Thatcher versus Clement Attlee, Barry Goldwater opposing Lyndon Johnson, Robert Taft against Harry Truman.

In the 1960s a consensus developed that poverty could and should be eliminated in America, and that it was the responsibility of the government to see to it that everyone who wanted a job could have one. This was enshrined in the Humphrey–Hawkins Bill, which, although it avoids committing the government to full employment, certainly points in that direction. What has happened to these attitudes? In the midst of unemployed resources, we are told that we cannot afford to satisfy people's basic needs.

In fact, there is a new consensus emerging – that the government has been growing too rapidly and must be cut back, not only to reduce the deficit, but to make room for private capital and private initiative, which are (supposedly) more efficient and more productive. As we have seen, these views have no foundation in fact, nor are they supported by theory.

But if what we have been saying is correct, why has public discussion been so confused? Why have both the Republicans and the Democrats taken up the issue of the deficit, leading the Democrats to abandon a large part of their heritage for a meaningless cause? Is it really possible that public discussion of a major issue could be so wrong-headed? (This is a little like asking whether the *New York Times* could be mistaken, or whether *Time* could publish nonsense.) The correct answers are, in fact, well known and are available (although in somewhat distorted form) in any good economics textbook. So why haven't they figured in the current discussions in the media? Why have virtually all major participants taken the view that the deficit presents a clear and present danger?

Part of the answer, no doubt, is that the president and the dominant party set the terms of political discussion, and their agenda has been to attack the role of the government, in which they had the support of a good part of the business community. But that can't be the whole story, because the opposition party could have challenged those terms. Yet this is exactly what they have not done. Instead, they have abandoned their own heritage in order to adopt what used to be the conservative position.

To see why, we shall have to look at the dominant cultural forces, at least as regards money-making and the market; in the US in recent years these undoubtedly arise from the business community. The ideology of the free market is at the core of American business's self-image. We had better take a closer look.

The Consensus on the Free Market

In most modern capitalist industrial countries, for example in Western Europe, the political parties of the Left throw down a challenge to the dominance of the market. The program of the Left involves control and regulation of economic forces by democratically elected representative assemblies; planning replaces the market over wide ranges of economic activity. And these programs, in place for years in the Scandinavian countries, in Holland, and to a lesser extent elsewhere in Western Europe, have greatly improved living standards, and have led to a falling off both in economic crimes and crimes of social resentment.

In the United States, by contrast, there is what can only be called a bi-partisan consensus on the virtues of the free market. Both major political parties are wedded to the market as the fundamental economic institution of the country. To be sure, the Democrats want to direct it and guide it, even at times to control it – but their policies *supplement* rather than replace the working of the market. There is no major political program in the US that explicitly challenges the hegemony of the market, in the way the parties of the Left do in Europe.

Let's first try to understand what this means, and then relate it to the current political debate over the role of government. In the US it is an axiom underlying any serious political discussion of the economy that the market should be left to work on its own unless there are pressing reasons to the contrary. (This, in fact, is the position John Stuart Mill took in the 1840s, and later abandoned in favor of a modified socialism.) There is plenty of room for heated argument over just what should be taken as a 'pressing reason', and how exactly the market's working should be modified when there are such reasons. But neither major party, and no minor party with any significant influence, advocates wholesale redistribution, nationalizing or otherwise socializing major corporations, suspending the market, or replacing it with large-scale planning.

So both parties and the media take it as self-evident that in general the free market is efficient, that is, that the normal working of competitive markets will bring about some sort of optimal allocation of resources. Labor, land and capital will be put to the best uses, and as a result everyone will be better off. Moreover it would be very difficult to achieve this any other way; the market has the great advantage over planners of being anonymous, so that personal rivalries and jealousies can't get in the way.

But we have already argued that the vision of efficient markets, in which flexible prices allocate scarce resources optimally, applies (if it applies at all!) to an earlier system, a small-scale, craft system, consisting of small independent farms and shops, which can have flexible prices because in this mode of production output and employment are stable. By contrast, today we have a capitalist industrial system that uses huge, scientifically based interdependent technologies, financed by a banking system that operates on a nation-wide and, more recently, a world-wide scale. In other words, the vision of efficient, price-flexible markets is inappropriate; believing in it therefore leads to mistaken interpretations of the world around us. We shall see that these mistakes are, in fact, serious; they have real costs. But, at the same time, this vision provides both political strength and legitimacy not just to conservatives, but to the business community in general.

Let's go back to the efficiency of the free market. This is so familiar that it sounds eminently reasonable, until you stop and think about it. What is says (among other things) is that the *distribution of income and wealth* that the market brings about is efficient and optimal. Now this is very hard to swallow. What's efficient, let alone optimal, about widespread poverty, particularly when it can be seen side by side with extravagant wealth being squandered on luxuries? Poverty means that human talents and resources are not being developed; children born in poverty are never taught the skills they need, and may never have the health or get the nourishment they need to take advantage of the meager opportunities they do come across. How can this be efficient? Talent and human resources are being wasted, on the one hand, and anti-social attitudes and resentment are being created on the other. Yet the claim that the market is the best method of allocating resources, means that it is the best way of allocating and rewarding labor and capital. So the market distribution of income must be the best. Or we have to reject the market in an absolutely fundamental area.

Of course, the obvious compromise is to attribute poverty to 'market failure', so that the role of the government becomes that of stepping in to make adjustments where the results reached by the market, even if efficient, are clearly inequitable. This concedes primacy to the market; it remains the central determinant of the nation's distribution of wealth and welfare, of opportunities and rewards, although it may need to be corrected from time to time.

From another perspective, what this does is to affirm individualism: what an individual has in the way of wealth is his (occasionally: hers) to

do with as he pleases. If you've made money, you can do what you like
with it; if you've inherited it, good luck – that was what your forebears
wanted, and they made it, so it was theirs to dispose of. Of course, there
are certain reasonable restrictions on what one can do, essentially
preventing any one person from interfering with other people's freedom
to do as they wish with *their* money and other assets. But if you use your
money to set up a business, to make more money, then you're the boss,
and you call the shots. (George Steinbrenner picks the players and the
manager; if you don't like it you can go watch the Mets. Or set up your
own team.)

Once again this is so familiar that we tend to swallow it without
thinking twice. So we usually don't notice some of the really indigestible
implications. Probably the most striking is that the whole story is cast in
terms of *individuals*, that is, actual people, whereas the real problems over
the activities of businesses and their impact on people and communities
and the environment arise in connection with corporations, which are
institutions. The reason for this anomaly, of course, is that the idea that
people have the right to do as they please with the money they have made
comes straight out of the individualistic social order of family firms and
family farms. *There*, in that context, it all makes sense (which is not to
say that there aren't serious problems, even there – for instance the
rights of women, since the system is one of patriarchy.) The central idea
of individualism is independence and self-reliance. The family farm was
very often capable of being almost completely self-sufficient, and the
small craftsman relied on others or on the market only for raw materials
and supplies, and sometimes for specialized tools. Often, of course, life
was better if you could buy on the market; this made it possible to
specialize, and specialization increased productivity. (Here is the basis of
the doctrine of comparative advantage.) But it was not necessary. Farms
and small communities were capable of supporting themselves: they grew
enough food, they cut wood for heat and fuel, they had the skills to build
their own houses and schools, to tend the sick and so on. (Remember *The
Little House on the Prairie*?)

An important implication of self-reliance is that responsibility for the
results of economic activity can usually be clearly attributed. If someone
builds up a business, he deserves the credit; if someone makes shoddy
goods, he deserves the blame. The contribution of a worker can also
normally be measured. Some workers will be better and faster than
others. Workers can be paid in proportion to what they contribute in output. This leads straight to the basic idea that wages in general are or
should be proportional to the worker's contribution, and, in the same
way, profit to capital's or management's contribution. There are troubles
with this idea even in the simple versions of traditional theory, but at
least it makes some kind of sense in a system of self-sufficiency.

However, the idea of economic rights and economic freedom – 'free to
choose' – cannot be carried over to the modern corporate industrial
economy. Today, most people work most of the time, not for themselves,
but for some giant institution. Nor are such institutions run by owner-

managers; owners are for the most part also institutions – banks, trust funds, insurance companies, other corporations, foundations and universities. Even many of what we call 'small businesses' today would have been regarded as huge in the nineteenth century. And they are increasingly managed by modern methods, that is, they are run as corporations.

As we have seen, modern businessmen certainly like to think of themselves in terms of independence and self-reliance. What's wrong with it? The point is simple, but very far-reaching, although once seen, it is obvious.

How many corporation executives are self-reliant – capable of growing their own food, and martinis, fixing their telephones and computers, or even their cars or exercise machines? How many businesses are self-reliant, or independent – capable of making their own tools, building their own factories and offices, producing their own raw materials? Some firms, a few, *are* significantly 'vertically integrated', that is, start with a raw material and take it right through all the refining stages to the set of finished products. But even these firms are not self-reliant and independent in the way a nineteenth-century family farm was – they don't produce the food and clothing for their employees, for example, and they usually don't produce their own light and power. (My grandparents made their own clothes and furniture, and also made candles, put up preserves for the winter, and lived in a house they had largely built themselves. In later years they bought many of these things, but all their lives they retained the skills to be self-sufficient.) In other words, the central fact about a modern economic system is that it is *not* made up of self-sufficient units trading surpluses over and above their own needs. That is the picture on which the supply and demand theory is based, and which underlies the ideas of economic individualism. But in the modern world the basic economic institutions are *interdependent*, rather than independent, and in general are forced to rely on *others* for basic inputs. *Self-reliance is, literally, impossible in a modern setting* – that is why the hippies in the late 1960s and early 1970s had to return to the poorest areas of the countryside to find pockets of the older system still surviving (as catalogued in the *Foxfire* books.)

In an interdependent system, in which economic activity is organized by large institutions, it's very difficult to say that a particular business or company has the right to do something because it's 'their' money. (They can move to Mexico if they want; it's their factory. They can dump the chemicals where they like, it's their land.) A modern business involves the life of the community: it depends on many other businesses for supplies, on the government for social and public services (police, fire, courts of law, public highways, sanitation, water supplies, etc.), and upon its workers for its reliability and productivity. Its success is the result of teamwork, to cite a well-worn management cliché. And for that reason it is very hard to attribute responsibility to individuals. It is very hard to say how much one member of the team has contributed. Neither wages nor salaries can be set in terms of such contributions, since they cannot be accurately measured. Moreover, the teamwork extends beyond just management, even beyond the boundaries of the company, or the local community. A modern product or process of production is the result of applying scientific principles to practical problems, but this in turn rests not only upon the scientific community, but also on the entire educational system that underlies and supports the scientific community. How can the contributions be separated?

In short, the public morality of the free market might make sense in an individualistic community of family firms and family farms (though there are questions even there), but it is not appropriate to an economy of giant institutions, based on an interdependent techology.

Still, it may be objected, this is all beside the point. Corporate executives may be bureaucrats indistinguishable from their counterparts in government, and equally integrated into the system – but what about 'entrepreneurs'? Surely, it is they who are supposed to be self-reliant and individualistic, not, of course, literally, but metaphorically. No one believes the frontier exists any more, but the entrepreneur is animated by its spirit, and through his adventurous innovation and risk-taking provides the driving force for the entire economy. In this sense, independence and self-reliance not only are very much alive today, but form the basis of whole new industries – computers, microelectronics, bio-tech, and so on. Moreover, it is these new 'sunrise' industries that hold the promise of restoring US world competitiveness. Entrepreneurship, then, and so the frontier spirit of the free market, is the key to the future.

Nothing could be more fanciful. The new technologies have all come out of the great labs and universities of modern science. They are built on, and literally inconceivable without, an extensive, state-subsidized network of scientific research and development. The application of modern hi-tech has often been entrepreneurial, but not so its development. Nor does entrepreneurship, in the sense of adventurous risk-taking, require the institutions of the free market, as corporate experiments with what has come to be called 'intrapreneurship' have shown. Innovation does require breaking out of the bureaucratic mold; it does mean taking risks and flying in the face of the conventional wisdom. And to get people to take such risks usually requires the prospect of substantial reward. The market is one way to do this, but it isn't the only way. And it is very wasteful, but that is another subject.

There is another problem, equally serious. If prices are set, as we have argued, by firms establishing a markup over their variable labor and raw material costs, where this markup is set at a level that will enable firms to meet their fixed costs and provide earnings on their equity (much of which may be retained for investment purposes), then the 'price mechanism' does not work the way the textbooks say. In fact, it doesn't even exist. So one of the costs of believing in the free market is that you have to systematically misunderstand the way the economy works, first as regards pricing and price-setting, but secondly as regards the way the levels of output and employment are arrived at. This is serious stuff. How can we manage the economy if we don't understand rightly how it works?

Answer: it's fine if we don't *want* to manage the economy; and what's more, or perhaps especially, if we don't want anyone else to manage it either. Who is the 'we' here, and why not manage the economy? Basically, the 'we' refers to the business and professional community, and those who identify with them, and the reason is simple: so long as American politics is united in a consensus on the virtue and necessity of a free market, capital will have a relatively free hand (not only in the US, but also in the US sphere of influence). Wealth will not be redistributed, US capital will be able to move anywhere in the world, public controls will be limited but private opportunities for money-making will not. The practical effect of supporting the idea of a free market is to maximize the field of opportunity, not the current earnings, of private business. Indeed current earnings may suffer in ways that might have been prevented by following Keynesian policies, for example. However, the price may be regarded as worth paying, and indeed the calculation is very traditional: the long-term position is improved at the price (if it has to be that way) of short-term losses. What could be more in line with our grandfathers' thinking?

This gives us some insight into current policy debates – deregulation, for example. The dismantling of the Keynesian policy machinery and of government regulation generally is a preventive measure, a way of de-clawing or de-fanging an incipient popular movement to control business and to prevent it from inflicting heavy costs on the people in the pursuit of its best opportunities for profit (for example, if the best chances turn out to be overseas, or in areas that don't generate much employment). If there are no experienced government bureaucracies, or well-seasoned government officials, then even if a populist or socialist movement won electoral power it would not be able to implement its policies, because the practical and experienced agencies would not be there and it would take years to build them up again. Moreover, if Keynesian policy machinery has been dismantled, business can stage an 'investment strike' and inflict unemployment on the country if it objects to the government's approach to the economy. This does not even have to be a planned movement or an overt conspiracy. It can be the result of an unspoken confluence of opinion – the 'state of business confidence'. If however, Keynesian policy machinery is still in place, then an investment strike can be counteracted by government spending and essentially broken by a system of tax penalties for not investing and incentives for doing so. So, if there are good reasons to expect the future to harbor some serious conflicts between the opportunities for profit and the welfare of the common people, it would be wise, from the point of view of capital, to dismantle and disperse the agencies that a popular or leftist movement would rely on to control and regulate the business world.

But there has to be more. Besides dismantling the state agencies capable of enforcing the popular will on business, there has to be some program for restoring profitability to capital. Where is accumulation to take place? How can the centers of capitalism, especially the US, be kept prosperous and strong?

In fact the business community has extremely simple answers to these questions. Accumulation will take place on the basis of consumer-driven growth, based, as in the past, on the auto-industrial complex, abetted by modern microelectronics and computers. The difference, however, is that a great deal of it will now take place in the Third World, or rather in newly developing countries (NDCs) of the Third World – South Korea, Brazil, Mexico, Chile, and so on. In these nations, a large and relatively prosperous middle class is ready for a consumer boom, specifically for an automobile boom. The market is there, and the labor force is large enough, skilled enough and cheap enough to carry it out. So, the pattern can be repeated, with the US and European companies licensing or producing through subsidiaries. This is the importance of free capital mobility and free trade. Nor do the companies want their new operations tied down in a maze of safety or anti-pollution regulations.

So, the answer to the question about how capital is to accumulate is easy. Capital must migrate to where the automobile and consumer durable product cycle is about to begin again. But that leaves the difficult question of how a strong and prosperous economy is to be maintained at the center of the system, in the US. Here again, however, the conservative perspective provides an exceedingly simple answer – through a military buildup. By greatly increasing domestic military spending and at the same time promoting military sales abroad, they hope to bring the economy back to somewhat less than full employment, thus keeping the industrial system strong, even if growth is no longer chiefly centered at home. Moreover, a degree of slack in the economy will help to discipline labor and weaken the consumer/environmental movement, while the military buildup will provide the center with the strength to defend its client governments and its investments in the newly developing countries of the Third World.

On the surface, the policy is coherent. But it has two flaws, each serious. First, the growth patterns of the NDCs are not altogether attractive, quite apart from questions of human rights. In general, growth has caused the emergence of a dualistic society: the accumulation of capital has not only brought high wages and modern technology, it has also destroyed traditional agriculture and older balanced ways of life, creating a mass of displaced, jobless, often homeless humanity, swirling in barrios around the great cities. Military dictators may be necessary for private capital to maintain its sway. Necessary, but perhaps not suf-ficient. Development generates its own contradictions and may throw up its own forms of government, and economic organization, based on indigenous culture. That is what happened in Iran, and it may well happen again in other places. Even earlier, Salvador Allende, and Chile, showed that a progressive, anti-capitalist government not only could get elected, but could carry out its program and increase its popularity even in the face of a massive undercover American campaign to 'destabilize' it. So the proposal to shift the center of accumulation to the NDCs of the Third World carries more than a little risk.

The second flaw is different. Prosperity in the US depends on growth in spending, but military spending does not *grow* in any natural and regular way. Once a level of military power is decided upon, a certain sum of spending will be required – but that is it. The weapons system then has to be maintained, but that is all. Of course the military–industrial complex has an answer: a new generation of weapons is developed as soon as orders have been completed for the old. 'Technological progress' makes the earlier weapons obsolete, and it will be claimed that, if we don't develop the new weapons, the Soviet Union will do so and take the lead in the arms race. (Very often the 'progress', aimed at sales rather than battlefield performance, has created baroque monstrosities that require continuous servicing and sometimes do not work at all.)

Moreover, even if new weapons systems replace old ones regularly, there is still no guarantee that military spending will grow at a rate that will sustain full employment demand (or even grow at all). The new systems could simply replace the old at the same or even lower cost, with the result that military spending would *shrink* as a percentage of GNP. Of course, this would be 'better' than if it fell to zero, which it would if the old (and often more workable) weapons were kept on. But this is an uncertain way to sustain prosperity, because, as we saw, the *level* of prosperity in capitalism depends on the *rate of growth* of investment and goverment spending. Prosperity should be grounded on something that contains an inner growth dynamic, preferably something that is not completely wasteful.

There is a way to make military spending grow, however, and that is to whip up war fever. Scare talk about the Soviet Union will do a lot. But it tends to produce a once-for-all hike, and then a new scare will have to be invented. Perhaps the best way to keep military spending growing would be to have lots of little wars – 'police actions' – carried out in the context of a permanent confrontation with the Soviet Union. For the point is not just to keep military sales up; it is also to preserve the Free World, the world, that is, where capital can move freely to where the markets are developing. Military spending will both keep these markets open and prop up the advanced economies as capital pulls out of them to invest in areas of future growth. It is wasteful and dangerous – 'cowboy capitalism' – but it does make sense.

So this is the bottom line: the business community and other profit-oriented groups find it in their long-term interest to maintain the ideology of the free market, even at the price of misdescribing the way the world we live in works. And why? Because there is a good possibility of a clash between the pursuit of profit and providing for the people. From what we have already said, it's easy to see: computerization may destroy more jobs than it creates; overseas investment opportunities may be much more attractive then domestic, because markets may grow faster there than in the US; overseas wages may be (are!) much lower than in the US, but the workers (in Korea, Hong Kong, Mexico, other 'export platforms') may be nearly as good; environmental controls may be much more necessary and strict in the US than there; or military dictators can create a more attractive investment environment there than in the US. And so on.

And the issue of the deficit? It fits right in. For conservatives, the government has to be cut back because otherwise we shall run the risk of all those dangers that deficit spending brings in its wake. On the other side, progressives try to use the issue of the deficit to attack the irresponsibility of the administration, on the one hand, and to reduce the budget of the Pentagon on the other. Both sides agree that the deficit poses serious dangers to the health of the economy, although they disagree on what are the best ways to reduce the deficit and avoid these dangers. And both agree that the market operates according to supply and demand, which means that it tends to produce socially optimal outcomes, in the absence of monopolies and other forms of interference, including that of governments. Both are wrong.

Not only are they wrong as a matter of fact, that is, about how prices are set and output and employment determined, but, as we have seen, they are wrong about the meaning of economic life, the social and moral content of economic decisions. For these are one thing in a context in which most people can be regarded as self-sufficient, and quite another in one in which no one can possibly be anything but significantly interdependent. In particular, in the first case it makes a good deal of sense to relegate the government to an essentially subsidiary role, a safeguard and a support system for those hit by unexpected disasters of nature, such as floods or hurricanes. But if the system is one of institutional interdependence, this makes no sense at all. Democracy requires that individuals have a say in the control of their everyday lives (which they do as a matter of course if they are self-reliant); so the institutions in which people work, or which otherwise dominate their lives, must be subjected to democratic control. Corporate hierarchies are military-type organizations, as we would expect, since they must defend their markets and raid those of others. But this means that the government, which we can control (to some extent at any rate) by democratic means, is the only agency that could conceivably wrench the great corporations out of their present patterns of behavior, and realign them. How to do this, and in what ways they should be realigned to return to people some measure of control over their everyday lives, are questions beyond the scope of this book. Our point here is simply that, if we are committed to the idea that ordinary people should have some say over the content of their everyday, working lives, and if we recognize that in modern society ordinary people are not and cannot be self-reliant, then it makes no sense to cut back the government. It is our most democratic institution, and it is the means by which we could establish democratic control over private business. And, far from the deficit being a barrier to this, deficit spending is one of the policy tools by which such control can be established. Nor, as we shall see in a moment, does the payment of interest on the national debt pose a problem, once the questions are posed in the right way. But the central issue has to be faced at the outset: who is to be master – private capital, that is, the business, banking and corporate community, or the general public, that is, the households of the working and middle classes? Of course, these overlap in many ways, and on many issues will find common ground. But the point is, who controls, who decides in a pinch? And on what grounds? Will it be elected representatives, expressing the interests of households (rich and poor), or will it be corporate boards, acting in the interests of shareholders, many of them institutions?

We know what the corporate approach is; we've had a chance to see it in action in recent years in many countries – virulently in Chile, Guatemala and the Philippines, more mildly in the US and the UK. And we have seen the dangerous dependence of this approach on military spending. In the final chapter we shall consider what an alternative policy would look like – not a compromise policy, but an all-out attempt to establish democratic control over the business system; a policy based on complete rejection of the free market and full recognition of the interdependence of economic life and its organization by large impersonal institutions.

10
Public Spending in a Demand-Constrained Economy

In a demand-constrained economy, public spending can be wise or foolish, appropriate or inappropriate, effective or ineffective, but – the paradox first pointed out by Keynes – *it cannot be more costly to the economy as a whole than doing nothing*. In a demand-constrained system, individual households and businesses are forced by economic pressures to economize, but the system as a whole normally operates with a substantial reserve of both labor and productive capacity. In a resource-constrained economy just the reverse is true: individual units have incentives to overspend, to squander resources and overrun costs, while the system as a whole suffers from shortages in the face of excessive demands. And, as we saw, in each case the system works so as to preserve its own nature: in the demand-constrained case, cost-cutting constricts effective demand, whereas, in the resource-constrained case, cost overruns further expand it.

This provides us with a new perspective on 'full employment', by which we no longer mean 5 per cent or even 4 per cent or 3 per cent unemployment as conventionally measured. Nor do we mean 90 per cent or even 100 per cent capacity utilization, as measured by one or other of the methods discussed in earlier chapters, although as a practical matter we shall use both. 'True full employment' instead will refer to a way of running the economy, rather than to a level of output; when the economy is fully employed in this sense, it will be *resource-constrained* rather than demand-determined. By this criterion the era of World War II constitutes the only case of full employment in recent history. (Even during the Korean War the women did not go back to work.) Achieving full employment, then, means moving the economy to a point just beyond which the characteristic problems facing it would concern chronic shortages, and the pattern of incentives facing firms would lead them to speed up delivery at almost any cost.

Why adopt a criterion that is unlikely to be achievable, for which there are no present measures, and that implies new problems for the economy? In practice we shall have to rely on conventional measures; nevertheless, to keep true full employment in mind will provide a sense of perspective: in most cases, the economy will still be a long way away from a condition of generalized shortage. The target, in fact, *should* be set just short of true full employment; for then the pattern of incentives will continue to be that of a demand-constrained system and business will still be cost-conscious. This will avoid the characteristic problems of planned economies – chronic shortages combined with incentives to behave wastefully. But, by moving the economy near to true full employment, the macroeconomic waste of underutilized resources characteristic of capitalism can be avoided. And, by doing it through government-generated growth in demand, at least some of the social waste characteristic of marketing and sales campaigns may be avoided. In these conditions, prices will still not be indicators of relative scarcities; instead they will reflect the capital requirements for expected growth. Since the government budget would only have to be balanced at true full employment, which is not desirable, a growing deficit, providing a growing demand stimulus, must be considered acceptable at any time.

'True full employment', then, is a theoretical ceiling – the topmost point that the trade cycle boom *could* reach. In general, there will be a practical ceiling, probably well below the theoretical maximum, at which a boom will tend to peak. Long before a condition of generalized scarcity arises, the boom will be cut short by the response to particular localized scarcities, which temporarily choke off growth – and this could be enough to lead to an accelerator-induced downturn, in the absence of planning and policy directives. This is also likely to be the point at which prices of primary products tend to rise, setting off inflation. But inflation in the industrial economy is not normally an indication of genuine scarcity; rises in primary product prices instead reflect the way their different cost structure responds to a rise in demand, and the effect is to generate a cost-shifting sequence of wage–price responses. To prevent this it is not necessary to keep the system operating at low levels; the basic requirement is a program of government 'buffer stocks' – stockpiles of primary products that will be used to prevent wide fluctuations in prices. This should be complemented by a program of low-interest loans for primary output expansion whenever there is substantial rise in demand. More of this later; the important point is that inflation is not a sign of excessive demand pressure, it is a problem of smoothing out market responses.

A full employment policy, in the sense just explained, in a world where transformational growth has ended, will have to be based on the state creating new demand, which means that deficit spending must be a cornerstone of policy. But deficit spending is only a beginning. A full employment policy will have to re-ignite investment, and that means it will have to generate new markets. So there will have to be a redistributive incomes policy as well, and this has to fit together with a world trade policy, with anti-inflation policy, and with a myriad other government policies, many of them affecting supply conditions. So we not only have to outline a policy for ensuring that aggregate demand will grow adequately to continue to employ everyone; we have to make sure that demand and supply policies are coordinated, and fit together into a whole package, so that efforts to bring about full employment do not backfire by setting off an inflation or ruining our balance of payments. This means taking a comprehensive policy approach to all aspects of the economy, and we shall see that this will run into conflict with the interests of capital. But first let's explore what is required for a recovery to full employment.

Transformational growth is not likely to be re-ignited by the unassisted market. First, the long-term basis of the process was the transference of activities and functions from the household to industry and the market – and for both the middle class and large parts of the working class there is little, if anything, left to transfer. That leaves the poor, but they can only be reached through policy measures. Second, we cannot simply rely on computers, bio-tech, or other new techologies. They *might* create a boom, but, then again, they might not. In any case, they clearly displace labor, not only in the blue-collar world of industry, but also in the white- and pink-collared arenas of office and sales work. To put it bluntly, the automobile has come to the end of the road, as far as growth is concerned, and, as yet, there isn't anything to take its place. The shift to the information economy is just beginning, and the computer, so far, just isn't a big enough household item – and in the near future, there is no reason to suppose that every household will need or be able to use one. (For one thing, not everyone can read, type and handle numbers well enough. And even voice-activated computers will require users who can think.) In short, there may well be a new era of transformation, and it may be a very profound one, but it is not just around the corner. Even more important, however, from what we can already see, the way it works is going to be different.

If functions cannot be transferred from the household to capital and industry, then perhaps we should raid – the state! That is one way of interpreting an important part of the conservative anti-interventionist stance. The private sector should take over schools, the mails, roads and bridges, highways and harbors, even policing. However, we have already seen that this introduces a pattern of systematic distortion: essentially public activities (in the sense we defined earlier) are privatized and thereby twisted out of shape, often at great social cost. This is not the road to prosperity.

We cannot expect to re-ignite traditional transformational growth (although we cannot wholly rule out that possibility, either.) What we can do, and rather easily, is complete the job. There are whole sections of modern society whose transformation remains more or less unfinished because they are still too poor to enter fully into the consumer society. No G.I. Bill ever assisted them, no war was ever won against their poverty. Yet given adequate incomes they would gladly enter the mainstream of the consumer society. They have the skills and the motivation. However, because in many cases they are distinct social groups, they would need products adapted to their specific cultural histories, and this would require product innovation and investment. In other cases, they already consume cheap versions of the goods; the move would be to higher quality. In other words, by substantially raising the incomes of the large poorer sections of the advanced economies, consumer demand could be set on a path of growth once again.

Such a strategy would rest on three pillars. First, it would be necessary to raise wages across the board, particularly for low-income groups. Note that this is *not* a policy of transfer payments. The aim is not redistribution; it is to expand the economy, but one important means of this expansion will be to raise real incomes in the poorer sections of the community – precisely because, being poor, they have the greatest need for additional consumption.

Second, complementing the policy of raising wages, the government would introduce an extensive program of well-paid employment in government service. Jobs would have to be developed in many fields, but there is a great deal of work to be done in restoring and rebuilding the infrastructure of the nation – bridges, harbors, roads, rivers, public buildings, parks, and so on. These jobs will set standards, both as to pay and working conditions. Of course, there will be objections, since such public works will be seen as taking jobs away from existing public employees and/or private contractors. But this is simply another example of the 'fixed output fallacy'. If the new strategy catches fire, and sets off a chain reaction of expansion, then there will be plenty of work for everyone.

Third, the state will have to develop an investment plan, on a large scale. And this means prodding private industry, with subsidies, tax breaks – and penalties for non-compliance. It would probably be easiest to develop this primarily in public goods, but to promote recovery and expansion the important point will be to generate high capacity utilization in a situation of high and rising wages. Then, if these wages cannot be passed along in prices, and if capital cannot migrate elsewhere, the result will have to be investment and technical progress. Capital will be forced to invest and innovate. Let's explore this further.

What Can Be Done?

So we need more than a new assessment of state expenditure and deficits; we need a new package of policies. The old Keynesian cookbook has run out of recipes; to judge from the record of the 1970s, it is not capable of coping with stagflation. But the failures of monetarism and supply-side approaches, which led to the crash of 1981–82, the weak recovery, and current high unemployment do not hold out hope for back to business as usual. In particular, we have to dismiss the traditional theory from consideration. It can give us no guidance in dealing with the problems of today. Let's reconsider the traditional prescriptions before turning to our new proposals.

Mainstream economics has always tried to strike a balance between the interests of capital and those of the state. Capital is out after profits and new markets, and wants to maintain its prerogatives in controlling and directing production, while the state is or should be concerned with the general welfare of the citizenry. Clearly the interests of capital and the citizenry can clash; equally, they can be complementary. (When capital and citizens conflict, it cannot be presumed that the state will always take the place of the citizens. But this is too complex an issue to deal with here.) Mainstream economics tries to find compromises whenever there are areas of conflict. However, this approach was a washout in the 1970s: the tradeoff between inflation and unemployment worsened, the conflicts over the environment and pollution intensified, the fight over the flight of capital to 'export platforms' in the Third World grew more rancorous, while the competition between the leading firms of Japan, West Germany, France, the UK and the US grew fiercer every year.

Monetarism, unabashed, is out to get the maximum freedom of action for capital in these circumstances. With no hint of compromise, monetarists try to repeal legislation and, where that is not possible, to undercut and weaken the adminstration of any and all forms of economic regulation. Recessions turn out to have a good side, from this perspective. They tend to put labor and consumer groups in their place, while tighter job markets and bleaker prospects generally dampen the militancy of the campuses. And so on; we need not repeat the full program.

Monetarism abandons even the pretence of supporting full employment. Supply-siders, by contrast, do hold it as a goal, but it is in practice subsidiary; full employment will come about through 'trickle-down'. The old-time Keynesian program supported full employment and active intervention, but it compromised with the traditional theory and today is in disarray. So we have to seek out new directions.

Very broadly, there are two places where we can look for a new set of policies. One is to seek a new form of compromise between capital, labor and the people. The 'social contract' and most proposals for incomes policies, along with most plans for reviving industry, fall under this heading. Labor must show restraint over wages and working conditions, the people have to learn to be less demanding and impatient when it comes to safety and the environment, while business, fattened up by subsidies, must move energetically to invest and expand. Labor's restraint will be rewarded by more jobs, as the economy grows, and eventually, as the new investment raises productivity, with higher wages. The consuming public will reap general prosperity, while the government (local governments, too) will take in higher taxes as a result of greater economic activity. Business, of course, gets lower costs, so higher profits. Everyone is better off. How can such a program be resisted? Why isn't everyone jumping on the bandwagon?

For one thing, subsidies and giveaways don't create markets. They are 'supply-side' proposals; they reduce costs. But no matter how low the costs, you can't make a profit unless you can sell the product. Of course, lower costs can be passed along in lower prices, but in an industrial economy, as we have seen, demand tends to be price-inelastic. The lower prices will do very little to expand the market. Only an expansion of incomes can do that, and the incomes that expand have to be among groups whose appetite for consumer products is not already heavily sated.

The economy has been in a prolonged period of slack, and no recovery can take place unless demand is stimulated.

Moreover, in the 1980s and even more in the 1990s, no one can be sure that 'giveaways' to business – wage restraint, deregulation, subsidies – will actually lead to expansion at home. Profits will rise, it is true, but it doesn't follow that business will invest these profits at home. In fact, it may take the money and run, moving its capital abroad, either by lending or in the form of direct investments. In the 1970s, favored places were Western Europe and the so-called newly industrializing countries – Brazil, Taiwan, South Korea, Singapore, Iran (under the Shah) – where markets for consumer goods were growing rapidly as a large and prosperous middle class emerged and consolidated its position. In the US, by contrast, market growth slowed markedly, especially for consumer durables, at the end of the 1960s. So, on the one hand market growth is slowing in the US while it is accelerating in other parts of the world. On the other hand, the pressures of population on space and resources, together with the accumulated pollution from a century of industrial production, have created an environmental crisis, with serious workplace and community safety problems. Regulatory 'giveaways' are more expensive than ever.

So the 'giveaway' route to recovery is not promising, though, of course, since it involves making concessions to capital, it will be strongly promoted and is the most likely to be tried. But, to repeat, it is unlikely to succeed for the simple reason that investment cannot easily be encouraged when market growth is sluggish. For example, if the underlying pressures for housing construction are weak, because of lower migration from the countryside to the cities and lower rates of family formation, then dropping interest rates will not have the same effect on construction that it did, say, in the 1950s. Moreover, as we saw earlier, consumer durable spending, the government deficit, net exports and private investment all grew more slowly in the 1970s than in the previous two decades.

Popular Domination of Business

So let's now look at another possibility, which will certainly not be popular with the business community, and so will face serious political obstacles, but which might benefit nearly everyone, including members of the business community in their capacity as consumer and homeowners. Instead of a new compromise between government and private business, a set of policies could be defined on the basis of *dominating* business. (Note that this still falls short of abolishing or expropriating it; these policies remain within the framework of capitalism.) Such domination would only be possible if based on a powerful and popular political movement of course, and would last only as long as such a movement held together. No such movement can presently be discerned on the political horizon in either the US or the UK.

Nevertheless, it is still worth sketching the outline of this form of economic policy.

What would political domination of business mean? Basically, it means limited planning, in the public interest, and controls. Why? It can be objected that the pursuit of profit by business *is* in the public interest, since it stimulates productivity and innovation. But this is in no way contrary to planning; planning should include planning to reward innovation and productivity. And the purpose of controls is less to enforce the decisions of planners than to prevent businesses from pursuing policies that are both profitable and against the public interest. Inflationary policies, environmental spoilage, unsafe working conditions, and all kinds of white-collar crime – fraud, misrepresentation, and the lot – these are the things that controls and regulation are supposed to prevent. Of course, the result can be a lot of red tape; but that is not so much a point against controls and regulation, as a complaint about badly administered controls and poorly designed regulations.

How, then, can control by the state be established and maintained? (Policies cannot be adopted that would tend to undermine the basis of control.) First, there has to be a secure, well-paid state bureaucracy, with high prestige and high morale; otherwise it will not be possible to carry out a complex and controversial policy. A priority, therefore, must be to build up the civil service and to institute training in the techniques for the control and regulation of business. State control and regulation today have a bad press; the 'efficiency of the free market' is almost an article of faith, while the popular culture worships in the temple of Mammon. Perhaps the tide is beginning to turn; some of the themes of the 1960s seem to be recurring. But a long period of stable prosperity and job security will be needed to encourage ordinary people once again to challenge the meaninglessness of their jobs and raise questions about the relationship between market success and higher goals. To be effective, this has to be supported by a political program centered on a party or a major faction within a party. Moreover, it has to be tied to a major and perceptible issue; fortunately – or, rather, unfortunately – one exists: the Environment.

Traditional price theory and conventional market practice take for granted the independence of market activities. One person's consumption does not affect another's; a business's production does not injure households or impose hidden costs on other businesses. Free market doctrines and current business practice both rest on this assumed independence. Less obviously, so does modern macroeconomics: a change in investment is not supposed to endanger anyone's consumption; today's consumption is not expected to undermine tomorrow's investment.

This independence no longer exists: today's consumption is undermining tomorrow's investment and business activities are regularly injuring households and harming other businesses. Chemicals poison the water table, exhaust fumes the air; industrial smog covers whole cities, while acid rain destroys forests. Neither in theory nor in practice can the free market take account of these costs, nor in many cases can experts accurately estimate them. Most important of all, they appear to be rising.

An environmental crisis is almost certainly approaching. It will have to be dealt with by regulations and controls.

This impending disaster can be converted into an opportunity for the state to assume a dominant position with respect to business. Instead of trying to impose regulations from the outside, the state's power to create money can be used to buy enough shares in major corporations to establish control and to install a civil service management. The tax laws can be adjusted to control the resulting massive build-up of private liquidity, which would tend to put downward pressure on interest rates – a desirable development for an expansionist policy, anyway. By establishing government managements in dominant firms, the government can set the competitive standards – for prices, profits, technology, product quality, worker safety, etc. – in the major industries. But the government firms, no less than the others, will still be subject to competition, and will still have to meet the market test in the struggle for sales. The system would remain demand-constrained.

Controls for Full Employment

To set up a full employment policy, there will have to be two kinds of controls – controls over prices and controls over movements of capital. Taking the first, this is not as formidable a task as it is sometimes made to appear. As Galbraith has said, it is not so hard to control prices that are already administered, and the prices of products manufactured by the 2,000 or so largest US corporations, comprising over two-thirds of US GNP, are all administered. *Politically* there will be furious resistance to a national pricing scheme, but *technically* the job is not so difficult. It requires coordinating the separate pricing policies of the giant corporations, while constraining overall price increases in the national interest, together with passing on the benefits of technological advances to consumers in the form of lower prices. For example, it would be possible to use the tax system to penalize price increases and to reward cost reductions. But a better system, on several grounds, would involve establishing government-owned 'yardstick' firms in all major industries. These firms would be sizeable enough to command a perceptible market share, would be subject to regular audit by the General Accounting Office (the results of which would be public), and would employ the most up-to-date technology. Their prices would then provide a competitive yardstick that other firms would have to meet. Working this out will not be a small job, but it was done successfully in World War II, when the government managed a large number of firms, and during the Korean War, when it relied largely on controls. Both were before the age of computers and modern communications. So it should be possible to do it all the better now.

A price control policy needs a complementary money wages policy. But here new considerations enter. When growth has slowed down, maintaining full employment will require a rise in consumption, which is most easily achieved by bringing about a rise in wages. Moreover, such a rise in wages can itself encourage both increases in productivity, as firms innovate to maintain their traditional profits, and new investment to provide the capacity to service newly affluent households. Here caution must be exercised – too great an increase in real wages will impose unacceptable costs on business, leaving too little surplus for investment, but too small an increase will not provide sufficient stimulus either to productivity or to investment. This poses the problem of finding an 'optimum' wage increase and developing a policy to implement it. Such a policy of encouraging high wages, perhaps by systematically and regularly raising the minumum wage and extending its coverage, will have to be supplemented by subsidies to innovation, e.g. through low-cost government loans, and by retraining programs for displaced laborers. A major consequence of such a policy will be a change in the composition of industry, because low-wage, inefficient firms – even entire industries – will have to modernize or go out of business. High and rising wages will also lead to increased imports, because of lower labor costs elsewhere. But they will force labor and management to innovate and increase productivity. Moreover, the 'weeding out' under this policy would be directed at technologically backward and genuinely inefficient firms, not at firms whose debt structure was lop-sided or whose markets tended to dry up in recession.

A policy of raising wages would, of course, immediately lead to capital movement. So the second set of controls needed would prevent the flight of capital overseas. Some capital mobility would be permitted; the point would be to regulate it in the national interest, rather than permitting capital flows to follow anticipated profits (profits that may never be realized – as in the loans to some 'developing' countries, which went into the pockets, and Swiss bank accounts, of corrupt officials).

Along with these controls, a policy of managed trade will be needed. Countries must not be required to generate recessions in order to bring imports down to the level of their exports. This will require strengthening and reorienting international institutions, like the World Bank and the IMF. Selective import controls must be permitted and balance of payments deficits must be financed without requiring 'austerity'. Again, it is not technically impossible to see how to do this: instead of penalizing the weak – those who run deficits – penalties could be assessed against the strong – the surplus countries – who could be required, for example, to pay into an international fund that would provide loans to finance the deficit countries during a negotiated period of adjustment. Instead of cutting back imports through austerity, deficit-running countries would be encouraged to modernize their export industries, while being permitted to impose certain agreed protectionist measures during the adjustment period. (Such measures reduce the *propensity* to import, and thus permit a country's imports and exports to balance at a higher level of national income.) At present, whenever there is an inbalance in world trade, world income must be cut back as deficit nations reduce incomes and employment in order to reduce imports. But this reduces incomes in the surplus nations, creating a built-in bias towards world stagnation, and, of course, in the long run weakening the deficit nations even more. This has to be changed.

Finally , as mentioned, an expansionary approach based on raising wages would require a considerable retraining and relocation program for workers, since it would strongly stimulate modernization and technological development, which perhaps always, but certainly with today's 'high tech', tend to displace labor and change the skill mix demanded in the labor market.

High and Rising Wages

Let's review the proposal for raising wages, setting it in the context of our other proposals. The basic idea is to raise the lower end of the wage scale substantially at regular intervals, first because low wages are generally paid by technologically backward industries and firms, precisely the ones we want to put pressure on, and second because low-wage households will be certain to spend the increase, and will generally spend it on important items – improved diet, medical care, transportation, housing. When the lower end of the wage scale goes up, of course, that will lead to demands for increased wages throughout the rest of the scale, in order to maintain traditional differentials. This will presumably put pressure on firms to raise productivity in order to meet the high wage demands, and upon workers to accept the kinds of job restructuring and/or mechanization/automation that is needed to raise productivity. Thus, the proposal generates pressure for productivity advance throughout industry, not only in the backward sectors.

Of course, any general and widespread advances in productivity, even with growing demand, will lead to the elimination of large numbers of jobs. True, new jobs will be created, but the skills and training required by the new will normally differ from those appropriate for the old. Hence one could expect considerable resistance to this program by organized labor. On the other hand, raising wages to high levels, as a matter of official policy, and making the rises frequent and regular, must be a policy with considerable appeal. Hence it should not be difficult to arrange for retraining and relocation programs, and for organized labor to accept labor-saving innovations, speed-ups and the like. Obviously, these must be safe and compatible with decent working conditions, but if they are then labor's energy should go into support for retraining and relocation programs, and into ensuring that the phasing out of jobs is done in a humane and reasonable manner, rather than into resisting technical progress. So a major retraining and relocation program will have to be a part of a wage-raising policy. And if a major investment effort is to take place in rebuilding the social infrastructure, this will be much easier, since temporary jobs for displaced workers can be found in this project.

How frequently should wage increases take place? The object is to create a new market and stimulate the investment to build the facilities needed to serve that market, on the one hand, and to provoke modernization of existing production facilities on the other. Since the object is to stimulate investment, the stimulus should be applied whenever investment is due for renewal. So the period between policy-induced wage increases should be the *average write-off period*. This period tends to be as low as three years, more normally about five years.

We have seen that any policy package designed to produce a recovery leading to a boom will require.

- some rebuilding of the nation's infrastructure
- some form of price control, or other lid on inflation
- ways of preventing balance of payments/foreign exchange crises.

No boom can be sustained without significant modernization and repair of the infrastructure. Any substantial recovery could reignite inflation by driving up raw materials prices; hence any recovery policy will have to include some form of price or wage controls. Finally, any stimulus to demand is going to tend to generate balance of payments difficulties, so will have to include proposals to deal with them. It is important to emphasize these last two points: either inflation and balance of payments deficits are controlled by keeping unemployment high, or, if there is to be prosperity, prices and imports will have to be controlled. There is no way out of this dilemma at present.

Now let's see how these policies would work out in the context of a demand slump with delayed replacement. (It is not appropriate here to work out the actual details. That would require careful and extensive empirical study of the affected industries – pay increases, dismissals, shutdowns, new investment, impact on markets, and so on. That is a different project. Here we are trying to show the plausibility of a radical policy to restore and maintain prosperity. Once the principle is established, the rest can be filled in.) The proposal is to raise the minimum wage – assumed to cover all employment – quite steeply, perhaps up to near the median. The object is to push pay scales up across the board, as firms and workers both try to re-establish the traditional differentials. Clearly time to adjust will be needed; the increase should be announced in advance and should take place in series of steps – with compensation and retraining provided for workers laid off or dismissed. As much as the bottom two-thirds of the labor force might eventually experience some rise in their take-home pay. At the same time, an easy money policy will advance funds to firms that propose to modernize and improve their productivity. These funds will cover the difference between the cost of the new equipment and firms' present depreciation funds, and (depending on the circumstances) may include grants or one-time loans to enable businesses to pay the increased wages while waiting for the modernization work to be carried out. (These loans will also provide the government lending agency with access to the books and records of borrowing firms.)

The policy should be designed to generate its effects in two stages. First, the initial impact should be such that *the total real wage bill increases*, so that consumer demand will be stimulated and activity in the capital goods sector increased. Second, as new plant and equipment is installed and comes into operation, the ultimate impact should be to raise productivity enough to more or less catch up the rise in wages. In short, a large new set of customers will be brought into important sectors of the consumer market, which will both raise activity there and tend to stimulate new investment in both production and sales facilities. So long as productivity more or less catches up, and so long as capital cannot flee abroad, there is no reason to fear that investment will be dampened – once the growth in the consumer market is evident – by the higher wage.

. The initial impact on employment will involve two negative and three positive effects:

Negative: (1) workers released by plants closing down (N_C)
(2) workers released by speed-ups, technical progress or learning by doing (N_T)

Positive: (1) Workers hired by 'best practice' firms as they expand to take over the markets abandoned by the firms closing down (N_B)
(2) workers hired in the capital goods sector to produce replacement goods or modernization equipment (N_K)
(3) workers hired in response to increased activity (N_A).

Putting our point in formula, we can say that the total initial effect on employment will be:

$$N_2 = N_1 - (N_C + N_T) + N_B + N_K + N_A,$$

where N_1 is the original level of employment. The original level of consumer demand was $W_1 N_1$, where W_1 represents the original average level of the real wage. The objective, then, is to choose a new level of the wage that, together with an easy money policy, retraining programs, and so on, will maximize the difference:

$$W_2 N_2 - W_1 N_1.$$

This, then, is the initial impact that is designed to raise activity levels in both sectors.

However, the ultimate effect will contain one changed term and one additional term. The additional term (N_D) is the labor displaced by the new equipment when it comes into operation. The changed term is N_K, which must fall to the level of employment required for regular replacement rather than replacement plus modernization. So, the ultimate formula for employment will be:

$$N_2' = N_1 - (N_C + N_T + N_D) + N_B + N_K + N_A.$$

Clearly N_2' will be less than N_2; hence $W_2 N_2' < W_2 N_2$. But if the additional displacement of labor just raises overall productivity enough to compensate for the higher wages, we should still expect to find that

$W_2N_2' > W_1N_1$. For the reverse to hold, it would have to be the case that overall productivity increased proportionally more than wages.

But in any case, the chief effect the policy is aiming for is neither of these. It is the stimulation of a new burst of investment, building factories, salesrooms and offices to supply the new demand created by the entry of a large, identifiable new group of customers into the consumer goods market. This is first created by the rise in the minimum wage, then made permanent by the subsequent rise in productivity that ensures that firms will continue to be able to pay the new level of wages. It is this effect that will set off a new round of self-sustaining growth.

Comparisons with Other Policies

Now let's briefly compare our policy package with its chief competitors – the monetarists and the Keynesians.

Monetarism restricts the growth of the money supply to a fixed target (usually bringing on high interest rates and a credit squeeze) plus deregulation of markets and a cutback of government. It is an austerity program *par excellence*. The virtues claimed are that it will stop inflation, maintain regular growth, encourage 'productive' rather than 'wasteful' uses of resources and 'weed out' inefficient industries, producing a leaner, more competitive, faster-growing economy. Now, let's compare them.

First, both monetarism and our program increase a crucial cost of doing business: austerity raises the cost of borrowing – and also creates uncertainty about the future course of interest rates; our program raises labor costs. A high rate of interest tends to exacerbate inequality in the distribution of income, and it has a direct negative effect on purchases of consumer durables and on housing starts. By concentrating income in the hands of the already well-off, monetarism both shrinks the consumer market and shifts the composition of output from necessities to luxuries, and so, by a common-sense criterion, generates waste. Raising wages, by contrast, especially at the lowest end of the scale, tends to improve the distribution of income and so widens the consumer market.

Second, both programs claim to 'weed out' inefficient firms. Monetarism does this by constricting demand while at the same time raising the cost of borrowing. The result is a kind of indiscriminate pressure on all firms suffering from a shortage of liquidity for whatever reason. Sales will be down and money expensive. A firm could go to the wall because its market was weak at a point when a large debt rollover fell due, *even though it was perfectly efficient*. Our proposal, by contrast, ensures that only firms that are technologically backward are hit with increased costs. For these firms, paying below-average wages, there will be cost increases – but their markets will be strong and modernization loans cheap. If they are capable of modernizing, they have both the chance and a strong incentive to do it. Only firms really not capable of improvement will have to go under.

Finally, of course, high interest rates encourage the use of cheap labor and the postponement of replacement, so it is the *wrong cost* to increase if the purpose of the policy is to induce technical progress.

Now contrast our program with an old-fashioned Keynesian 'full employment' policy: low interest rates, a sizeable deficit – whatever is necessary – and various kinds of *ad hoc* controls to prevent prices and imports from getting out of hand (something like the Attlee government's program). Both policies stimulate demand, but the Keynesian program does not specifically address the question of the *growth of markets*. It merely runs a deficit – which will stimulate demand, but it does not create a new market. By contrast, our program targets a set of households and raises their incomes substantially. This creates *an identifiable new group of consumers* to supply which there will have to be new production and sales facilities created.

Keynesian policy works exclusively on demand; it creates no supply-side pressures. Our policy, by contrast, puts pressure on employers to modernize, as well as helping to provide a market, on the one hand, and low-cost loans to underwrite technological up-dating, on the other. Keynesian policy not only never addresses the supply-side question; it tends to promote full employment through military spending, which absorbs scientific resources *and* leads to costly, non-competitive, 'baroque' technological developments. Moreover, Keynesians often try to encourage investment by means of special tax breaks and other investment incentives. But these incentives are not usually tied to productivity growth or any other index of modernization or technical progress. In fact they are quite often counter-productive in that respect: the special 'incentives' actually enable business to continue to operate outmoded techniques and to keep on running outmoded plant and equipment. Our proposal does away with all that.

Objections

There will certainly be objections. Let's look at some of the more obvious ones.

● *'It would simply set off another inflation.'*

But not if the price control board works. That means it must be well staffed and well funded. Moreover, it must have the power to impose penalties for violations, which, however, it will waive if within a certain time the offender firm shows a certain improvement in productivity. Another factor preventing inflation will be the competition from firms already operating or moving into best-practice techniques and paying high wages. These firms will stand to take markets away from inefficient firms that try to pass along the wage increase in higher prices. Prominent among the competitive best-practice firms will be the government-owned 'yardstick' firms; since these will normally be the price leaders, it will be difficult for the others to establish higher prices.

● *'It will simply lead to flight of capital overseas.'*

Without doubt there will have to be controls or exit taxes on the movement of capital; this must be part of a system of managed protection. But besides the controls – which will be all the easier to manage if other advanced countries *also* adopt a wage-increase policy – there will be real incentives to capital to remain. There will be a growing full employment market, a labor retraining and relocation program, no labor objections to the introduction of new technology, improved social and economic infrastructure, and, finally, low-interest loans for modernization and technological improvements.

● *'It will make US industry non-competitive in the world.'*

First, it would not if other major countries adopted similar policies. Secondly, if and to the extent that the policy succeeds in stimulating technical progress, the US position will be unchanged or actually improved. US resources and tax dollars will no longer go to support outmoded and inefficient industries. They will be scrapped and resources will be shifted into the areas in which productivity is the highest and, within these areas, into the hands of the most efficient firms using the best-practice methods of operation. So, in fact, it is a way of improving the US world competitive position.

● *'The world crisis is due to a falling rate of profit and raising wages can only exacerbate this.'*

Not if raising wages also raises both demand and productivity. It all depends on choosing the right circumstances in which to raise wages in the right way. Nobody denies that in some circumstances some kinds of wage increase would prove disastrous.

● *'It will lead to unacceptable concentration of industry.'*

But austerity programs also lead to concentration. The point is that the power of capital would be subjected to many checks and controls, and the efforts of business would be channeled to making technical innovations.

● *'Raising wages will cause losses to shareholders through bankruptcies. This is unfair to capital.'*

But austerity programs also cause losses to shareholders, and they do not bring about technical progress, nor do they stimulate the growth of markets and a return of prosperity. And austerity programs are unfair to workers.

● *'Raising the minimum wage will cause unemployment among minorities and teenagers.'*

At the outset a large public works program is needed simply to repair the infrastructure – whatever kind of recovery program is undertaken. This can cater especially to teenagers and minorities and others displaced from backward sectors, until the boom is under way and they can be reabsorbed in the expansion.

To establish the new, higher wage the government will have to offer subsidies and low-interest loans for modernization to firms that, first, agree to modernize and submit a plan, and, second, agree to hold the line on prices. Once a few large firms agree, competition will make it difficult for the rest to raise prices. This means that the high-wage policy ultimately rests on expansionary fiscal and monetary policies. In a moment we will see how such spending can always be financed by a profits tax.

But, first, note an important consequence of low interest rates: the currency will be weakened and will tend to fall. This will make it more expensive for capital to take flight, and it will also tend to reduce imports. Some imports are necessities and can't be cut back, but, as these become more expensive, businesses will search for domestic substitutes, or will try to invent synthetics. Either of these can be expected to lead to increased investment spending. So the elements of the policy package tend to reinforce one another.

Now we must ask, is growth based on a redistribution that creates new markets really transformational growth? It certainly is not the sort of transformation we were talking about when we discussed the impact of the automobile and the internal combustion engine, although the transformation did involve redistribution. But if this is not the real thing, will it be enough? If the system requires transformational growth, will redistributional growth do instead?

There were broadly two sets of reasons why transformational growth is required to sustain prosperity. On the demand side, there is the tendency for consumer markets to saturate and stultify unless new groups are brought into them or new products are found to replace or enhance existing ways of managing the household. On the supply side, deposits of raw materials and energy will tend to become depleted, and the environment polluted or congested, unless new technologies generate new products and processes, relieving the pressures. Transformational growth creates new sectors, new products, new jobs, new cities; and destroys the old. The redistributive measures proposed above are obviously not going to bring about anything of the sort – unless there are new products and new technologies waiting in the wings. If there are, then our program will call them right to the center of the stage. Even in the absence of new technologies that are expansive in nature, the redistributive program outlined here does deal with two central problems – one on the supply side, the other on the demand side.

Taking the first. The program, of course, does not propose any new sources of materials or energy, but it does envisage rebuilding the social infrastructure, which will help considerably in managing, conserving and making the best use of the resources we have. In addition, new product designs for new consumer groups can economize on depleted materials. At least equally important, the program provides strong incentives for business to modernize, to introduce best-practice technology, and to save on labor costs. That is, it provides both cost pressures and the pull of a booming market. If a business can get its costs down, then it can be sure of selling. Nor can it hope to avoid the troubles and rigors of cost-cutting (cutting back on managerial staff, for example, or holding the line on top management salaries) by passing these costs along to consumers. Prices controls are there precisely to prevent that, and will keep prices at the level that will earn the normal rate of profit for the best-practice technique. Hence the program will tend to call forth technical progress. Of course, it does not follow that the innovations will be extensive in character (in the special sense defined earlier); that depends on the innovations themselves, and what causes people to have ideas is still unknown.

When it comes to the demand side, however, the program is on target. The problem with steady growth is that, with a given income distribution, markets cease to grow. The high-wage program is designed continually to bring new groups into the consumer market. Hence it directly targets the origin of stagnation: the failure of markets to grow, which results in a slowdown of investment (and a tendency to look abroad for faster-growing markets), leading in turn to a slowing down in the growth of productivity. So, by establishing a policy that deliberately raises the family incomes of the lowest paid – leaving it to the market and collective bargaining to re-establish the normal pattern of wage differentials – whenever consumer growth appears to be slowing down, we meet this problem head on.

There are limits, however. As the poorest elements in society are raised to the levels the middle classes have reached now, we can expect their consumption to begin to grow more slowly than their income and also to change character, shifting from demand for private consumption goods to (often politically expressed) demands for improved public goods. Thus we may find that even regular and repeated redistribution cannot sustain consumer-driven growth indefinitely. Moreover, the technical progress induced not only raises productivity, it does away with jobs. Up to now, most observers have agreed that the creation of new jobs brought about by new investment would offset the elimination of jobs by labor-saving technology. Yet there is no inherent reason why this should continue to be so. Indeed, as we saw in Chapter 7 (pp. 175–78), 'introverted' innovations will tend to displace more workers than they generate employment for, directly and indirectly. So we may find that in the relatively distant future both the demand for products and the technology for supplying them will tend to be such that the number of jobs will fail to grow, or even decline. In the extreme case, jobs and work could diminish dramatically in favor of automation, in which event the link between income and work would have to be severed. But this question will have to be left to another time.

The Financing of the Deficit

A central pillar of such a program will clearly have to be deficit spending by the government, because the modern economy characteristically runs with a shortage of demand. High employment will therefore normally require a stimulus. Can deficits be run year after year without ill effects? Does it matter how they are financed? Who will bear the burden of the debt?

Let's begin by considering a new complaint, that the interest burden of the present and future deficits will be too great for the country to bear. This worry is wholly unwarranted. The 'burden of interest' can be lifted completely by an appropriately designed tax. Remember what the problems are with taxes: a tax should not provide disincentives to work, or to investment, nor should it reduce demand by consumers, given that we want to stimulate demand. A tax that falls on corporations and the wealthy fits the bill. Let's now reconsider a proposal for financing the British wartime debt made forty years ago by Michal Kalecki, the famous Polish economist, then in exile and living in England.

Kalecki's objective was to design a form of taxation that would provide the funds to service the debt without creating distortions in the use of capital or adversely influencing production or employment. To this end he proposed a 'capital tax', the rate to be set in the same proportion to the rate of interest that the national debt stands in to the value of total capital of all forms. (Note that these must be aggregated by comparable methods, e.g. using the same price indexes, but since ratios are involved it doesn't matter whether calculations are done in real or nominal terms.) To put it another way, the rate of the tax on capital applied to the whole of capital held in private hands, whatever the form (bonds, stocks, actual plant and equipment, buildings and real estate, savings accounts, any form of wealth), would be such that the taxes raised would equal the interest cost of the national debt. If we were to write it as a formula, with i as the rate of interest, D the national debt, K the total national wealth, and t the tax, then

$$iD = tK, \text{ or } t = i(D/K).$$

Since the tax falls on capital or wealth whatever the form in which it is held, it will not have any influence on the decisions as to how best to allocate capital to its various potential uses. For the same reason it will not affect the inducement to invest – funds held idle must pay the tax just as surely as wealth embodied in plant and equipment. Moreover, with such a tax in place, changes in the amount of the national debt have no influence on the aggregate activity of wealth-holders. An increase, say, in government borrowing (everything else the same) means an increase in the interest income accruing to the wealth-holding class and wealth-holding institutions; but it also implies a rise in the capital tax, which just covers the additional income. Hence, under such a scheme, not only the inducement to invest but also the propensity to consume of wealth-holders will remain substantially unaffected by changes in the level of the national debt.

Even if there were persistent budget deficits and so a growing national debt, so long as the debt grew at the same rate as capital as a whole the rate of such a tax would remain stable, or would move only with changes in the interest rate.

The amount of capital tax paid would be deducted from income in the same way as depreciation, before the income tax is figured. Thus the yield of the income tax will be reduced, but this will be exactly offset by the additional income tax from the additional income accruing as interest on the national debt. So once again the scheme will be neutral – aggregate after-tax income will be unchanged.

To simplify administration, certain modifications are desirable (some of which Kalecki himself suggested in the British context): not to impose the tax on holdings of wealth below a certain size; to collect it by taxing the capital of enterprises and persons, not including shares and corporate bonds in the wealth accounting (since these are claims against the real capital of enterprises); and, if the administration of the tax were to prove too difficult, e.g. because of problems in valuing certain kinds of wealth holdings, to replace it with an equivalent tax on unearned income (income from capital). Such a tax would fall on gross capital income, that is, before depreciation, but *all* investment, whether for replacement or for expansion, would be deductible (if investment exceeds income, the deduction carries over to future years); as a result the tax would not affect the expected gross rate of profit on an investment, and so would not affect the inducement to invest.

Without a wealth tax of this sort, the burden of servicing the national debt will be borne by wage- and salary-earners and by corporations paying taxes on their earnings, under either present arrangements or under the new (1986) tax bill. The working population and active businesses will be taxed to pay exceptionally high interest charges to holders of essentially idle financial wealth. Such taxation can be expected to reduce aggregate demand and is arguably both an unfair burden and an undesirable incentive pattern.

So far, neither the US administration nor its orthodox critics has considered a wealth tax. Yet the proposal has clear advantages. For example, the conservative ideal of a 'flat tax' burdens the necessary household expenditures of the poor more heavily than is fair or socially wise, while leaving income that supports luxury spending by the rich untaxed. A wealth tax falls for the most part on income that will figure among the 'withdrawals' from the stream of expenditures, and it falls wholly on those who can afford to pay. It might be objected that a capital tax would lead to a flight of short-term foreign capital, which has been attracted by high interest rates, because it would reduce the after-tax earning rate. But, in fact, short-term capital mostly goes to finance the deficit on current account, and does not depend on the interest rate. Moreover, a small capital outflow, as long as it's not a panic, may be desirable, for it will tend to bring the dollar down, which is essential for the recovery of US exports.

The long term
A well-designed tax, then, can prevent the debt from being a burden, thus permitting deficit spending to provide a continual stimulus whenever needed. But can it go on? What happens as the debt accumulates?

The simplest way to answer this is to consider the case of a steadily growing economy, in which year after year there is a deficit, so that debt accumulates at the same rate that the total capital grows. Let us assume that all wages are spent and all profits invested; then the growth rate will equal the profit rate. But in that case competition will ensure that the interest rate on government bonds (i) will have to equal the growth (g) and profit (r) rates: $i = g = r$. Then interest on the debt will equal the annual deficit, since that is the growth of the debt, and $iD = gD$. For taxes to just cover the interest on the debt, the tax rate must fall on capital, and be set as just explained. Then, whatever the level of the deficit, it can be financed by borrowing, and the interest can be paid by imposing an appropriate and neutral wealth tax. This situation can continue indefinitely, so long as all parts grow in the same proportions. (If part of the deficit were financed by money creation, of course, the wealth tax would be reduced proportionately.)

The Political Question

The preceding is only a sketch; it is not complete and is intended only to be illustrative. Yet we have seen enough to ask, is it impossibly utopian? Surely the political force necessary could never be amassed?

Expanionist policies, and especially policies requiring controls, face a special problem. We saw earlier that what is good for the system as a whole normally runs counter to the perceived best interests of individuals and businesses. It is difficult to persuade people to accept expansionary policies, since they run counter to 'common sense'. To promote full employment and growing prosperity, we have advocated:

- *raising wages* – but to a normal business low wages mean low costs, making it possible to cut prices and expand, making it possible to hire extra hands, and so on;
- *protection* – but free trade makes it possible to get the best deals and the lowest prices, to look for the most advanced designs, increases the size of the market, etc.;
- *reducing savings* – but saving protects the future of the household or business, providing a fund for emergencies or opportunities and a reserve in bad times;
- *running deficits* – but debts are dangerous, have to be repaid eventually, and are a burden in bad times.

'Common sense' dictates that in times when demand falls short of capacity, so that there is unemployment and distress, wages and deficits should be cut, savings increased and every effort made to promote free trade. Individual firms and/or households would benefit from such policies; by analogy so would the economy as a whole. A shortage of demand translates into a shortage of income, which means belt-tightening – and, paradoxically, this only makes things worse. But how can individuals, instinctively reacting to crisis by cutting back, be expected to support government policies of extravagance? They *can* be persuaded, because it is ultimately in their own interests, but it will be necessary to admit, even to emphasize, that *the system is inherently paradoxical* – and celebrating the virtues of the free market, even as a matter of pure theory, will have to be dropped.

However, many features of the program are already in place in many capitalist countries. Industrial policies and job retraining are a crucial feature of the Japanese economy. High wages, with real wages *leading* productivity, have been policy in Singapore. Price controls have repeatedly been used, though on a temporary basis, in most major countries, and import controls have been and are ubiquitous. Easy money and fiscal stimulus are Keynesian commonplaces. And Keynes himself long ago proposed changing the rules of the international trade system to stop penalizing the deficit countries, and replace the stagnationary bias with expansion. Now we must change from drawing on these measures as part of *ad hoc* crisis management, and begin to weave them into a comprehensive, integrated, expansionist policy program.

There isn't space here to develop these ideas further. The point is rather that a comprehensive alternative to austerity is not only conceivable, but practically feasible. However, it requires political domination of capital by the community – rather than compromise with capital, let alone domination by capital, as in the strategy of radical plutocracy that we see today. Yet, so long as liberals and neo-liberals ally themselves with the opponents of government spending and regulation, they cannot develop a coherent program for full employment. Full employment requires deficit spending and government encouragement of high wages, in a context where price controls can be drawn into play when inflation threatens. It means that democratically controlled political institutions must be in a position to compel the business system to pursue the public interest. This doesn't mean force or a police state or anything of the kind. It means setting up new businesses or taking over existing ones by buying their stock, and competing, to demonstrate new technologies and compel private business to adopt them, to control prices, wages and conditions of employment – by setting the pace. It means using the government's powers of taxing and spending, and its powers of persuasion. An important element will be to offer business high profits; no one should ever go broke selling to the government. A combination of the stick and the carrot – that is the idea.

So long as the business system is the dominant player, full employment will not be achieved, except occasionally and by accident, as the by-product of some other process. It is an act of political will that is required, more than a commitment, a determination to bring the business system under the control of the people. Actively to dominate capital – that is the crucial element in any policy package that sets out to achieve full employment!

11

Postscript:
The British Experience

GEOFF HODGSON

The relative decline of the British economy is an internationally appreciated fact. But there is less of a consensus on the causes of the decline, and even less on remedies. It is argued in this chapter that, whilst there are long-term causes involved in the downward slide, the slowdown in the growth of demand in the British economy partly caused by policy, is a major factor in the further deterioration of recent years. The chapter is divided into three sections: first an account of recent events with an attempt to locate them in an international and comparative context, second an analysis of some rival explanations of the recent downturn, and third a discussion of some of the consequences. The argument will show that cutbacks in public spending adversely affected prosperity in Britain.

Events

Oscar Wilde once remarked that Britain and the United States are two nations divided by a common language. From the vantage of the 1980s it might well be observed that in addition they are divided by a common economic policy. In nominal terms at least, since the election of Margaret Thatcher and the Conservative Party to office 1979, and the election of Ronald Reagan to the US Presidency in 1980, both countries have followed a set of monetarist, pro-market and pro-privatization economic policies associated with Milton Friedman and others of the New Right.

The substance, however, is much more complex – in terms of both the context of their operation and the policies themselves. A key point is that although the long-term trajectories of development of the two economies have similar shapes – both rising unevenly to a long period of world dominance and prosperity, then entering a slow decline – the US lags a half century or more behind Britain, and is only just beginning its relative descent. Compared with competing capitalist nations, the US economy for most of the last hundred years has been in relative ascendancy, reaching its overwhelmingly dominant position in the world economy in the 1950s and 1960s. It is only in recent years that the US has faced a serious industrial and technological challenge from other countries such as Japan. British economic hegemony, in contrast, was undermined long ago.

Layers of decline

There are several levels in the explanation of Britain's decline, layered upon one another: at the most basic level, there is a long-term relative decline dating back to the Industrial Revolution; at the second level there is an acceleration of the relative decline since the Second World War; a third level involves a recession with a period of *absolute* decline after 1979 (the subject of this chapter).

After pioneering the first Industrial Revolution in the late 1700s and early 1800s, Britain's manufacturing output had already been overtaken by Germany and the United States by the start of the First World War. By the late 1940s Britain's relative position had further deteriorated. Its share of manufacturing exports (of the eleven main industrial countries) fell from 33.2 per cent in 1899 to 29.3 per cent in 1948 (House of Lords, 1985, p. 23).

When the world economy boomed in the 1950s and 1960s Britain very rapidly lost its share of world markets to reconstructing and newly ascendant nations: by 1969 it had shrunk to 11.2 per cent, and in 1979 it was 9.1 per cent. This postwar decline is put into international perspective in Table 11.1. This shows that the relative decline of the British economy has been much more severe than that of its main competitors. Whilst the United States lost about one-third of its share of world manufacturing trade from the early 1950s to the mid 1970s, in the same time period Britain lost well over half its share. The gainers in this period were, in descending order of importance, Japan, West Germany, Italy and France. It is no accident that the latter four countries have not been content simply to rely on market forces; they have adopted some degree of planning in their economic and industrial policy since the Second World War. In contrast, in Britain and the United States the policy of *laissez-faire* has been taken much more seriously by government and the business community.

Whilst the British and the US economies have both been in a process of relative decline, they are not equal in their wealth and resilience. It is important to stress that when Margaret Thatcher became Prime Minister in May 1979 the British economy was much weaker, both relatively and absolutely, than the US economy inherited by Ronald Reagan when he

Table 11.1   *Shares in world exports of manufactures (%)*

	Average of years	
	1951–55	*1973–77*
United States	25.8	16.8
United Kingdom	20.5	9.1
West Germany	13.1	21.1
France	9.4	9.7
Japan	4.4	14.2
Italy	3.5	7.1

Source: National Institute Economic Review, various issues.

Table 11.2 *Comparative levels of productivity, 1950–79*
(US GDP per person–hour = 100)

	1950	1979
United States	100	100
Canada	78	85
United Kingdom	56	66
Sweden	55	81
France	44	86
West Germany	33	84
Italy	32	70
Japan	14	53

Source: A. Maddison, *Phases of Capitalist Development*, Oxford: Oxford University Press, 1982, p. 98.

came to power just 20 months later. Whilst US gross national product grew by an average of 2.4 per cent per annum from 1973 to 1978, in the UK growth in the same period averaged only 0.9 per cent.

There is much understandable concern about the slow comparative *growth* rate of productivity in the US. It should be pointed out, however, that US absolute productivity levels are still relatively high. Table 11.2 shows the differences between US productivity levels and those in other major industrialized countries. Productivity in the UK has been consistently well behind since the Second World War. Partly as a result, Britain is well behind the United States and many other European countries in terms of the average level of consumption of its inhabitants.

The question of the causes of the long-term relative decline of the British economy over one hundred years or more cannot be discussed in detail here. It can simply be noted that broad support seems to be emerging amongst economic historians for the view that the cause is to be found in the rigidity of British institutions (see, for example, Elbaum and Lazonick, 1986). This, in turn, is partly explained by the fact that for over two hundred years mainland Britain has not suffered the disruption of invasion, revolution, or civil war, hence has never rebuilt its capital structure.

Since the ferment of the Industrial Revolution in the first half of the nineteenth century, practices and structures in British industry have shown a limited propensity for adaptation and change. As a result technological innovation has been slower, leading to less need for firms to invest in order to modernize. On the household side, institutional rigidity manifests itself in the relatively slow pace of introduction and diffusion of new products, again leading to slower home investment. Faced with relatively slow market growth, on the one hand, and little pressure to modernize to keep competitive on the other, British capital moved abroad in search of investment opportunities – taking both its multiplier and capacity-creating effects with it. The empire assured the safety of capital, and the imperial preference system its market, but the result was that the domestic British economy grew less rapidly than British capital. Cosseted by the existence of the world's largest empire and all its inbuilt imperial preferences, for over one hundred years British industry remained structurally atomistic and wedded ideologically to the virtues of *laissez-faire*. When Britain emerged from the Second World War with her world hegemony and empire fatally undermined, she was unable to compete with the dynamism of newly reconstructed industrial countries such as West Germany and Japan.

While the Conservative administration of Margaret Thatcher cannot be held responsible for many of the British economy's inherited problems, it will be argued here that it has a primary responsibility for the further fall in Britain's relative position and for a severe and damaging downturn from 1979 to 1982.

Our first task is to give an account of some of these more recent developments. This will be followed by an analysis and evaluation, in the light of Professor Nell's arguments in this book.

The Thatcher Regime

From the point of view of the development of British economic policy, Margaret Thatcher's election to the leadership of the Conservative Party in February 1975 was almost as important as her decisive electoral victory just over four years later. The change in the leadership of the Tory Party was not simply the replacement of one person by another, it marked the victory of the New Right over the traditional Right in that Party.

Since 1944 all three major parties in British politics had expressed a commitment to consensus politics, a mixed economy, and the goal of full employment. The Labour government of 1974–79 to some degree undermined these commitments, and had more than a mild flirtation with monetarism. But with the transformation of the Conservative leadership in 1975 all three commitments were to be decisively abandoned by the Opposition with a new ideological turn.

With greater effect than their US counterparts, the Thatcherite Conservatives were able to blame the very poor relative performance of their domestic economy on the Keynesian consensus and 'excessive' state intervention and public expenditure. Relative to the US, such an argument had a greater resonance for two reasons: first, because of the greater severity of Britain's postwar decline, and, second, because of the greater vocal, and to some degree practical, commitment to socialist and Keynesian measures.

However, the experience could easily be perceived in different terms. Since both Britain and the United States are mixed economies, it is possible, if desired, to blame either the public sector or the private sector for the crisis. It is far too easy to choose a scapegoat simply according to one's ideological disposition.

At this point, the Conservative Party proclaimed the objective of reducing public expenditure and state intervention on the grounds of both improving the British economy and 'setting the people free'. With a clear majority in the 1979 election the Conservatives could then attempt to put their policies into effect.

Slamming on the brakes

An immediate attempt was made to bring down public expenditure, and on the industrial front various efforts were made to shift the balance of power away from organized labour. The immediate objective was to bring down the rate of inflation (retail prices rose by 13.3 per cent from 1978 to 1979), but these measures were also in line with medium- and long-term objectives concerning a change in the structure, composition and efficiency of the economy as a whole. It was proposed that Britain should return to the 'Victorian values' of hard work, self-reliance and entrepreneurship.

In the 1979 Conservative Budget the Chancellor drastically reduced the top rates of income tax for the wealthy, and reduced the standard rate of income tax from 33 to 30 per cent. On the other hand Value Added Tax was raised to 15 per cent. The inherited target rate of increase of the money supply ($£M_3$) was lowered, in line with a proclaimed 'tight' monetary policy. In November the Minimum Lending Rate was raised to 17 per cent as part of a deflationary package of monetary and fiscal measures.

Targets for growth in the money supply were further lowered in 1980. In that year projections for cuts in government public spending were published, showing a planned fall from £74.5 billion in 1979/80 to £70.5 billion in 1983/84. Although these measures attracted some criticism from the Far Right, in that they were insufficiently severe, they represented a clear deflationary move compared with the normal stance of the 1970s.

THE SECOND-WORST SLUMP IN HISTORY

Partly as a result of the high interest rates, and partly because of confidence in the pound due to the North Sea oil bonanza, the sterling exchange rate climbed upwards, reaching a peak in 1980–81. The competitive position of the British economy was severely disadvantaged internationally by the high value of the pound. Combined with the vigorous deflationary measures, anyone but an extremely blinkered monetarist could have envisaged disaster.

By the beginning of 1980 the UK economy was hurtling downwards at an alarming rate. From 1979 to 1980 the gross domestic product fell by 2.6 per cent (constant prices). However, the slump was even more severe in the manufacturing sector. From December 1979 to December 1980 manufacturing output was reduced by no less than 15 per cent. It is difficult to find a historical precedent for this rate of decline. The biggest rate of decline in the Great Depression of the 1870s was less than 6 per cent, between 1878 and 1879. In the 1930s the maximum annual reduction was 6.9 per cent, between 1930 and 1931. Only the collapse of 1920–21, when manufacturing output slumped by 22 per cent in a year, compares with that of 1979–80.

The consequences should not be forgotten. The official unemployment figures show a rise from 1.4 million in 1979 to 2.5 million in 1982. Despite frequent downward revisions in the method of estimation, the annual figures have continued to rise, reaching a level of 3.2 million in 1986. As yet there is no clear sign of them coming down.

The number of bankruptcies rose rapidly during the recession. In 1983 yet another record was set of almost 13,500 company liquidations – almost three times as many as in 1979. As production collapsed, Britain's international trading position deteriorated. In 1983, for the first time in history, the first industrial nation imported more manufactured goods than it exported. In that year Britain's share of world manufacturing exports fell to an all-time low of 7.9 per cent.

By conventional economic criteria, one of the very few clear successes that could be claimed for the Conservative policies in its first four years of office was a large reduction in the rate of inflation. The annual rate of increase in the Retail Price Index peaked in 1980 at 18.1 per cent. By 1984 it had been brought down to 5.0 per cent. This is an achievement of a dubious sort. The rise in the exchange rate further cheapened imports of primary products whose prices had collapsed in the world slump; and the lower costs gradually permeated the economy. But the damage to exports was catastrophic. Historic unemployment, a rise in poverty and social disorder, and terrible damage to the nation's industrial base were the high price paid for this 'solution' to inflation.

Explanations

Was the world recession to blame?
Being confronted by its own figures on the scale and devastation of the post-1979 slump, the government responded with a mixture of two arguments. The first was to suggest that recovery and prosperity could not come without some initial dislocation: the suggestion being, in line with 'Victorian' philosophy, that the painfulness of the deflationary measures showed that they were working. The second was to argue that the British depression was due to a world slump, experienced by most other industrial countries. The evidence suggests, however, that there is little support for this argument.

If we consider the major seven OECD countries (namely the USA, the UK, Japan, West Germany, France, Italy and Canada), their aggregate GDP or GNP from 1979 to 1981 grew by 2.2 per cent. Yet in Britain it fell by 4.3 per cent. Total employment in the major seven grew by 0.6 per cent in those two years, yet in Britain it fell by 6.9 per cent (OECD, *Economic Outlook*, July 1982, Table 5). In the OECD as a whole, unemployment reached a peak in 1983 at 8.7 per cent, and it has declined slightly since. In Britain unemployment stood at about the OECD average at 5.7 per cent in 1979, rising to 13.1 per cent in 1983, and it has continued to rise to date (figures quoted in Tomlinson, 1986, p. 12). Consequently, the severe recession experienced by Britain cannot, at the outset, be blamed on any recession in world production, employment and trade.

Furthermore, there are figures to suggest that the actions of the Conservative government actually exacerbated the recession, once the

Table 11.3 *General government financial balances:*
Increase (+) or decrease (−) in deficit as a percentage of GNP/GDP

	1979–80	1980–81	1981–82	1982–83	1983–84	1984–85
United States	+ 1.8	− 0.3	+ 2.9	+ 0.3	− 0.7	+ 0.5
Canada	+ 0.9	− 1.1	+ 3.4	+ 1.2	+ 0.1	+ 0.2
United Kingdom	+ 0.0	− 0.7	− 0.5	+ 1.4	+ 0.1	− 0.4
Sweden	+ 0.8	+ 1.2	+ 1.2	− 1.0	− 1.8	− 0.9
France	− 0.9	+ 2.0	+ 0.9	+ 0.4	− 0.3	+ 0.5
West Germany	+ 0.3	+ 0.8	− 0.4	− 0.8	− 0.6	− 0.7
Italy	− 1.5	+ 3.9	+ 0.7	− 0.2	+ 1.1	− 0.1
Japan	− 0.3	− 0.5	− 0.4	− 0.1	− 0.8	− 1.0

Source: Derived from OECD, *Economic Outlook*, December 1985.

downturn in Britain had begun. Table 11.3 shows that the UK general government financial balance took a deflationary shift which was greater than the average in the other major OECD countries in the crucial period of 1980–82. From 1980 to 1981, as the UK economy was tumbling into a deep hole, the fall was accelerated by a deficit reduction that was exceeded only by Canada. Other countries such as Sweden, France, West Germany and Italy were actually reflating at the time. In the next period (1981–82) the US and Canadian governments both did a U-turn and made a pronounced reflationary shift. Excluding the UK, only West Germany and Japan took a deflationary shift in that period. Yet Britain, a much weaker economy by comparison, made the most severe deflationary move of all the major OECD countries.

It was not until 1982–83, in the run-up to the general election, that the Thatcher government briefly reversed its progressively deflationary policies for the first time. Arguably, from a Keynesian viewpoint, it is no accident that the British economy began to climb out of its deep recession in 1982 and 1983. These were precisely the years of the government's quick pre-election reflationary fix. It is remarkable how monetarist ideology can be quietly shelved, and the most deflationary of governments can assume Keynesian qualities, when elections loom near.

Is high public spending and taxation the problem?
In general, however, the Conservative government feared Keynesian remedies for the slump, and was prepared to witness a chronic decay in the UK manufacturing base while it waited for market forces to come to the rescue. In taking this view it was inspired by a belief that the growth of the public sector in the UK was a serious problem, and a further public stimulus to effective demand would make it worse. This is what the traditional theory teaches.

In addition the government was committed to a so-called 'supply-side' strategy, which put the emphasis on tax cuts as an 'incentive' to work and invest. It is reasonable to ask if the problems of the British economy can be

Table 11.4 *International comparisons of*
taxation and public expenditure

	Total taxation as % of GNP at factor cost			Central government Expenditure as % GDP		
	1973	1978	1983	1973	1978	1983
United States	31.5	31.4	30.8	20.8	22.1	26.3
Canada	36.9	35.2	37.4	n.a.	20.5	24.1
United Kingdom	36.4	37.7	44.2	31.8	37.0	41.4
Sweden	47.0	56.3	58.6	29.4	40.0	48.4
France	40.7	44.7	51.0	32.0	38.2	44.7
West Germany	44.2	46.2	46.1	24.6	29.2	31.1
Italy	29.9	35.9	46.7	31.8	41.1	52.4
Japan	22.5	24.7	29.9	n.a.	n.a.	n.a.

Source: Central Statistical Office, *Economic Trends*, London: HMSO, May 1986; International Monetary Fund, *Government Finance Statistics Yearbook*, New York: IMF, 1985.

seen in these terms, and if cuts in both public expenditure and taxation would offer a means of recovery. One of the best ways of attempting to answer this question is to compare the UK with other countries.

The changes in overall taxation and general public expenditure are put in some international perspective in Table 11.4. It is clear that, whilst total taxation has risen dramatically under the Conservative government, in 1983 it was still significantly lower (as a percentage of GNP) than in Sweden, France, West Germany and Italy. All these economies have so far out-performed Britain in the 1980s. Furthermore, taxation has increased to a similar extent in France, Italy and Japan, yet none of these countries has experienced a large downturn in output in the early 1980s, and their performance has been far superior to that in Britain. Japan, for instance, increased its real value-added output in manufacturing by 7.9 per cent from 1979 to 1983.

Comparative figures for public expenditure are also presented in Table 11.4. These have to be treated with some caution as they are central government expenditure figures and they do not take account of differences in the structure of government in each country. Nevertheless, they tell an interesting story. For all the major OECD countries for which figures are available, central government expenditure rose steadily from 1973 to 1983. In addition, there seems to be no support for the view that high public expenditure impairs economic performance.

Whilst central government spending increased by 4.4 per cent of GDP from 1978 to 1983 in Britain, it increased by 4.2 per cent in the US, 6.5 per cent in France, 8.4 per cent in Sweden, and 11.3 per cent in Italy. The three highest public spenders on the list for 1983, namely Sweden, France and Italy, have economic growth rates of output and productivity for recent years that are much greater than the fourth highest spender, namely the UK. Moreover, their levels of unemployment are significantly lower.

Table 11.5   *Changes in expenditure, UK, 1977–85*
(annual percentage change, inflation-adjusted market prices)

Years	Total spending	Total consumer spending	Central and local government spending	Gross fixed investment	Gross domestic product*
1977–78	3.6	5.5	2.3	3.1	2.9
1978–79	3.8	4.5	2.1	2.9	2.2
1979–80	− 2.5	− 0.3	1.5	− 5.0	− 2.1
1980–81	− 1.4	− 0.2	0.2	− 9.5	− 1.1
1981–82	1.9	0.9	1.1	4.3	1.0
1982–83	4.1	4.0	1.9	5.7	3.8
1983–84	3.6	2.2	0.8	9.1	1.9
1984–85	3.6	3.5	0.4	1.8	3.8

* Expenditure-based estimate, adjusted to factor cost.
Source: Central Statistical Office, *Economic Trends Annual Supplement*, London: HMSO, 1987.

There is no evidence here that high central government spending leads to economic stagnation, as New Right economic theorists presume.

Was the recession caused by a slowdown in demand?
Having shown that the deterioration in the British economy in 1979–82 cannot be explained by a slowdown in world trade or the deflationary policies of other major nations, or by its general levels of public expenditure and taxation, we turn to the argument that it was caused largely by a cutback in domestic aggregate demand and a deterioration in the trade balance. The latter was adversely affected by an excessively high sterling exchange rate, propped up by very high levels of interest. Both the domestic and the trade policies were inspired by monetarist theory, and it is in eagerly accepting this creed and many of its implications that the Conservative government's responsibility lies.

Table 11.5 shows the main subdivision of domestic spending and reveals the changing pattern of aggregate demand from 1977 to 1985. Figures for the overall growth of the gross domestic product are included for comparison.

By far the most important single component of effective demand is consumer spending, which accounted for 48 per cent of total expenditure in 1980. After rising at a rate of around 5 per cent per annum in the latter years of the 1970s, consumer expenditure went into reverse in 1979–80 and 1980–81, and rose only slowly in subsequent years. Rising unemployment meant a dramatic cut of real incomes for millions of people, and wages and salaries for those in employment did not rise with sufficient rapidity to prevent the demand slowdown.

Turning to the question of government expenditure, it was clearly a Conservative objective to bring this total down. Although the government did not succeed in meeting its own public expenditure targets, the growth

Table 11.6   *UK trade surplus as a percentage of
gross domestic product*

Year	Surplus %
1977	3.8
1978	3.3
1979	1.6
1980	2.6
1981	3.2
1982	1.9
1983	0.9
1984	0.2
1985	1.2

Source: Central Statistical Office, *Economic Trends Annual Supplement*, London: HMSO, 1987.

rate was brought down from above 2 per cent in the late 1970s to only 0.2 per cent in 1980–81. Thus the Thatcher government brought the growth in state expenditure virtually to a standstill at one of the deepest points in the recession – a time when by Keynesian criteria the government should have been increasing its spending.

The most dramatic fall in expenditure was in gross fixed investment, which in 1980 accounted for 21 per cent of gross domestic product. After growing at around 3 per cent in the late 1970s it fell by 5.0 per cent in 1979–80 and 9.5 per cent in 1980–81. This, combined with the fall in consumer expenditure, accounts for more than two-thirds of the fall in aggregate effective demand in the 1979–81 period. The large fall in investment must have been associated with a near-collapse in domestic confidence and a substantial downward revision in expectations. The explanation is unlikely to be a general loss of confidence in export markets; the most severe and apparent decline in demand was within the UK.

The picture would not be complete without some consideration of the balance of trade in these years. Effective demand for products of the UK economy consists in part of demand for UK exports from abroad. This has to be set against domestic demand for imports from other countries. Exports exceeded imports for each year from 1977 to 1985 and the difference represents a positive component of effective demand.

However, as Table 11.6 shows, the trade surplus as a percentage of GDP was more than halved from 1978 to 1979. Although it rose to 3.2 per cent of GDP in 1981, it did not again reach its 1978 level. This was despite the bringing of North Sea oil into full flow. Thus the balance of trade deteriorated right at the outset of the slump. Furthermore the trade surplus was achieved through the additional export of financial and other services,·plus North Sea oil. It thus concealed a much more serious deterioration of Britain's position in world markets. As noted above, from 1983 Britain was importing more manufactured goods than it exported.

The decline in domestic manufacturing industry is portrayed in Table

Table 11.7   *The decline of the UK manufacturing sector
(volume terms, 1979 = 100)*

Year	Total manufacturing output	Manufacturing gross fixed investment	Gross domestic product
1979	100.0	100.0	100.0
1980	91.2	86.4	97.5
1981	85.7	64.9	96.0
1982	85.9	62.8	97.8
1983	88.3	63.7	100.9
1984	91.8	73.9	103.7
1985	94.5	75.5	107.0

Source: Central Statistical Office, *Economic Trends*, London: HMSO, May 1986.

11.7. Whilst by 1983 gross domestic production had crept back to its 1979 level, the manufacturing sector was showing signs of more lasting damage. By 1985 manufacturing output was still well below its 1979 level and manufacturing fixed investment was about one-quarter lower. Thus the so-called 'supply-side' strategy of the Thatcher government in fact resulted in the greatest damage to the real supply side since British industry was bombed in the Second World War.

Outcomes

Limited Room for Manoeuvre

The monetarist and deflationary policies imposed by the Thatcher government on the slumping economy augmented a serious recession from which the government emerged with a highly limited room for manoeuvre.

The failure to address the real underlying problem – the contracting economy and its ailing manufacturing base – meant that as time went on the government had fewer resources in real terms.

By 1983 monetarism had been abandoned in all but name; but the government had renounced the Keynesian policies of demand management, and rejected any interventionist industrial policy to restructure British industry. So was there an alternative strategy?

The government could allow effective demand to rise in a short pre-election fix, but it could not do this in a concerted and sustained manner for fear of losing its credibility. The refusal of reflation and industrial stimulation meant that the government therefore had little alternative but, in Harold Macmillan's words, to 'sell off the family silver'. One by one, each nationalized industry was put on sale by hawking its shares, giving the government much-sought revenue and some scope for tax cuts. Of course it is argued by the Conservative Party that privatization itself will promote efficiency and growth, but the government has produced no evidence that this will in fact be the case. The only clear benefits are in one-off government revenue terms.

Another resource for the government, but this time an accident of geology rather than ideology, has been the massive revenues from the drilling of North Sea oil. However, it has frequently been argued that the money has simply been spent on dole payments for the vast numbers of involuntary unemployed. Arguably, the government's own deflationary and monetarist policies mean that the great potential benefit of North Sea oil has been largely frittered away. Furthermore, it has also been argued with some force that the economy would be in an even more perilous state if the oil had not been discovered. As Professor Sidney Pollard writes:

In 1974, just before the oil began to flow, Britain's expenditure on oil imports, in hard-earned foreign currency, was £3.7 billion; today the contribution of oil to exports and import substitution is of the order of £16–17 billion. The mind simply boggles at the chaos and destruction which the absence of that income would cause in Britain, given the usual reactions of the Treasury to a payments deficit, had we not been saved by our own oil. (1984, pp. 55–6)

Across the other side of the North Sea is another country that has a share of the oil. But Norway has not adopted such a deflationary stance, and in 1984 its unemployment rate stood at 3.0 per cent and its GDP growth rate averaged 3.9 per cent for the period 1973–84. By contrast, percentage unemployment in Britain is more than four times as much, and growth has been less than a third of the Norwegian rate. Instead of promoting investment and future prosperity, in Britain the oil revenues have been used to prop up an ailing economy.

Since the weakening of the OPEC cartel, the oil price has fallen to well below its former level. Whilst this has led to a loss in revenue for the Chancellor, it has been argued in some quarters that the lower oil price will act as a stimulant to the world economy, thus helping British exports. Be that as it may, North Sea oil production is likely to peak in the late 1980s, and a God-given source of revenue will be removed.

Future Prospects

It seems from the government's current stance that its strategy is to use the oil and privatization revenues as a kind of booster rocket to bring a renewed 'supply-side' strategy into orbit. It is hoped that the revenues will enable the standard rate of income tax to be brought down. It is further hoped that tax cuts will stimulate the economy, as the 'supply-side' theoreticians propose. They are praying that when the oil runs out, and there is nothing more that can feasibly be privatized, the British economy will be sufficiently healthy to prosper, like Japan, without succour from its own natural resources.

The prospect of success for this strategy is not at all good. Japan prospered by adopting a long-term industrial strategy: it has a financial system that promotes the long-term financing of its indigenous industry; it has restructured its industrial relations along more participatory lines; and it has massively expanded its education and training so that its workforce is ready for the new, knowledge-based industries that are the bulwark of future success. Relative to Japan, and indeed even to all other advanced capitalist nations, Britain's record is the poorest on all these counts. Even if the 'supply-side' strategy could work – and there are convincing theoretical arguments that it will not – it is indeed highly risky to base the post-oil prosperity of the British economy on a tax cut and a prayer.

Bibliography

Arrow, Kenneth and Hahn, Frank (1971), *General Competitive Analysis*, San Francisco: Holden-Day

Azarchs, Alex (1987), 'Labor supply and the multiplier', Discussion Paper, Pace University, New York

Barro, Robert (1986), *Macroeconomics*, New York: Wiley

Blinder, Alan (1979), *Economic Policy and the Great Stagflation*, New York: Academic Press

Bowles, Samuel, Gordon, David, and Weisskopf, Tom (1987), 'Power and profits: the social structure of accumulation and the profitability of the postwar US economy', *Review of Radical Political Economics*, Summer

Branson, William (1979), *Macroeconomic Theory and Policy*, 2nd edn, New York: Harper & Row

Bruno, Michael and Sachs, Jeffrey (1985), *Economics of Worldwide Stagflation*, Cambridge, Mass.: Harvard University Press

Chandler, Alfred (1977), *The Visible Hand: The Managerial Revolution in American Business*, Cambridge, Mass.: Harvard University Press

Davidson, Paul (1978), *Money and the Real World*, New York, John Wiley and Sons

Eatwell, John and Milgate, Murray (1983), *Keynes' Economics and the Theory of Value and Distribution*, New York: Oxford University Press

Economic Report of the President (annual), Washington, DC: US Government Printing Office

Elbaum, B. and Lazonick, W. (eds) (1986), *The Decline of the British Economy*, Oxford: Clarendon Press

Feldstein, Martin (ed.) (1980), *The American Economy in Transition*, Chicago, Ill.: University of Chicago Press

Foster, John Bellamy (1986), *The Theory of Monopoly Capitalism*, New York: Monthly Review Press

Friedman, Milton (1970), 'A theoretical framework for monetary analysis', *Journal of Political Economy*, vol. 78, pp. 193–238; reprinted in Gordon (1974), pp. 1–63

Friedman, Milton (1973), *Unemployment and Inflation*, London: Institute of Economic Analysis

Galbraith, John Kenneth (1952, 1980), A Theory of Price Controls, Harvard University Press

Galbraith, John Kenneth (1978) The New Industrial State, Boston: Houghton Mifflin

Galeano, Eduardo (1983), *Days and Nights of Love and War*, New York: Monthly Review Press

Garegnani, Pierangelo (1970), 'Heterogeneous capital, the production function and the theory of distribution', *The Review of Economic Studies*, vol. 37, no. 3, pp. 407–36, and 'A reply', p. 439

Garegnani, Pierangelo (1978/9), 'Notes on consumption, investment and effective demand: I and II', *Cambridge Journal of Economics*; reprinted in Eatwell and Milgate (1983), pp. 21–70

Gordon, Robert (ed.) (1974), *Milton Friedman's Monetary Framework*, Chicago, Ill.: University of Chicago Press

Hahn, Frank (1973), *On the Notion of Equilibrium of Economics: An Inaugural Lecture*, Cambridge: Cambridge University Press

Hahn, Frank (1981), 'General equilibrium theory', in Daniel Bell and Irving Kristol (eds), *The Crisis in Economic Theory*, New York: Basic Books

Hahn, Frank (1984), *Money and Inflation*, Cambridge, Mass.: MIT Press

Harcourt, Geoffrey (1972), *Some Cambridge Controversies in the Theory of Capital*, Cambridge: Cambridge University Press

Hollis, Martin and Nell, Edward (1975), *Rational Economic Man*, Cambridge: Cambridge University Press

House of Lords (1985), *Report from the Select Committee on Overseas Trade*, London: HMSO

Kahn, Richard (1931), 'The relation of home investment to unemployment', *Economic Journal*, pp. 173–98

Kaldor, Nicholas (1985), *Economics without Equilibrium*, Armonk, New York: M. E. Sharpe

Kalecki, Michel (1943), 'The political aspects of full employment', *Political Quarterly*; reprinted in Kalecki (1971)

Kalecki, Michel (1971), *Selected Essays on the Dynamics of the Capitalist Economy*, Cambridge: Cambridge University Press

Keynes, John Maynard (1973), *The Collected Writings of John Maynard Keynes*, ed. A. Robinson and D. Moggridge, Cambridge: Cambridge University Press

Laibman, David and Nell, Edward (1977), 'Reswitching, Wicksell effects and the neo-Classical production function', *American Economic Review*, vol. 67, no. 5, pp. 878–88

Lowe, Adolph (1976), *The Path of Economic Growth*, Cambridge: Cambridge University Press

Mandel, Ernest (1978), *The Second Slump*, London: New Left Books

Marshall, Alfred (1961), *Principles of Economics*, 8th edn, ed. C. W. Guillebaud, London: Macmillan

Marx, Karl (1973), *Capital*, vols I and II, New York: International Publishers

Marx, Karl (1981), *Capital*, vol. III, New York: Vintage

Mayer, Thomas (1960), 'The distribution of ability and earnings', *Review of Economics and Statistics*, vol. 42, May, pp. 189–95

Minsky, Hyman (1986), *Stabilizing an Unstable Economy*, New York: Twentieth Century Fund

Nell, Edward (1972), 'Two books on the theory of income distribution', *Journal of Economic Literature*, vol. x, no. 2, pp. 437–53

Nell, Edward (1973), 'The fall of the House of Efficiency', *Annals of the American Academy of Political and Social Science*, vol. 409, pp. 102–11

Nell, Edward (1980a), 'Value and capital in Marxian economics', *The Public Interest*, Special Edition; reprinted in *The Crisis in Economic Theory*, ed. Bell and Kristol, New York: Basic Books, 1981

Nell, Edward (ed.) (1980b), *Growth, Profits and Property*, Cambridge: Cambridge University Press

Nell, Edward (1980c), 'Capital and the firm in neoclassical theory', *Journal of Post Keynesian Economics*, vol. II, no. 4, pp. 494–508

Nell, Edward (1982), 'Growth, distribution, and inflation', *Journal of Post Keynesian Economics*, vol. V, no. 1, pp. 104–13

Nell, Edward (ed.) (1984a), *Free Market Conservatism*, London: Allen & Unwin

Nell, Edward (1984b), 'Structure and behavior in classical and neoclassical theory', *Eastern Economic Journal*, vol. XI, no. 2, pp. 139–55

Nell, Edward (1986), 'On monetary circulation and the rate of exploitation', *Thames Papers in Political Economy*, London: Thames Polytechnic

Nell, Edward (1987a), 'On deserving profits', *Ethics*, vol. 97, no. 2, pp. 403–11

Nell, Edward (1988a), *Keynes after Sraffa*, London: Allen & Unwin

Nell, Edward (1988b) 'Accumulation and capital theory', in George Feiwel (ed.), *Joan Robinson and Modern Economics*, Boston: Kluwer-Nijoff

Nell, Edward (1988c), 'On long-run equilibrium in class society', in George Feiwel (ed.), *Joan Robinson and Modern Economics*, Boston: Kluwer-Nijoff

Pasinetti, Luigi (1977), *Lectures on the Theory of Production*, New York: Columbia University Press

Pasinetti, Luigi (1981), *Structural Change in Economic Growth*, Cambridge: Cambridge University Press

Pollard S. (1984), *The Wasting of the British Economy*, 2nd edn, London: Croom Helm

Roberts, Paul Craig (1984), *The Supply Side Revolution*, Cambridge, Mass.: Harvard University Press

Robinson, Joan (1937), *Introduction to the Theory of Employment*, London: Macmillan

Shaikh, Anwar (1984), 'The rate of profit and the theory of crisis', New York: New School for Social Research

Snelling, Richard (1984), 'The deficit's clear and present danger', *The New York Times Sunday Magazine*, 17 January

Steedman, Ian (1977), *Marx after Sraffa*, London: New Left Books

Tomlinson, J. (1986), *Monetarism; Is There an Alternative?* Oxford: Blackwell

Weintraub, Sidney (1978), *Capitalism's Inflation and Unemployment Crisis*, Reading, Mass.: Addison-Wesley

Williamson, Oliver (1975), *Markets and Hierarchies*, New York: The Free Press

Index